D0053590

Kill the Silence

Kill the Silence

A Survivor's Life Reclaimed

MONIKA KØRRA

HARMONY
BOOKS · NEW YORK

Copyright © 2015 by Monika Kørra

All rights reserved.
Published in the United States by Harmony Books,
an imprint of the Crown Publishing Group,
a division of Penguin Random House LLC, New York.
www.crownpublishing.com

Harmony Books is a registered trademark and the Circle colophon
is a trademark of Penguin Random House LLC.

Library of Congress Cataloging-in-Publication Data
Korra, Monika.
Kill the silence : a survivor's life reclaimed / Monika Korra.—First edition.
1. Korra, Monika.   2. Rape victims—United States—Biography.   3. Rape
victims—Rehabilitation.   4. Rape trauma syndrome—Treatment.   I. Title.
HV6561.K66 2015
362.883092—dc23
[B]   2015009127

ISBN 978-0-8041-3962-5
eBook ISBN 978-0-8041-3963-2

Printed in the United States of America

Book design by Claire Vaccaro
Jacket design by Jess Morphew
Jacket photograph by Larry Sengbush

10 9 8 7 6 5 4 3 2 1

First Edition

For my family and dearest friends—the guiding stars of my life.

Thank you for showing me that love conquers hate in every way;

thank you for giving me my lovely life back!

Contents

Prologue

December 23, 2013

I sit at the frost-rimmed window. Outside the snow falls in gentle arcs through the gray light of a Little Christmas Eve Norwegian day. I smile. The lights of our just-decorated Christmas tree color the nearest flakes, transforming them into a kind of flowing spectral rainbow. The glass is cold to the touch as I attempt to wipe away some of the moisture that has built up, a by-product of the fragrant dish that my mother has simmering on the stove to later serve to my sister, my father, and me for lunch. The sweet smells of the pork sausage and dill are carried on the draft from the poorly sealed glass-and-wood windows. What I'm really looking forward to is the porridge we'll have this evening, a renewed tradition from childhood in which whoever ended up with the bowl that had the almond in it got presented with a marzipan pig as a prize.

Though it is barely noon, I know that my window of opportunity to get outside will close quickly. With my base layer already on, it takes just a few minutes to fully dress before I grab my skis, poles, and boots and head toward the door. I say good-bye to my mother on my way out. She is seated on a chair in the living room, enjoying the newspaper and an extra day off of work two days before Christmas.

"Ha det bra, Mamma." I wave to her as I head for the door.

"God tur, Monika. Kos deg på ski," she responds, wishing me a good ski trip without even turning to look.

My mother knows me well. Not many people would want to go outside in such weather, especially with the temperature so far below freezing, never mind choose to put their body through the exertion that I'm about to. But I've never let what most people do define me.

As I drive to Budor, the skiing area where I've spent countless hours propelling myself on cross-country skis around hundreds of kilometers of trails, I think about the conversation I had with my mother earlier that morning. I was having trouble with a zipper on my favorite Swix running/skiing jacket. I tugged and tugged at it, but its teeth wouldn't release their grip. In frustration, I muttered about the stupid thing, louder than I probably should have, and stamped my feet.

My mother came up to me and held out her hand. I handed over the jacket.

She pinched her face in concentration. "This is as stubborn as you are. It only wants to go where it wants to go and doesn't like anyone insisting too strongly."

As she coaxed the zipper down, she reminded me about the time when I was a little girl just starting out on skis. Like most kids in Norway, I was strapped into a pair of cross-country skis as soon as I could walk. Unlike most one-year-olds, who fell, cried, and held out their arms to be picked up when they couldn't keep their balance, I only cried if someone tried to help me. I was going to do it on my own or there was going to be hell to pay. I joked that that was because I wanted to be like Anette, my older and only sibling, who was four when I was first put on skis, but my mother shook her head.

"You were always so headstrong, in a good way," she added, smiling. "It's helped you more than hurt you."

Arriving at the trails, I think about how some things have changed and how others have not. I've had to learn to let other people help me over the last few years. Anette is still someone I look up to and admire, but I've become less competitive with her in many ways. We've always been close and supportive, but the dynamic of our relationship has shifted. Though I was thousands of miles away from her when the attack occurred, and it is impossible for anyone who hasn't been subjected to what I was to ever completely close the gap between the raped and the non-raped, Anette, my friend Ida, and my mother have been as close to being with me stride for stride since that horrific night as it is possible to be. I had always wanted to race ahead of everyone, to be the first to the finish line, and it still feels odd to me to let others stay with me, to maintain my pace, to resist the urge to sprint away.

When I was younger, very few people ever said my name, Monika, without using the word *lille* or "little" in front of it. That was natural, I suppose, given that I was always the shortest and slightest of my class-mates and fellow teammates and competitors. I spent my childhood try-ing to keep up with my sister and her friends, on skis, on Rollerblades, while running around our property in Løten playing *gjemsel* ("hide and go seek") and *hermegåsa* ("follow the leader"). Maybe that was where I'd become so goal oriented—if I didn't keep up with Anette and the other kids, I wouldn't get to play. And I always wanted to be a part of the action. I didn't just want to play; I wanted to win.

I pull into the parking lot at Budor, close to the lodge. I look through the gloaming and see the platter lift. Its swing-set seats and curved metal poles look like baited fishhooks. They climb the hill, oscillating slightly in the wind. Empty. The scene could have been sad, like a dilapidated amusement park standing empty in the off-season, but instead it cheers me. If the parking lot's sparseness and the lift's emptiness are any indica-tion, I'll have the Nordic trails mostly to myself.

I snap into my bindings, wind the handles of my poles around my wrists, and set off. The snow on the trail is well packed, and each of my kicks is accompanied by a satisfying squeak. The trail climbs from the base near the simple lodge. I bend slightly at the waist and thrust my arms directly ahead of me while bringing my leg forward, before propelling myself up the slope. My father waxed my skis for me the night before, and I'm pleased that I am both gaining good traction and also enjoying a bit of a glide. If the skis had been too slick, I would have lost momentum going up the hill, losing a bit of distance with each stride. I don't like slipping back, losing at anything, not even a little bit.

Soon the trail levels off a bit, and I move into a smooth rhythm. As I pick up speed, the wind numbs my cheeks and ears. My breathing settles into a good pattern, and I can feel my heart rate climb. About a thousand feet ahead of me, I see where the trail enters the forest, a tunnel of trees carved out of the mountainside. I give myself one minute to get to the first of the trees and kick into a sprint.

Training for an endurance sport demands that you be comfortable being alone—whether that isolation is in your mind or literally so in your training. Your coach can provide you with guidance; your family can stand on the sidelines and cheer you on, or cheer you up later when you have a bad result, but ultimately the responsibility for how you per-form lies on your shoulders alone. You're the only one who truly knows your own limits; you're the only one who can truly assess how much you tested them.

By inclination, I'm a social person and love the company of others, but I have always needed my independence; I need to have time by myself and with my thoughts. When I'm alone with my thoughts I'm better able to solve problems, put events into their proper perspective, do all the work necessary to build the kind of mental strength you need to succeed as an athlete and as a person. At those times I'm both my harshest critic and my most caring comforter—I know when I need a kick in the butt and when I need a shoulder to cry on. Too often I've struggled with com-municating those needs to others.

As I speed along, I feel a lightness come into my heart. I am outside in the crisp winter air, nimble as I glide between the snow-frosted trees that seem to embrace me, and I allow my mind to wander.

Four years earlier, almost to the day, I also came to Budor. That was the Christmas just after the attack. I was so wiped out by the anti-HIV drugs I was taking that it was a struggle to get out of bed at all. I was so tortured by memories that not even my sister's presence in my bed was sufficient to make me feel secure enough to surrender to sleep. I didn't like the idea that what had happened to me was bringing everyone else down, and I tried to be even more cheerful as a way to reassure everyone that I was okay, but I wasn't.

That Christmas in 2009, I felt friction in every part of my life. I just wanted everyone to believe that I was the same old Monika, that nothing had changed. I clung to the belief that the essential parts of me—my tenacity, my work ethic, my hunger to prove to everyone that I had what it took to take on any challenge—were still there. Those traits rubbed against another part of my reality—that the culture I was raised in emphasized a different set of values, and subtle forces were telling me that I should fit in and not fight.

The trail leads to a slight depression, a cut in the mountainside that leads sharply down and then equally sharply up an incline. I dig my poles in deeper, settle back on my heels to maintain my balance, and am soon on more level ground again.

That Little Christmas Eve back in 2009, with everyone in my family hovering over me, blanketing me with well-intended concern and compassion, I grew claustrophobic. Their hovering began to feel intrusive; it was as if I couldn't make any movement without someone noting it, assessing it, pondering its potential deeper meanings. I felt as if I were a specimen in a jar, floating in a fluid of their and my own fears and anxieties. I was as angry and hurting, both over what had happened and because I did not want to be so fragile, so helpless.

I can't blame them for thinking of me that way. They saw through the façade I'd tried so hard to erect around myself. I was a wreck—physically and emotionally and spiritually sore and spent. I'd been a competitor all my life; I hated to lose, but when I did, I'd always manage to find some element of the competition to give me hope for the future. That could mean having a chance to evaluate my performance, to set new training goals, or simply to enjoy being out in the environment giving my body a chance to express itself. But after the rape, I found nothing hopeful about what had been done to me. I saw no lessons, only injuries that had been inflicted. I worried I might never recover. It was as if my body, the thing that in many ways gave my life meaning, was lost to me. Being in my childhood bedroom, surrounded by ribbons, trophies, and other marks of achievement, only reminded me of what I'd lost, what had been taken from me; the accolades were no longer signifiers of any kind of victory.

On Christmas Eve, 2009, I had gone to Budor because I had experienced a loss greater than any other in my life, and the only way I knew how to move beyond it was to train harder than ever. I turned to what

I knew best—the same way I responded after a race that hadn't gone as I'd hoped. First, I would experience panic and the desire for wish fulfillment—I wanted to get back out on the track immediately and do everything different, fix every mistake. I was certain that a bad race meant it was over—my running career, my chances of progressing, everything gone. If I could just get out there again, maybe no one would notice that I'd failed.

Over time, I'd learned that first reaction wasn't the best reaction. No good could come of rushing right back out there. I needed to give myself time—time to reflect, to analyze, and to plan a better strategy. I also came to understand that my career wasn't over, that the stakes of every race weren't that high. We all have good races and bad races. I couldn't outrun my mistakes or pretend that they hadn't happened. I had to learn from them. What was the point of enduring if all you were going to do was repeat the same mistakes and wind up back at the starting line having learned nothing?

I'd come to think of it like this: We couldn't ever expect to have a completely pristine, track-free trail of snow to ski on. Those other marks would still be there, showing where our missteps were, where we'd not taken the most efficient line around a turn, but that was okay. We'd eventually settle into a groove and make the fastest progress.

That morning in 2009, my parents had both gone off to work; Anette was no longer living at home, and I was alone. I decided that I needed to get my body back into its familiar routine. I got out of bed and struggled just to pull on my base layer. It was as if the polyester and spandex had been transformed into some kind of super fabric that resisted my muscles' efforts to overcome the forces of their friction and resistance. As I pulled and tugged, I sat down on the bed, breathing hard and crying, remembering how someone else's force had stripped me of my dress, my bra, and my underwear.

If I felt like my power was diminished now in the simple act of clothing myself, then what had taken place on the night those three men overpowered me? What they had stripped from me couldn't be measured on a stopwatch. I knew that I would need to achieve a series of victories if I was ever going to reclaim some of what had been taken from me. And in that moment, I realized that getting dressed and going to Budor was going to be the first. I knew that more than my body had been damaged, but that is where the harm had begun, and it was there that I was going to begin to heal.

The Christmas of 2009, I attacked the trails at Budor with a fury that seared my lungs and strafed my quadriceps and my hamstrings. I beat my way across the snow and the climbs, teeth gritted, snarling and slipping, sometimes spinning in place and then recklessly hurtling downhill once past the apex. For three hours, I burned calories and bridges hoping to put as great a distance between that night and myself as I possibly could. I remember stopping at the crest of one hill, my heart pounding, my chest heaving, nearly every fluid in my body pouring out of my eyes and nose, and thinking that I didn't want to go back there—not back to Dallas and the scene of the crime and not back home, either. I just wanted to ski on forever, stay lost in those woods and mountains, allowing the cold and the wind to numb me past sensibility and reason.

Now, four years later, I power up those hills and fly on the downhills and am thrilled with the feeling of speed and being on the edge of control and my limits. I can feel myself, my body—that essential part of me, who I am and how I view myself—returning bit by bit.

Just as I begin to think about turning around to retrace my path back to the lodge and my car, the path bursts out of the trees. The snow has stopped and the wind has picked up, creating a soft swishing of tree branches that is the only sound. I look to the west, down the slope and across a snow-covered valley where Norwegian fir trees poke their tips out of the drifts like beard stubble. The sun stands balanced on the distant tree line, a bright glow illuminating the sky, spreading a swath of light toward me. To the east, another light shines. The moon has risen in almost perfect parallel to the sun, a great circle the mottled orange color of an ember coming to life, burnished and silhouetting a stand of trees. I have a choice now. I can turn around and retrace my steps, move toward that setting sun and return home; but instead, I take a deep breath and watch as the frigid air sets fire to my exhalation.

Settling into my stride, I kick and dig, moving forward slowly and then gradually crossing larger and larger distances with each stride. I am confident that above me, the moon is rising and the stars are beginning to emerge, that those constant beacons will be there to guide me if I lose my way. I am full in the knowledge that I still have miles to go, but that, no matter which direction I choose to travel, many, many more things will make themselves available to get me home safely again.

I'm certain that my parents will know that not so *lille Monika* is still outside, doing what I need to do. They and the porridge will be warm and waiting for me when I arrive. But whether or not there is an almond in my bowl, I've already won. I'm not back to who I was, but a different, and better, version of the person who walked out of a party and into an early-morning nightmare four years ago.

DECEMBER 5, 2009, was the most horrific day of my life. I wish that I could say that what I experienced in being kidnapped and raped was an isolated incident of random violence. Sadly, the statistics point to a devastating alternate truth: On the day I was raped, 1,870 other people in the United States endured the horror that I did.

In choosing to tell my story, I hope to shatter the silence that often follows attacks like the one I endured. The paralyzing feelings of guilt and shame that accompany being raped last far longer than the assault itself. Just as rapists often tell their victims to shut their mouths, society can do something similar to victims. I hope that by sharing my experiences I can help others who've been raped, as well as their family members, friends, mental health experts and counselors, gain a new and better perspective from someone who was there and is now here. The silence does not have to linger forever. I'm fortunate that I was able to utilize many of the skills and traits that I developed over the years as a competitive runner to aid my healing.

I still have some ways to go, but I'm not that young woman who didn't want to be here anymore. I am here, and I have a voice and I want to be heard.

FOR THOSE WHO have struggled with adversity, who have experienced things that they wish they could undo or leave behind, those who are haunted by their past, I am here to say that there is a way through. We will all face challenges in life, but we have to refuse to allow those feelings of fear, guilt, and shame to hold us back or to victimize us again. We can use those experiences, as horrible as they might have been, to make us stronger than we ever dreamed possible. I hope that in reading my story you'll find some keys to unlocking your own strengths and abilities. You may not be a runner like I am, but you can begin to move more freely in your world and in your own way. You can find peace and take pleasure in simple acts. You can recover what was taken from you. Your life can be better than it ever was before, knowing that you have strength inside you to overcome any obstacle.

I was victimized, but I refuse to be called a victim.

I've been sad, but I won't let anyone feel sorry for me anymore.

I've been raped, but I will never let that define who I am.

CHAPTER ONE

Stillhetens Timer

S *tillhetens timer.*
Quiet hours.

I sat on the couch wishing that the mandatory quiet time imposed in the dormitories during the week of final exams could be enforced in our apartment complex. Through the thin walls, the first notes of the Black Eyed Peas' "Boom Boom Pow" thumped from my neighbor's apartment and made my water bottle dance on the end table. I set aside my textbook for my Health Psychology class, shut my eyes, and pinched the bridge of my nose.

My lids scratched across my eyes as I tried to blink my vision clear. I briefly wondered if our neighbors were suggesting that the lyrics to the song they were blasting were an example of limbic language, the topic I'd just been reviewing in my notes. I looked down at the page and saw that there was more fluorescent highlighting than plain text there. That was a sure sign that I was getting too tired, that my efforts weren't producing good results. I was just about to complete my third semester in Dallas at SMU, and another sure sign of fatigue was when my rapidly and much improved English seemed to fail me and I spent too much time tearing through my English/Norwegian dictionary or Google. Before I could convince myself to buckle down and study for another few hours, my roommates Kristine and Viktoria came bouncing into the room. They danced around to the soundtrack our neighbors were providing, laughing as they pulled me out of my chair for an impromptu dance party. The studying-induced tension that had crabbed my neck and shoulders seemed to flow out of the ends of my fingers.

When the song ended, I sank back onto the couch and reached for my book and highlighter. Kristine grabbed my wrist to keep me from retreating back to my studying, and we jumped around the room in time to Lady Gaga's "Just Dance."

Kristine shouted the song's title at me over and over, her Cheshire grin and sparkling eyes playfully admonishing me for not letting go of my work ethic completely. I tried to let go of the guilt I felt at not sticking with my books, and Kristine and I played a kind of game of tug-of-war as she pulled me back out onto our makeshift dance floor and I tried to drag her toward my security blanket of books and papers on the couch.

The music ended abruptly and Kristine and Viktoria collapsed to the ground and lay on their backs beating their fists against the carpet in exasperation.

"I didn't want that song to ever end!" Viktoria said.

Then they giggled and surrounded me, hugging pillows to their chests.

"We have to get ready," Kristine said. She held her watch out to me so I could read the display.

I had agreed to go with them to a party, but my eyes involuntarily took in my study materials.

"N-o-o-o-o!" they said in unison.

"I k-n-o-o-o-w!" I teased back.

"Then let's g-o-o-o-o!" Viktoria said, ending the conversation.

In the shower, I thought about how different that scene had been, how the year before I wouldn't have been dancing, or if I was, I would have been dancing alone and completely self-consciously. When I first arrived on campus in Dallas, I'd had no idea how I was ever going to find my way to my classes, let alone how I'd manage in the city. I knew that coming to the U.S. was going to be difficult. I'd been thrilled when the coaches at SMU offered me a scholarship to run track and cross-country, but the transition to life in the U.S. hadn't been easy.

English was never my best or favorite subject, and in my first encounters with people here, I was puzzled by even the simplest interactions. The first time I went to a grocery store in the U.S., I was overwhelmed by the rows and rows of strange food items towering over me. As I wandered the aisles, looking for some familiar colors and shapes of packaging, I averted my eyes whenever another shopper glanced my way and smiled. Back home, we'd only do that if we saw someone we knew, but I didn't know any of these people. Why were they regarding me as if we were acquaintances? When it was finally my turn to check out, the young woman behind the counter, a blonde with ringlets of curls and a teardrop tattoo beneath her right eye, smiled at me and said, "Hi there! How'reyoudoingtoday?" I understood the first part, but the second was a rush of sounds that had me wondering what it was I was expected to do next.

"Hello," I said, and immediately dug in my purse as if I wasn't sure where my credit card had gone.

As she scanned the items, I tentatively extended my hand to take them and watched nervously as she placed them in a bag. When she was done, she asked me, "Can I take these to your car for you?"

I understood the words "take" and "car" and was puzzled for a second. Was she asking me to give her what I had just purchased?

I shook my head and said, "No. I do this. Myself." I wondered if there was something about me that made her feel that I needed help.

The truth was that I did, but I wasn't going to ask for it.

I do this.

Myself.

Those words were my motto, and they guided my actions throughout my first days at SMU. I couldn't explain to that woman that I didn't have a car, but I walked home from that grocery store with my head held high. I'd accomplished what I'd set out to do. That sense of accomplishment didn't last long. During those earliest days, I wasn't just confused and bewildered; I was homesick. My mother and I talked nearly every day to combat that for the first few weeks, until she received the first phone bill.

Luckily, we soon discovered Skype and could once again communicate freely.

I had worried all semester that I had made a mistake by coming to the

States. During the first week of school, I barely understood a word my professors said. I tried to take detailed notes, but my English wasn't fluent to begin with, and now I was contending with strong Southern accents and dialects on top of it. How would I ever learn?

Luckily, that part did get easier over time. I understood more and wrote down more—in fact, I wrote so much that I was copying down my professors' lectures almost verbatim until a friend suggested that I ease up a little on the notes and trust my listening skills.

Unlike most beginning college students, who indulge in their freedom and party too much, I probably studied too much. I was lonely but was so focused on keeping my grades up for my scholarship that I spent all of my time either in training or studying, so I didn't really notice how much time I was spending by myself.

Academically I was on the right course, and I made the top five squad of the cross-country team, which meant that I got to compete in all the big races right from the start. But I kept to myself in the dorms and rarely went out with the other girls. It wasn't until Kristine arrived in my second semester that things changed.

Kristine Eikrem Engeset was one of the world's elite middle-distance runners. She was someone I'd met in competitions in Norway and admired very much—all the young female runners looked up to Kristine. You couldn't help but admire her for her beautiful hair, the toned legs, and her body of steel. Not only was she likely to make our Olympic track team, she was even a model for PUMA after she ran in the World Championships in 2007. She appeared on huge posters worldwide with the Jamaican sprinter Usain Bolt, the world's fastest human being. I could only dream of attaining such notoriety and such an impressive record of success on the track.

Before I moved to Dallas, I didn't know Kristine well enough to call her a friend. I had heard they were trying to get her to SMU and was thrilled when she finally arrived for what was my second semester of freshman year.

It turned out that we had a lot more in common than just being runners from the same country. I went from being thrilled to have her running alongside me at a competition to seeing her as a true friend. She made me look at the world differently; as famous as she was, she never took herself too seriously, and definitely never put on airs. We became such close friends because we shared many of the same values and dreams— marriage, children, making ourselves and the world a better place.

In the fall, we moved into an apartment with Viktoria, a high jumper on the team who came from Estonia. I felt like my life in Dallas had really begun; it was great to have someone from home to talk to, to share the experiences of moving this far away and trying to fit in to a different culture. The three of us shared a common sense of discipline, but the two of them showed me that finding a balance in life was important. With their help, I opened up a bit more, and realized how much I missed getting to know different people and learning about their backgrounds and perspectives. Oddly, the less I obsessed about school and track, the happier I was and the better I was able to perform.

As I got ready to go out with my roommates that night of our impromptu dance party, I felt grateful that I had them there to remind me to enjoy myself a little. Though I'd gotten into the shower a little after 9 p.m., three women in one apartment all trying to get ready at the same time means nothing is moving quickly. By 10:15, I was still sitting and waiting for Viktoria and Kristine to emerge. I had put on a dress and a pair of heels, feeling a bit naughty about going out, especially with the end of the semester so close. I liked that edgy feeling of stretching my boundaries a bit.

At 10:30, we were finally ready to go. Viktoria took one more look at herself in the mirror near the door, applied her lipstick, and said, in her best American movie hero accent, "Let's roll."

Of course, we couldn't really "roll" without the aid of our friend George, who was waiting in his car to take us out. George was a good-hearted guy whom we had all come to think of as a kind of surrogate older brother. He met Kristine first, at a PUMA store where he worked. He noticed her tattoo and started a conversation. They connected as friends, and I could tell that he had a slight crush on Kristine. I mentioned that to her, but she shrugged it off. Kristine didn't understand the power she had over men, and unlike some women who pretend to be that way, she truly was oblivious to the effect she had on males. But it was no surprise to any of us that George had volunteered to take us to the party and was going to stick around.

I'd only known George for a couple of months, but I enjoyed his company. He helped me with my English, a lot of times with slang or odd expressions, and I loved how his eyes would grow wide and his bottom jaw drop a bit when I asked him about terms like "bromance," "FOMO," "schwa," and a few others that I'd overhear or see in a text or an e-mail. Viktoria was in the front seat next to him, and she turned to look at me. "Who's going to be there tonight, Monika?"

"Kevin told me about it. I don't really know who is going to be there. People from some of the other sports, I think."

"And who's Kevin?" George used his exaggerated I'm-your-father-and-you-should-tell-me-everything voice.

I rolled my eyes at Kristine, who grunted a laugh and continued texting someone.

"He's on the soccer team. We have Sports Management class together. Anything else you need to know?" I pretended to sound like an irritated teenager, but I wasn't, and George smiled at me through the rearview mirror.

I've always hated walking into parties, that feeling that every eye is on you, but when we got to Kevin's place, the music was loud and people were either dancing or standing around talking busily to one another. We slipped in and, feeling bad for George, who stood there watching as Kristine waded through the bodies in the living room toward the sounds of laughter and cheers and disappeared into what must have been the kitchen, I remained there with him for a few minutes. We both stood there with that I'm-having-a-good-time fake grin plastered on our faces.

We tried to talk, but with the music and the voices so loud, it was hard to hear. We made disjointed conversation about our plans for the upcoming holiday. We drifted toward the kitchen in pursuit of Kristine and Viktoria. They were both standing on one side of the kitchen table, Viktoria holding the Ping-Pong ball in her hand, squinting at the cups that sat at the other end of the table as targets. She released the ball and it hit the lip of one cup, bounced into the air, and found a home in another. The room erupted in cheers and groans, and Kristine and Viktoria engaged in an arms-to-the-ceiling victory dance and fist bumps.

They saw George and me and waved us over. I was never much of a drinker, and one half cup of beer later, the sour vegetable taste still in my mouth, I excused myself from the game. The alcohol seemed to be working, as the dancers now far outnumbered the conversers, and a loose conglomeration of bodies moved around the living room. I was reminded of films I'd seen back in Norway of neurons firing and attaching and detaching in the brain, little flits of movement and flashes of light from cell phone cameras. I joined the group, losing my self-consciousness in movement.

I was surprised, then, when George approached me to tell me that he was going to leave. I looked at my watch. It was a quarter after twelve.

"I'll be back," he said, leaning in close. I could smell something on his breath, not alcohol, not tobacco or pot. His tongue was an odd reddish color and I realized he was sucking on a throat lozenge. I wondered if he was sick.

"To get you guys," he said, finally making himself heard.

"If you're sick you should just go to bed," I protested. "You don't have to come back just for us."

"I do," he said. "I want to and you need me to."

We made plans for me to text him when we were ready to be picked up. Only then did I realize why he was so insistent. I'd had a similar conversation a few weeks earlier with my boyfriend.

Robin lived just across the street from my apartment complex, and we'd spent a quiet night watching a movie. When I told him I was going to go home, he jumped up and started to work his feet into his shoes.

"I'm coming with you. I want to make sure you get there okay."

Another female athlete who lived in the same complex as Kristine, Viktoria, and I had been raped a few days before. We were all shocked and saddened, and I knew it was important to be vigilant, but I didn't want Robin to worry too much about me. I made some joke about my speed and the hundred or so meters from his door to mine. "If anyone tries to attack me, I'll get away. Don't worry."

Robin's expression hardened into a frown.

"I'm sorry," I told him, "*and* I'm serious."

"I'm not going to let that happen to you."

I was touched by his kindness and concern. I was, in fact, crazy in love with this tennis-playing marvel from Sweden. In April of 2009, a friend had asked me to accompany her to a tennis match. Maybe it was the red bandanna that Robin wore to keep his long hair back; maybe it was the combination of grace and power that he exhibited as he covered the court and blew serves past his opponent, or the intensity of his expression on the court, so different from the warmth of his smile when we first met; but he caught my attention as soon as I saw him. His being from a Scandinavian country was a plus; the cultural familiarity was more than just one of those early-days-in-a-romance searches for things we had in common.

That night, I kissed Robin good night and dashed home.

A little after 2 a.m., I was ready to leave the party. I texted George asking if he could come get us. I let the inexhaustible Kristine and Viktoria know that our guardian angel was on his way. Then I collapsed onto a couch and waited for George's phone call to let us know that he'd arrived.

Sitting there, I thought about how fortunate I was to have found two soul mates at SMU. In Robin and Kristine, I'd come across two people who knew me nearly as well as anyone. Ida and I were very close, but with her back in Norway, and me here in the U.S., I felt really fortunate to have Kristine in my life. I didn't doze off, but it seemed like only a second later that George phoned me. I told him we'd be right out.

We opened the door to a gust of wind and cold. The three of us linked our arms and hands and made a short-skirted dash toward George's car, all of us laughing and making it's-really-cold-out-here sounds.

"I can't wait to get home and into my warm bed," Kristine said.

I was just about to tell her that I agreed when a black vehicle pulled into the parking lot alongside George's Toyota sedan. I saw the driver lower his window; I assumed he needed directions or would ask after someone else from the party.

A second later, I heard a scream and felt Kristine's grip on my hand tighten into a death grasp.

Cold metal jutted against the right side of my head. Somehow, I knew it was a gun. I went limp at the feeling of hands on my arms and the back of my neck. My body was being stretched in two directions—toward Kristine and toward the SUV. Its chrome wheels glinted in the street light. Voices shouted, the men's in anger, Kristine's in desperation.

The cold sensation at my neck ceased, and I saw—first out of the periphery and then fully across the field of my vision—the weapon move in Kristine's direction. I felt every hair on my body stand on end and a bead of cold perspiration run down the side of my body.

"Let go," I said to Kristine. Her eyes wide and her mouth agape but silent, Kristine released my hand. I watched as she stood there, arm extended, like a relay runner reacting to a failed handoff. A thought flickered briefly in my mind.

I'm alone. I'm going to have to do this myself.

CHAPTER TWO

A Black SUV

Thoughts, sounds, and images all ran through my head, colliding with one another. The one constant was the hands gripping my biceps and around my neck, my struggle to breathe, the feeling of near weightlessness as I was half-dragged and half-lifted across a short stretch of pavement. Though it was only seconds before I was tossed into the vehicle I'd seen pull up, I was aware of flailing when my feet lost connection with solid ground. Then my face was pressed into the carpet, the rough fibers scratching at my cheeks and lips, the sour smell of something I couldn't identify, something like body odor and chemicals, stinging my eyes and throat.

Above me, voices seemed to be swirling. I tried to count them, to note the differences in their tone, but at times they seemed to blend into a single accented voice. Their words were all layered on top of one another, but I could pull them apart.

"Stay down or we'll shoot you!"

"Don't you try to move!"

"We'll kill you!"

"Please," I begged the three men. "Please don't kill me. Please don't. I don't want to die!"

I couldn't be sure if I had been heard. The engine added its roar and I lay there as the car bumped and shuddered over what may have been a curb before the ride smoothed and the men's voices stilled. We drove straight ahead for what must have been miles. We turned right a couple of times, and the road grew rougher. My neck ached with the effort to keep my head from bouncing too painfully against the hard floor.

I repeated my pleas, and when I got no response, I added, "You can have whatever you want. Just let me live."

It was as if my words set them in motion. A hand grabbed my arm and I was pulled roughly upward. I swung my legs to gain some balance and sat with my back against the second row of seats, my feet beneath the third. Somehow, I'd managed to hold on to my cell phone during those opening minutes of the ordeal. Even before the thought could fully form in my head that I could use it, another hand grasped me around the wrist and shook my entire arm. More out of shock and surprise than pain, I dropped the phone. One of the men picked it up and stuffed it into his pocket. I thought of all the numbers of the people I knew and loved that were stored on that phone. I hoped that I would have another opportunity to speak to every one of those people again.

I could make out one voice better, mostly because it was the loudest, the most shrill. One of the men was down on one knee beside me. He held the gun in one hand. As the vehicle turned, he seemed to lose his balance and he was bouncing back and forth between the two rows of seats. Each time he swayed back and forth, he grew angrier, louder, and more impatient. The gun passed across my face. I needed no reminder that it was there.

"How old are you?" that loud voice asked. Before I could respond, he added, "And don't lie, because I have a gun."

"Twenty," I said. I was too afraid to lie. I hoped that if I told the truth, things would turn out better for me. A moment later, they seemed to. I could hear my phone ringing, a distant but distinct jangling of fake bells.

I craned my neck and could see the man in the middle seat moving around. He brought the phone up to his ear and raised his hand in the air like a teacher quieting a class. We all obeyed. After a few seconds, I yelled out, "Please don't kill me!" louder than necessary, just so whoever was calling could hear my voice and know I was still in that SUV. I heard a voice coming from the cell phone, but then the man hung up.

The gun crossed my vision again. "I will do this. You be nice!" A thin smile sliced the man's round face; his red-rimmed eyes bulged from their sockets. His free hand scraped across his close-cropped hair and then massaged his blunt chin. My eyes went back to the gun.

I felt as if I was shrinking, that each time he raised his voice at me or pointed the gun my way, I was disappearing inside my clothes, like I was a snail retreating into my shell. I put my hands up as if to ward off his words, but each one felt like a blow to my flesh.

He pawed at my coat and kept shouting. I thought it was best to cooperate with him. I turned my back slightly and raised my arms so that he could remove my jacket. I wrapped my arms across my chest, and even that seemed to make him fiercer. He pulled my right arm toward him. He fumbled with the clasp of my watch; I started to move to help him, but he slapped my hand away. Next, he took two of my rings, sliding them off easily.

The third ring, a thin silver band that I'd had since I was a little girl, fit snugly. A childhood girlfriend, Nina, had given it to me when I was ten. It had a small plastic diamond on it. How I wished that diamond was as real as the ones I'd seen on the fingers of the women of Dallas, that its value would be enough to satisfy these men.

I flinched as he tried to scrape it past my knuckle, my flesh bunching up like a closed flower. I looked at his forehead and saw the same image there—pinched flesh. Though I couldn't see his eyes, I watched as his lids and brows twitched.

"Give it to me now!" he yelled. "Don't fuck with me!"

I twisted the ring off my finger and dropped it into his palm. He rocked back onto his heels and let out a heavy sigh. If he was so angry about such a small and essentially worthless thing as that ring, what might he do to me later? Still, he refused to look at me. I watched as the tendons in his jaw pulsed and he chewed at his lips, his expression twisting into a grimace I'd seen when runners were approaching the finish line.

I knew that we were only getting started.

Please see me, I thought. Stop what you're doing and see that I am a human being. I'm not just some thing that you can steal with no more thought than a shoplifter.

In answer to my silent plea, he brought his hand close to my face. I flinched, thinking that he was going to strike me. I shut my eyes and gritted my teeth. Instead, I felt a slight tug at my ears, the flat of his hand briefly touching my cheek. In another context, that gesture would have been a sign of a welcome and desired intimacy and not a violation. A tear leaked from my fiercely shut eyes. It felt hot, as if I had a fever. It made me aware that I was cold and shivering.

I opened my eyes and saw him staring at my earrings, appraising them. He frowned and then shook his head.

"*Basura*," he said, and tossed my earrings over his shoulder toward the two in the front of the vehicle.

The other men laughed.

I didn't have much time to think about what he might have said. More than anything, I was shocked by the sound of the men laughing. How could they?

As bad as they all were, the man kneeling astride me was the worst. When he finally looked at me, I could see nothing in his eyes. I saw no anger. I saw no pleasure. I saw nothing, a deadness that I'd never seen before in my life. I drew my legs in close to my chest and wrapped my arms around them, buried my face in the hammock of my dress's fabric.

In the next instant, I was on my back on the vehicle's backseat. The man I'd come to think of as the Worst One stood above me. He grabbed the hem of my dress and pulled it up, thrusting his hand between my legs. I twisted away, but he bent over and leaned his weight on my hip bones, pinning me there. A flash of memory came back to me. I was in a laboratory classroom and on a tray in front of me was a frog that we were about to dissect. Its flayed skin was pinned to the cork lining of the tray.

"Take it off."

He eased some of the pressure off me, and I did a kind of sit-up as I pulled the dress over my head. Growing impatient, he grabbed the back of my bra and yanked it over my head. My arms entangled in the elastic and fabric, I couldn't maintain my balance and I fell back, the buckle of a seat belt digging into my shoulder blade. A few seconds later, he had my underwear off.

"Don't fight me. This is what you want. You like this."

Could he really believe that?

I didn't fight him. He dragged me toward him and onto his lap. I could hear him unsnap his pants and lower his zipper. I willed myself to do what I'd been doing for years as a runner—to let go of my body and ignore the signals of pain it was trying to send to my brain. As he thrust himself against me the first time, I imagined that I was in a pack of runners jostling for position, the body contact not really registering, my eyes focused on the meters of track just ahead of me, the lane lines. The crowd on the outside and the other competitors in the infield all reduced to shadows and indistinct sounds. One terrible thought passed me and overtook my vision of a clear track ahead of me—that gun. I knew that I could outrun and survive anything except a bullet.

For me, the finish line was the moment when I was going to be turned loose from these men. I was going to do whatever it took to get there.

The Worst One thrust his hand upward at me, but he couldn't penetrate me. He muttered something angrily in Spanish and tossed the gun to the man in the front seat, the one I'd heard them say was the boss. I pressed my head against the seat back in front of me. I shivered as I heard his breathing grow more rapid. Still not inside me, his anger increasing by the second, he finally shouted, "I know you know how to do this, so don't pretend you don't!"

"I'm sorry," I said. "I think it's just that I'm nervous. Please, just let me go."

I'm sorry? For being difficult to rape? It was absurd, and yet it was all I could think to say to keep me alive. I knew that I only served one purpose for him then. If he failed to get what he wanted from me, I'd be more dispensable and easier to kill.

The road noise came to a stop. The engine fell silent. I heard a door open and close, and then another. I heard the other two shuffling around, drawing nearer.

I tried not to think of what the Worst One would do to me after he succeeded. And I didn't know how to make my body respond so that he could do what he wanted to do and let me go. As much as I was trying to outrun any thoughts of my friends and family, I couldn't help but let them catch up. Only hours before I'd been studying, while on my laptop's screen a photo my best friend in Norway had sent to me just two weeks earlier sat watching over me. It was of her newborn son. I was days away from returning home to see them all. I knew that Mama's and Papa's hearts were bursting with joy, they were so eager to see me again. I couldn't do anything to ruin that for them, spoil everyone's Christmas. Kristine and I had talked endlessly about the upcoming season, how she was going to run a personal record in the fifteen hundred meters, earn all-conference. The two of us would qualify for the Olympics, hang out in London, become poster girls together.

The Worst One finally forced his way, but it didn't soften his anger at all.

"Make some sounds! Show me how much you like this," he ordered.

I did as he asked, but what he took as sounds of pleasure were actually sounds of revulsion. My stomach turned and I felt the lone beer I'd drunk rise in my throat. I worried that if I vomited on this man, I'd only make things worse for myself. I forced myself back onto the track. Unlike the way it was there, though, time had lost all meaning for me. In a race, I always knew how far I had to go, how I had to pace myself. In that cramped area with those three men, I had entered some zone where time and space had collapsed on themselves. I was there and I wasn't. Time was compressed and elongated. Nothing I had been able to count on in the past was working; all was uncertainty. In running the steeplechase, I always knew exactly where the hurdle and the water pit were; I timed my steps precisely to use my left leg to lead, my right to trail behind. I tried to focus on my breathing, the technique I used to get over that obstacle as cleanly as possible, to get my proper cadence back.

I felt a presence in the vehicle. I also heard a very faint voice telling me that I was going to be okay. I opened my eyes, but it was still just the four of us there, yet that feeling that someone else was there watching over me lingered and gave me hope.

Weakened and distracted and temporarily unable to fight against it,

I thought of Robin. His kind words of concern gripped my throat and my heart. I knew I'd done nothing wrong, that I'd been careful and yet somehow this was still happening. My reassurance to him that I could run away from any attacker felt hollow now. I wanted to kick and scream and lash out at these men, but shock and fear seized control of my limbs; my brain told me one thing, but my body didn't respond.

Robin was the first man I'd truly been in love with, and I'd somehow managed to mangle things. I quickly chased that sentiment away. He would understand, surely he would. After all, he was the man who, the summer after we first met, had arranged a surprise visit to Norway to see me. We had been using Skype to keep in contact, and we'd established a set time each day when we'd both be available. One late afternoon, I logged on and waited for the Skype ring to sound. I waited and waited, but the Skype screen sat empty. I went downstairs, and Mama told me that I just needed to be more patient. Back upstairs nearly a half hour later, I heard the doorbell ring and faint voices. I left my bedroom and walked down the stairs. Halfway I caught sight of the familiar red hat, wrapped my arms around Robin, and told him, as endearingly as I could, "You idiot."

In that moment with those three men, all I wanted was to be with Robin as far from that place as possible.

I knew that Kristine, Viktoria, and George must be out of their minds with worry. Had they called Robin? What was going through his mind just then?

"Kiss me."

Given that it was the Worst One who'd said that, given that I'd just been thinking about Robin, the contrast was too much and those words roiled my stomach once again. His request was the most invasive part of the whole thing—I had already let him take over my body, but now he wanted me to look him in the eyes and show him affection, share that intimacy with him?

I turned my head away, tried to tuck my face beneath my arm. Grabbing my hair, he yanked my head back to his. I felt the barrel of the gun being pressed to my temple. My bladder burned, and in taking a sharp inhalation of breath, I could smell and taste the man's putrid breath. I balled up my fists and wanted to strike out at the Worst One. In my moment of hesitation, he seized the opportunity and pressed his face against mine, his lips working senselessly and greedily.

The other two men laughed, and I pulled away long enough to look at them.

"Turn your head! Don't look!" the man I started to think of as the Boss said. The gun convinced me to do what I was ordered to.

Why can't I look now? Will this be my moment to die? Is he about to shoot me in the back of the head?

If they didn't speak, if they didn't make a sound, it was easier for me. I'd learned about dissociation in my Psychology class—how your mind has the ability to withdraw from a terrible place. Since I was consciously trying to do exactly that, I knew that I wasn't psychotic. I was using this as an appropriate coping mechanism. Pierre Janet. A French philosopher and psychologist. He was the one who came up with the term. I shut down that stream of thought, unwilling to consider all the ways in which something could be final.

This was something that happened in Stieg Larsson novels and to people on the news, not to me. I involuntarily saw flashes of those news clips—the photos of the women found dead after being abducted and raped. Did women ever survive this? What would it feel like when they shot me, and who would find my body?

Done with me, the Worst One pushed me away from him and pressed my head back down into the filthy floor.

"Don't you move," he spat.

As an athlete I had devoted my whole life to movement. I loved the feelings of freedom and exhilaration that running produced in me. I also felt so in control when I was running, that my speed was solely dependent on my muscles' effort and my will. What chance did effort and will stand against three men and a weapon?

"My boss is coming now, so behave," the Worst One said. "Don't even try to turn your head. Don't look at our boss. Just give him what he wants. You don't want to disappoint him."

He continued to push my head down. I heard the "boss" step out of his seat, then the jangle of a belt buckle letting me know what the Boss had planned. I couldn't believe that the man who had just raped me was using that word, saying that another man was his boss. I wondered briefly if that was how he justified in his mind what he had just done to me.

In the minutes that followed, I would find out. It wasn't as if they had a well-thought-out set of work orders to complete some job in a neat and orderly fashion. Amid much conversation among them, what sometimes sounded like squabbles and infighting, they raped and sodomized me—singly, in pairs, the three of them working together to subdue me, to break me.

With my head pushed down most of the time, I didn't know who was doing what after that first encounter. But I briefly made eye contact with the third man, the one who took the longest to join in. He looked almost sorry. Could that have been it? Was there remorse in his eyes, or was I imagining it? Was I hoping that somehow, if there was at least a tiny shred of decency among the three of them, then somehow that might redeem my faith in people? If I could hold on to that thought, then maybe this all might end with me escaping with my life?

But he laughed right along with the others, and he slapped me on the backside and joined them in their gang rape. Somehow, though, I got the sense that he was going along without wholeheartedly wanting to. How could someone be so weak to just go along with something like this? If he had any conscience whatsoever, *why didn't he stop them?*

When they spoke to one another, it was always in Spanish, so I couldn't understand a word. The Worst One did most of the talking to me. When I thought they might be done and the driver started the car again, the Worst One made it even more horrible—he wanted oral sex.

"Do it. Suck me. I know you want to. Open your mouth, but don't bite me!"

No.

I didn't think I could. I was again so on the verge of being sick that I didn't think I could physically do what he was telling me. And yet there was a gun, and this was the price of my life. What would I have done to keep my life? *Anything.* I paid for my life in horrors, in disgust. I paid with every piece of me. Through it all, though, the sense that another presence was there with me and watching me took hold. I was a Christian in the strictest sense, baptized and confirmed, though not a regular churchgoer, but it seemed to me that the presence and the voice I heard in my mind and in my heart was some otherworldly being.

The Worst One held my hair and pushed my head up and down. And when he was done, they all laughed together again. Was this the end?

"Please, can't you just let me out here?" I asked.

More talking and yelling in Spanish, with less laughter this time. With my heart in my throat, I waited for a door to open—but when it did, the Boss and the Worst One got out. The third one sat half-turned in the seat, his gun hand draped lightly over the back, all his fingers loosely spanning the grip. I briefly wondered how long it would take for him to aim and fire. Through the open door the sound of the other two relieving themselves on dry leaves reached me.

While they were gone, the third one offered me back my clothes. My dress, then my bra. Then he held up a black clog and asked, "Is this yours?"

I shook my head, barely able to contain my anger. I felt as if someone were pressing a sharp tool to each of my temples.

I had a better sense of what kind of job the Boss and the Worst One and the third one did.

I shrugged my way into my dress, and the third one sat there staring at me, stupidly holding the shoe like a salesclerk wondering if I might like it.

"That isn't my shoe. I don't want it. I don't care about my stupid shoes either. Just let me out of here!"

He lowered the clog and then it thumped to the ground. He sighed, confirming for me that he was the weakest one—not the third one any longer, but the weakest one. I wasn't afraid of him. He wouldn't do anything to me unless the others were there. But he also wouldn't disobey them; he wasn't going to let me go free until they allowed it. In some ways that made me despise him even more. I imagined the conversation they might have had earlier that evening.

"We were thinking of going out and kidnapping and raping someone. Want to join us?"

A shrug. Pursed lips. "I guess so. I don't have anything else to do."

How pathetic. Furious, I stared at him, all of me wanting to shake him and say, "How could you?"

He dropped his eyes, and I felt some small measure of victory.

That feeling didn't last.

It became clear that the other two weren't happy with him. The Worst One pointed at me and shook his head and then snatched the gun from the weakest one and used it to gesture toward the front of the vehicle. The weakest one rubbed his chin and then stood outside the car with his arms spread wide as if to say, "What did I do to deserve this?" He remained there, his slumped posture accentuating the belly that hung like a hammock.

I didn't think it was possible, but in that moment, I found him even more despicable than before. How could he believe that in any way he was the victim, he was the one who had somehow been wronged?

A moment later I was naked again. The engine started and we were moving, the Boss and the Worst One taking turns with me again.

When they were through, after they'd dressed themselves again, the Boss sat in the seat in front of me. The Worst One sat beside me. He set the gun on the seat, just within his reach.

"Where are you from?"

It took me a moment to be sure I'd heard him correctly.

"I'm not from this country. I'm not American," I told him. It seemed important not to give him anything more of myself than necessary, so I held on to my Norwegian background as a secret. I wanted to give him just enough so that he knew that I was a person; maybe that would make a difference in their decision.

"Where do you live?"

"In an apartment."

He engaged in more small talk, like we were on a date, and I replied almost automatically, revealing as little as I could, keeping my tone flat, like we were two strangers on a bus and he was interrupting my reading and I hoped that he'd get the message.

After a few minutes, he lapsed into silence.

"Please, just drop me off anywhere," I said, enunciating each word as precisely as I could, not angry, not pleading, simply speaking in as determined a manner as I could.

Even through their Spanish, I got the gist of their conversation—they

were talking about what to do with me next. The weakest one wanted
to call my friends and tell them where to find me. The other two didn't.
They were talking about Oak Cliff and then asked me if I knew where
it was.

"No," I told them. "Please, may I have my dress back?"

They kept my shoes and underwear, but the Weak One handed me
my phone and my dress again. I hadn't even put the dress over my head
when they grabbed me and covered my eyes in duct tape. I flinched at the
stuttering sound of it as they unrolled it, wrapping my head several times.

I felt the SUV come to a stop. I heard a door open; felt hands on my
back; then small stones stinging my knees. The wind and the chill air bit
at my skin. I tried to rise, but my legs refused to support me at first. I
struggled to get into something like the position a sprinter takes in the
blocks. After that I was able to stand. I wobbled and shivered, but still
afraid of what they might do to me, I didn't tear at the tape holding me
in darkness.

"We know where you live and how to find you, so don't even try to
tell the police!" the Worst One threatened. Then he slammed the door.

I took a few steps, then heard the crackle of their vehicle's tires following me. I tried to move faster, but my feet rebelled. Had the men just
been waiting until I was outside to shoot me, so there wouldn't be a mess
in the SUV?

Again, I felt hands on my back. Again, they were pushing me. I hit the
ground hard, unable to break my fall. A hand grabbed my wrist and lifted
my arm before slamming it to the pavement. I heard my cell phone clatter
and then another order.

"Run!"

I took off, blindly running. I didn't care or know in what direction I
was moving. It felt exhilarating to no longer be held in place, no longer in
that vehicle. All I wanted to do was to put time and space between those
men and me.

Doors slammed behind me again. I ran and ran as straight as I could
until I no longer heard the sounds of their car, until I felt less sure they
would come back and shoot me. I ran, and I was *alive*. The voice I'd been
hearing all along telling me that I was going to be all right had been tell-

ing me the truth. Feelings of relief welled up from my stomach and for a few moments I was no longer cold.

Several minutes passed before I felt it was safe to remove the tape. The adhesive had secured itself to my hair, and every tug at the stubborn tape felt like my scalp was being pricked with dozens of needles. I abandoned that effort and just pulled the tape below my eyes. I blinked to clear my vision.

Shaking and numb from shock and the cold, I resumed running along the side of the road, finally realizing that my dress was still in my hand. I stopped and pulled the dress over my head and made myself stand still for a moment, fighting against my body's urgent call to just keep running. I needed a plan to get myself home, but my thoughts took off in a million different directions.

How could I flag down a car? How could I trust that the men inside the car wouldn't want to rape me? How would I look to someone passing by? They'd think I was drunk or crazy, someone wandering around at that hour barefoot in a dress with no coat. Wouldn't they be frightened of me?

You have to do this, I told myself. You don't have any other choice.

Another thought stabbed at me. What would happen when people found out what had been done to me? I wondered if I would lose my scholarship and have to leave school. I loved being at SMU; I loved the life I had in Dallas, my friends, Robin. What if all that was going to be taken away? What if my parents refused to let me return to school, didn't trust any longer that I'd be safe in the U.S.? Maybe I should just get myself home, not tell anyone what had really gone on, make up a story that the men were just playing a joke on us, trying to scare the college kids.

I shivered, and it was as if my body was taking control again, letting my brain know that it needed help, that all my delaying was getting in the way of being taken care of.

I saw approaching headlights and then the outline of a car, and a lone figure silhouetted behind the wheel. I retreated deeper into the shadows farther onto the shoulder. Not with one person. Better if it was a couple. The cold was starting to really get to me. I worried that hypothermia had begun to affect my thinking process. I had to get inside somewhere.

A string of cars came toward me. I dashed to the edge of the road, screaming and waving my arms. The first car in line got within fifty meters or so, and I backed away, the sound of the frightened voice in my head drowning out the more sensible voice.

You can't trust anyone.

In the distance, a traffic signal went from green to yellow to red, its colors bleeding across the pavement toward me.

The next green light, I told myself. I repeated the same charge-and-retreat process three times. That was enough, I told myself when the image of the three men—the Worst One, the Boss, and the Weak One—appeared in my mind.

To my left stood a row of three darkened houses. From somewhere, the sound of a dog barking carried on the wind. I hoped that meant that someone else was awake at that hour, someone either coming home from or going to work. Without pausing to think, I made my way to the first house. The sound of my fist rattling against the storm door startled me. I banged again, harder this time, and stood running in place, taking tiny steps and hugging myself like a kid just out of a bath.

In my impatience, I looked along the trio of houses. From the corner of my eye, I saw a dark shape. I turned fully and saw it was a black SUV. Its tinted windows hid whoever might be inside it. Why would anyone choose to drive something like that and with those windows? They had something to hide; they did things they didn't want anyone to know about. Rapists used that kind of car.

I ran away and to the next house, where I again banged on the door. No one answered. I moved to the third house, but again, no one answered. I imagined that if I was the one inside and was startled awake by a loud noise, I would wonder if I had been dreaming, or maybe I'd be too afraid to answer. I thought it best to try each house again in the same order as before.

The ground underneath me was ice. The only way I could get warm was to run, so I set off running again, avoiding the passing cars, talking to myself the whole way.

You've come this far. You can't give your life away now out of fear.

It felt like I was playing a version of Russian roulette. The next person in a car could be my savior, or maybe he would be another man with a gun who would rape me. I wanted to see my family and friends again, and I didn't want to die out here in the cold.

More than anything, I wanted to be in Robin's arms again. I remembered how it felt when he held me, how safe I felt. I needed to feel that kind of reassurance, experience again the sense that nothing existed outside the two of us. In those moments when he enveloped me, I felt invincible. I needed to experience that again.

I knew what I had to do; I just couldn't seem to get my body to do it. I stopped running for an instant. I bent over and balled my fists and punched at my thighs as a way to get my body to respond, to break out of the numbness.

A block later, I spotted a man walking in the opposite direction on the other side of the street.

"Please help!" I called. "I need you to help me!"

He looked and said something I couldn't understand. He continued moving toward me, but then he paused and leaned against a stop sign. From the way he canted his body at a nearly obtuse angle, I could see that he was drunk. He could not help me.

"Never mind! I'm okay! Just turn around and keep going wherever you were going," I said foolishly, thinking it was best not to offend him.

He didn't listen. I ran a few paces and looked behind me. He was trailing behind me.

Now I *had* to flag down a car. Not only had I just been raped, but now I also had a drunk man following me. I couldn't afford to let my fear take over again. This time, I ran alongside the road and waved my arms and shouted loudly when a car approached. But it didn't stop.

I tried to brush it off. Another car, and I did the same thing. Again, the car passed me by. How could it be?

I had finally found my nerve, and then I lost my faith. One after another, cars drove right past me, ignoring the girl wearing nothing but a dress, with duct tape all over her face, begging for help. I will never forget the woman who looked right into my eyes without blinking and drove away, not even slowing down.

Is this what it has come to?

Nothing made sense anymore. The world was turning its back on me, and I couldn't let it. I had to do something drastic to make someone stop, so I stood right in the middle of the road. I planted myself there and waved my arms.

Instead of stopping, the cars just swerved around me.

I couldn't believe it. I wanted to cry, but the tears didn't come. Exhausted and in shock, I felt like my brain was about to shut down, when, at last, I heard a woman's voice.

"Are you okay?"

I turned and there she was, leaning her head out of her car window on the side of the road. Relief washed over me. I was going to be rescued!

"No, I need help. Can you help me? I got raped and I need help now."

She just stared at me for a few seconds and then said, "Oh. Sorry, but my car is broken down here. I need help, too. But if you keep running, there's a police station further up the road."

I didn't know whether to laugh or cry. I looked past her and saw someone slumped over the passenger seat, saw the shattered windshield, and wondered briefly what had happened to them that put them there that late at night. Those thoughts took off.

I'd been running for more than two miles. Out of energy to run, I walked right down the middle of the street with no sense of logic or sanity. I felt sure I was losing my mind. Was anything even real anymore?

All I wanted to do now was to get home. I thought to myself, No one has to find out about this. I just have to go home and go to sleep and not tell anyone, and I'll be able to forget this night. Someday. I just have to find my way home.

But then another thought made me remember why I *couldn't* stay silent about this:

The shoe.

A white van passed me. I had given up on hoping for anyone to stop, but then it turned around and came back toward me. I felt a bit of hope, right until I saw that there were three men inside. All three of them got out of the van. This couldn't be happening. They were coming to rape me!

I took off running again, continuing even as I heard a man say, "Calm down! We're going to help you." How could I trust him? Any of them?

My mind fought with itself—this could be my chance, or it could be another horror. I turned back toward the men and shouted, "I need help!"

As I did so, I kept moving away from them, keeping that good head start in case they made a move toward me. Each time they stepped toward me, I shifted back. It was as if we were opposite poles of a magnet, invisible forces directing us.

"Just stay there. We called the police and they're on their way." The man's voice was calm, matter-of-fact. I wanted to believe him. At that point I was like a wounded animal, feeling cornered. Part of me believed these men were something I could trust in; a larger part of me wanted nothing to do with them. The man who spoke held his ground, and we stood there eyeing each other. All I could see were three potential rapists.

We stood there for a few moments, all of us frozen in place. I'd begun to shiver, and I realized that more than anything in that moment I needed to pee. The scene grew more surreal when another car came flying toward us. A red-and-blue light flashed on its roof and in the headlights. The door was flung open, and a man stood in the open space with his arms locked in front of him. All I could see were those colored lights glinting off his weapon. The policeman dropped one hand, and it disappeared behind the door. A moment later he held out a badge.

I had a brief moment of clarity. Kristine and the others had to have called the police. They told the authorities about the three men. Now here I was with three men looking like they were confronting me. I had to make it clear what was going on.

"No! No! They're helping me."

Before the officer could respond, the sound of tires squealing added to the chaos. The three men were all trying to say something, offer some explanation, but another voice rose above theirs.

"You need any help, Officer?"

I sank down again and rested my hands on my knees. I don't know how many seconds lapsed, but as I rested there, my chest heaving, my heart racing, and my mind overloaded, I felt like I'd crossed the finish line at the end of a race completely spent. Except race officials and my coaches were rushing toward me telling me that I had to get back out there. I still had another lap to go.

That impression was broken by the sound of another voice.

"I'm a police officer, ma'am, and I'm here to help," it said.

"I don't believe you. I don't know who you are," I said. "I want to speak to a *woman*. Stay away."

Still looking at the ground, I saw a shaft of light twitch to my right and then move off. I looked up and followed the spotlight up to a circling helicopter. The distant whup of its rotors was soon joined by sirens and more flashing lights.

For the first time, I began to cry. I looked up; above the helicopter, a sliver of moon and a few stars lightened the night sky. Through my tears the lights flickered and brightened. Shoulders quaking, I let my arms dangle at my side, felt the tension leaching from my body with each heaving sob.

This wasn't the night I was supposed to die.

"I'm Officer Shivers. James Shivers. You're safe now."

I nodded dumbly. Another man approached, holding out a coat to me. I nodded again, and he draped the coat around my shoulders. He stepped back and just stood there while I nestled inside it.

"Thank you."

I looked up at him, and he met my eyes briefly and nodded.

"No need for that." I could tell that he was struggling to figure out what to say. "My pleasure" or even just a simple "You're welcome" somehow wouldn't have seemed right.

Officer Shivers led me toward the police car. There, another policeman, this one dressed in a uniform, approached.

I eyed him suspiciously.

"We'd like to ask you some questions about what happened. Why don't you take a seat?"

He gestured toward the car. I saw the mesh grillwork that separated the sets of seats, the guns in the passenger seat.

I pursed my lips and shook my head.

"No. Not in there."

I saw another officer whisper in the ear of the man who had spoken to me.

"I understand. It's cold out here. We want you to be comfortable. I'm sure you want to help us find these men. We need your help to do that."

I considered that for a moment and took a tentative step toward the car. With each step it was if my adrenal glands went further into action. I felt my pulse quicken, the lobes of my ears grow warm; my vision sharpened, and all I could see were the weapons the officers wore.

Eventually, I was able to take control of my mind and my body. I allowed a paramedic to examine me. I reached up and felt the tape in my hair. I looked at him pleadingly, but he shook his head and gestured toward where the police were standing. I was going to have to stay exactly as I had been for the last two hours for a while longer. My face felt numb and swollen, and I heard a high-pitched hollow ringing in my ears.

When the man's gloved hand touched my chin and my cheek to tilt my head back, I flinched and shut my eye against the light he shined into it.

"Sorry," he said. Again, as with the second officer, something about his tone and his demeanor let me know he thought that his choice of words was inadequate. "I think we'll leave the tape on for a while. I'd hate to mess your hair up."

He tilted his head toward me, moved it from side to side. He spent the rest of his time examining my head, shining a light in my eyes, asking me to follow the beam from side to side. I had to answer questions about my name, the date, where and when I was born. I kept telling them that I was fine. All the time I was thinking that I wanted to go back to where the men had dropped me off—the area hadn't been familiar to me, and if we waited too long to return there, I'd forget how to reach it.

"We just want to be sure that you're not hurt," one of the paramedics told me. That was obvious enough, and I asked to be allowed to speak to someone in charge.

Finally, one of the uniformed police officers came over, and I pleaded with him to let me take them back to the site. Now, mostly assured that these people were here to help me, I climbed into the back of the police car. I guided them to the intersection of Barry Avenue and Upshur Street, close to where I'd been dropped off. As we drove there, they asked me a few questions about what the men looked like, and I did the best I could to answer. They asked me about my cell phone, and I told them that after I'd been pushed out of the van one of them came after me to take it away.

My head was spinning at that point, and I only wondered briefly why my cell phone mattered to the police. I knew it mattered to me. The idea of those men having access to me and to my friends and family soured my stomach. I felt like I did after a hot summer workout, as if my head were floating above my body, unconnected to what it was experiencing. I recognized that I was feeling dehydrated—it had been hours since I'd had anything to drink. I sat in the car while the policemen were busy. They next drove me past the house where the party had been. I didn't want to look up to see if the lights were still on, if the partygoers were still at it. The contrast between then and now felt too severe.

We drove on to the hospital. I sat in the backseat and watched as the lights of other cars and the passing buildings flickered by. After a few minutes, the sound of the police radio turned into white noise, no different from the sound of the wind rushing past the window I leaned my head against, the thrum of the tires. I felt a strange calm come over me at that point. I saw myself as if looking down from above—a small blond girl in an oversized coat and a rumpled dress, barefoot and shivering. Yet she was smiling. I knew why. She'd made it. I'd made it. The images that had flickered now seemed to have slowed. I was bathed in light for longer and longer periods of time. I could see that my face was slightly swollen and bruises colored my otherwise pale skin. Still, the face was mine, recognizable to me.

I didn't have a choice about what had been done to me, but I could choose what happened next. I hadn't been killed. I couldn't begin to formulate an idea of what would happen next, but I was alive. Whether I lived or died had briefly and frighteningly been out of my hands. Now I was once again in control, and I loved how that felt.

CHAPTER THREE

Tomorrow

Those good feelings lasted as long as it took me to walk from the ambulance and into the emergency room of the Parkland Memorial Hospital. Two policemen escorted me down a dimly lit hallway. A few chairs sat in rows facing a television set that dangled from the ceiling. The screen's illumination puddled on the worn floor. Even at that hour, several people sat in the waiting room. Their eyes grew wide at the sight of me. I tried to turn my back to them. I smelled something sharp and ammonia-like, and it stirred in me some distant and indistinct memory. I couldn't identify the source of that new anxiety. I'd always had good doctors back at home and had little fear of needles or anything like that.

A lone woman sat behind a high counter. She looked at me briefly before turning away. She slid a clipboard to me across the counter. A pen slithered along with it, then leaped over the edge, held in midair by its tiny ball chain.

"Fill these out. Make sure you check both sides. Sign here and here." She slashed an X on each of the pages.

The pen swung back and forth. I clumsily grabbed at it, my muscles still numb from the cold and exhausted by my exertions and sleep deprivation.

One of the officers led me through a set of swinging doors and into a long hallway. A pair of chairs sat side by side. I pulled the coat as tight around me as possible and set the clipboard in my lap. I wondered if something was wrong with my eyes. The printing on the pages was blurred. I realized then that my legs were twitching involuntarily. I watched almost fascinated as my quadriceps rippled like tiny waves.

The patient intake form asked for the usual information. Name. Address. Phone number. I knew the answers, but I felt like I was trying to write them down with the handle of a broom. I could barely sense the feel of the pen against my skin, and I watched as its top spun and staggered while I scrawled my answers in a script that was unfamiliar to my own eyes.

Then I reached the question asking the reason for my visit to the ER, and it was as if no language I spoke could help me. Somehow, writing down the word "rape" made everything that I'd fought so hard to that point to survive inescapable, permanent. I don't know if it would have been any easier to speak that word to someone else than to write it down, or if it was just my frozen clumsiness, but of all the words I had to write, that one came out the least legible.

I stopped looking at the forms to ask what I'd asked of the police. "Can you please call my friends? I need to see them."

The officer who'd been with me had been replaced by a man in plainclothes, a detective.

"Not just yet. We'll get them here. They have some work to do, too."

I wondered at that; what work would they be doing? And was what I was doing now some kind of work as well? Was that all this was for everyone, some kind of job?

I took a deep breath to compose myself. I did, in fact, have a job to do. I had to get this form filled out. Then, I hoped, I would be taken to some place where I could warm myself and clean myself up. Along with wanting to see my friends again, I was overwhelmed by the desire to brush my teeth. The thought of having that man in my mouth sickened me.

I leaned over to rest my elbows on my thighs and tackle the rest of the questions. I looked past the form and saw my feet. They weren't quite as bone-pale as the rest of me; they had become splotched with red, as if because I had developed some kind of rash and not just because my blood was only now able to leave my core to heat my limbs. As I finished the forms, I could feel the pinprick sensation of my fingers and toes thawing. The familiar sensations reminded me of home.

I had to push that thought away. I didn't want to think of my parents. I glanced at the clock. It was four in the morning here. That meant that my parents were about halfway through their workdays. I tried to picture them, my mother at her desk reviewing papers, with a cup of black coffee beside her; my mechanical engineer father sitting in front of a machine, squinting as he diagnosed a problem. My father was one of the handiest men I knew, whether it was one of our cars, an appliance at home—he could fix anything. I used to think that he could speak to machines, get them to tell him what ailed them. I wondered if how I was now broken was something he could sense and help with.

"Did you notice any distinguishing scars or marks on the man—" The detective stopped. I thought maybe he recognized my look of frustration. I didn't want to answer any questions at that point. I wanted someone to be with me and comfort me.

I was wrong. The detective looked at his notebook and continued, ". . . the man you called 'the Boss.'"

"They called him the Boss."

"The Boss, then. Anything striking about him."

It took me a moment to fully understand what he meant by "striking."

I sat with my elbow on the chair's armrest and closed my eyes trying to picture the Boss; instead all I could do was feel the frozen tips of my fingers against my temple, how my hand shook and vibrated my skull.

"I didn't really see him. The other two kept telling me not to look at him."

This pattern continued. I tried to fill out the forms, wondering what I could possibly put in place of a Social Security number. How could I explain in that little blank that I wasn't from the U.S., didn't have that number, and had now lost whatever sense of security I might have once possessed. I also didn't have my phone. I'd never been good with memorizing people's phone numbers. I always relied on my phone for that. Even now, if I wanted to call Kristine or Viktoria or George, I wouldn't be able to. I gave the police their full names and hoped that they could get the numbers.

I needed someone's assurance that I was safe, that I was going to be okay, that someone understood at least a little bit what I was going through.

I'd just finished the paperwork and handed it to an officer when I heard a woman's voice. "Are you cold?"

I looked up. A woman in a blue nurse's uniform stood in front of me. Her eyes were kind and framed by blond hair the color of my own. She didn't smile at me, but her expression revealed her concern.

My lip quivered and I tried to speak, but I couldn't get the words out. Instead I just dropped my eyes to my lap and sat there with my fingers working as if they could form the words my mouth could not.

"How about if I get you a blanket?"

"Please. Yes," I said, watching as she strode away from me, alternately brightening and dimming as she passed beneath the fluorescent light fixtures. I sat in silence, the hum of the bulbs above me a raspy static.

The woman reappeared. Instead of just handing the blankets to me—she'd brought two—she held them spread open to me. Like a small child stepping out of the bath into her mother's swaddling arms, I stepped into the blankets and the woman's embrace. She closed her arms around me, and the two of us stood there entangled in something that we both understood was needed, if we hadn't said exactly why.

I started to cry then, sobbing spasms that tore at my throat, tears of sadness, gratitude, and fear. Her arms stayed wrapped around me, offering me the first real bit of comfort I'd experienced since the man had offered me his coat. Then I experienced a moment of panic.

"This coat," I said. The woman released me and I stepped back. "How will I get it back to him?"

Confusion flickered briefly across her face.

"I'm sure it's fine," she said. She lifted the edge of the blankets like a bride's train so that I could sit again. I brought my feet up onto the chair and sat hugging my legs, trying to restore some warmth and feeling.

"It's not mine. The jacket—" I managed to speak those words calmly, but then it was as if I were back in that SUV going through it all again. Words and tears came out of me in a torrent. I had no idea if I was making sense. It was as if I was vomiting up the entire experience, trying to purge myself of any of its foul poisons. The nurse sat with me, alternately holding my hand and leaning in to squeeze my shoulders. In the absence of my friends, this woman helped me hold myself together until they could arrive. I thought again of Robin and so desperately wanted to be in touch with him; that pain was worse than any physical discomfort I experienced.

The nurse, whose name I forgot almost as soon as she told me, listened until I had calmed myself again. My breathing returned to normal and my crying stopped.

"Listen, Monika, you're going to be all right." She held my hand and knelt in front of me, nodding, her eyes locked on mine. "I know it. I can see how strong you are. I have other patients that I have to see. But I'll be back." I knew it was my mind playing tricks on my body, but as soon as she left, shivers again overtook me.

I sat there wondering what was next. All I wanted to do was to see my friends and go home.

I looked at the clock. It was now 4:30. I asked the detectives again if I could call Robin. The two of them looked at each other, and the older one, a bald man with Vandyke facial hair, finally nodded his approval. He handed me his phone and I dialed the number, anticipation rising from my belly to my head. All I heard was the ringing on the other end. A dozen possibilities of where he might be ran through my head. Robin could be a very sound sleeper. I knew he'd been exhausted from studying so much. I shut my eyes and pictured him in his room, sleeping, as he did, sprawled across it, one arm tucked beneath his chest. In my mind, I was there with him, nudging him gently, watching as his eyelids fluttered and then opened, his expression a mix of surprise and pleasure, a smile spreading across his lips like curtains parting. Early-morning sunlight sliced through the blinds and the smell of coffee warmed the room.

I let the phone ring and ring but left no message. How awful would it be for him to hear a disembodied voice saying those words, asking for help, letting him know the hours of agony he'd not been there for?

Someone from the hospital, another person in quiet shoes and what seemed to me to be pajamas and a robe, stepped around the corner, and my vision of Robin disappeared. The person indicated that we should follow. I shuffled along in my blanket cocoon. The room the person led us to was windowless and cramped. A chair and an examination table sat opposite each other. A basin and a small cabinet lined another wall. That same ammonia-like smell I'd sensed when I first came into the hospital reached my nostrils. I sat in the chair, trying not to look at the table.

Two men, strangers to me, resumed asking me questions about what the three men had done to me, their voices indifferent, clinical, asking me where and how and how many times. They used textbook words and the tone I'd imagine someone taking inventory at a clothing store might use to come up with a tally. I just wanted the voices to stop, so I answered the questions, though it seemed to me that I'd already told them everything so many times before. A lengthy pause was filled by the sound of footsteps, more than one person, talking and then a quick laugh. A moment later, a doctor stepped into the room.

She introduced herself, but it was just syllables and sounds to me. She began an explanation of what she was going to be doing with me. She pointed to the examination bed and said that I could lie down. I did, wrapping myself up in a blanket, finally feeling some warmth. She'd only just started when a knock at the door stopped her. Another investigator sidestepped into the room. He held a camera out. I shed the blankets and stood as he took photographs of me from various angles, stepping toward and away from me, standing, squatting. The flashes jabbed at my eyes, and I flinched each time.

It seemed as if he paid particular attention to the duct tape that still clung to my neck and hair. I felt as if I was a package that had arrived damaged, partially torn open, and visual evidence was necessary to be granted a refund of some kind.

When he was done, the woman picked up where she had left off. Finally she asked me, "May I begin the examination now?"

I shrugged. I wasn't sure just what was required of me or what she was stating was going to happen to me.

Her eyes flickered from mine to the one detective who remained in the room.

"Even if you choose not to prosecute, to go forward, it is a good idea to have evidence collected. I'll also be examining you to see if you've sustained any injuries. Do you understand?"

I told her yes. I couldn't have guessed how thoroughly I was going to be probed.

I stood on a section of examination table paper and awaited further instructions. After removing my dress, I was asked to place it in a paper bag. I was told that would avoid contamination. I knew what the word meant but didn't fully grasp how it applied in this case. I hadn't thought at all about potentially being exposed to disease. I was so out of it, I wasn't even thinking clearly about it being used as evidence.

Once I was outfitted with a paper gown, the general examination began. The woman's voice led me through the process, but I wasn't hearing much or even feeling much at all as she checked each of my limbs. She startled me a bit when her face popped up in front of mine and I watched her gaze narrow as she stared at my mouth and face. I flinched when she asked me to spread my thighs and shined a light there. She swabbed across my genitals and anus with some liquid that had me back shivering from cold or fear or both.

I tried to picture myself back home, running through the woods, the smell of pine and grass and the feel of sunshine on my face. Every time I was just about there, something invaded—the tug of a comb through my pubic hair, the speculum inserted into me, questions asked about ejaculation, terms like "motility" and "staining."

When I sensed that she was just about through with me, I finally said what was most on my mind at that point: "I need to take a shower. Please, can I take a shower?" I felt so dirty. My skin crawled with the feeling of the sweat and smells and fluids of these men all over me. It was a deep disgust that I was desperate to rid myself of. They were still *on me*.

"Not yet," the examiner said. "There's still more testing to do. You can take a shower when you get home."

"Please," I begged, clasping my hands together. "I feel so sick."

"It won't be too long," she said.

"Can't you get one of my friends here to sit with me?"

She referred me to the policemen in the hallway, who again told me that my friends had to stay at the police station for now, and that they had tried to call Robin but couldn't get through.

"Then call one of my other friends!" I said. "Call someone else from my school. I want someone I trust here with me."

"It's the middle of the night—"

"Someone will answer."

I had no idea how loud or shrill my voice was. It was as if my emotions were like little children running around the room, occasionally and randomly making contact with the others and me.

As angry as I was with the police for not meeting my request, I was frustrated with myself for not having those numbers memorized. In Norway, phone numbers have eight digits paired in four groups of two. The ten digits and the three-three-four grouping in the United States made no sense to me. Keeping contact information stored in my phone gave me one less thing to have to worry about. Now I was lying on my back staring up at the ceiling, clusters of digits floating around me, and me unable to grab them and put them in their proper order. I blamed myself for not having adapted better, but learning the language was hard enough.

The university's offices were still all closed, Robin was asleep, my friends were still at the police station answering questions, and I was lying there in a thin hospital gown—the paper one had been exchanged for a faded cloth one—feeling as much like a prisoner as I was a victim. I couldn't stop shaking. I wasn't allowed to leave, not allowed to wash off, not allowed to make a phone call, forced to fill out an endless array of paperwork that I didn't understand, forced to wait around in a cold room for hours so I could be poked and prodded and questioned some more. I couldn't stop shaking.

When the doctors stepped out and left me alone in the room, I heard several of the policemen in the hallway laughing. At first I was furious, wondering how anyone in that circumstance could find anything funny at all. Logically, I knew that these men were doing their jobs, that they were at work, but still I felt my cheeks and ears burning with anger. I told myself that that response wasn't going to do me any good. Instead, I had to use that anger to get through this thing. I needed focus and energy, and being upset was something I could use to my advantage. I'd been in shock for hours, if not physically then at least emotionally. I took it as a good sign that something had awakened me from that state.

Eventually, someone from the Physical Evidence Unit came to "collect" the duct tape from my hair. I'm normally not particularly vain, but at that point, with every other humiliation and frustration that I'd suffered, each snip of the scissors and the sound of my hair being placed in a plastic bag nearly made me lose my composure completely. I gritted my teeth and shut my eyes while my legs twitched and bounced, wanting to carry me away. I had to remind myself that in the end, this was all going to be worth it. I'd be able to go back to doing what I loved, running and competing, hanging out with my friends, being a part of the team. This was like a workout. Painful but necessary. All part of attaining a larger goal. I had to dig deep. Digging. That's what we'd always been told, finding something inside ourselves the extent of which maybe we didn't even know existed. I'd been doing that my whole life.

Sitting there, watching a small vial fill up with blood, I wondered what else was going to be taken from me that night. I couldn't stop now. I had to tap into who I was at my core, keep my eyes fixed on those points near and far. That's how I was raised.

In Norway, kids grow up with outdoor sports almost from birth. Parents pull their kids in sleds until they can walk, and once their balance develops sufficiently, the toddlers are fitted with skis right away. My older sister became a runner, soccer player, and cross-country skier in her youth. I followed in her footsteps. As we got older, Anette came to love yoga and meditation and singing and dancing, and focused more of her attention on those activities while I became even more dedicated to the pursuit of medals, ribbons, and lower and lower times in races. Skiing was my main sport. I loved being able to propel myself at great speed, leg kicks and arm thrusts overcoming the snow's friction, its seeming desire to hold me back.

I started running at the age of fifteen, and I didn't like it at first. I felt clumsy and awkward, missed the sensation of a single glide eating up meters of distance. I competed in races over the summer just as a way to train and stay in shape for ski season, but I soon fell in love with running for its own sake. Before long, I was competing in both about equally.

My coaches had suggested that it was time to choose one or the other, but that didn't make it easier. I loved both. My high school in Norway was a special school for students who hoped to become professional athletes. We studied all the basic academic subjects, but with a sports angle wherever possible, and with plenty of time during the day to train in our respective sports and to learn more about *how* to train. Because I hoped to make the Olympic team one day, I took my sport very seriously. I was accustomed to running in the mountains or through the woods on nature trails. That's how it was at home; people didn't run along sidewalks or in the streets, alongside cars. Part of the joy was the feeling of communing with nature.

One day in 2008, as I walked in the door after riding home from school on my scooter, my mother came running over, talking so quickly that I couldn't get a grip on what she was saying. Someone had called and it was something about running—that much I got, but the rest of it was just high-pitched, excited chirps.

"Slow down, Mom," I said. I took off my coat and asked her to explain it again.

"Magne called."

I recognized the name immediately. Magne trained many elite runners in Norway, including Silje Fjørtoft. I'd idolized Silje for a while now. She was one of the top female runners in the country, and I'd followed her career closely. Her times were always improving, and I knew that some of her success had to do with having Magne as her coach.

"He just got back from Dallas," my mother said, her smile widening, "He was visiting Silje, and he said she's having such a good time at Southern Methodist University. Well, they've been talking all about you at the school, following your race results on the Internet, and they want to offer you a scholarship!"

My mother looked at me mischievously, and I stood there staring back at her blankly.

I hadn't really considered going to the U.S. on a scholarship before. I knew that Silje had moved to Dallas, but I didn't really understand that she was there to run and had her tuition paid for. In Norway, no college athletic programs or athletic scholarships existed. The only way for me to continue running in my college years was through a club team, separate from the university. I had already applied to a university in Oslo as a Physical Therapy major, something that would be an extension of my life as an athlete. But this opportunity in Dallas would mean that I could study *and* run, with all of my costs covered. I didn't have any doubts—it was the chance of a lifetime, and I wouldn't let it pass me by.

After the first phone call with the coaches at SMU, I looked up the school's website. I regretted not studying my English more diligently, but the photos on the site told me all that I needed to know. I saw a mix of old and new architecture, some buildings that looked like they could have been the capitol, their columns and façades reminding me of the National Theatre or the university in Oslo. I loved winter and I knew that Dallas was in Texas, in the southern part of the country and that it would be warm, but I'd always have snow and home.

What made me absolutely certain I wanted to go were the photos of the athletic facilities there—the amazing track, the enormous weight rooms, trails to run on at White Rock Lake.

A few doubts crept in. I knew I was a good runner and I had placed well in competitions, but I was not yet elite. I called back Magne and kept him on the phone for about an hour, just making sure that this was all real and that he wasn't confusing me with a different runner. I could hear the laughter in Magne's voice as he tried to assure me. We went on talking, and like the barrier I'd jump in the steeplechase, the conversation changed each time I asked again and again, "Really? You're sure?" My parents had told me my whole life that hard work paid off. It wasn't that I didn't believe them, but I couldn't believe that it could pay off in such a huge way.

Dave Wollman, the head coach of SMU's track-and-field team, called a few days later to confirm the offer. It would be the same scholarship that Silje had gotten: 100 percent tuition coverage for all four years. I could barely contain my excitement. Me? Little Monika from Løten, Norway? Were they sure they had the right person? They'd had good experiences with other Norwegian runners and they wanted to "invest" in me, he said. Like most Americans, he was adept at using big words and fancy phrases that I didn't yet understand. When I did open my mouth, I was tongue-tied—both from joy and because of my broken English. I have no idea what Dave thought of me on that first phone call; I imagine he was thinking that I might be a good runner, but not the smartest young woman ever to attend the school. I had no way to respond when he told me that he was glad that I was going to be a Mustang, other than to say, "Yes. You also."

I trained even harder in preparation and had the best season ever that summer. I competed in the European Cup, the Norwegian Championships, and the Junior World Championships, and that was a very big deal for me. In the Norwegian Championships I even earned a medal. I tried not to think about how much I would miss Anette and my mother and father. I was going to be able to do something that I loved, but I wasn't sure what it would be like to be so far away from those I loved. I told myself that in a way you had to be selfish to be successful as a runner.

In mid-August, I had a farewell party with my friends, and then, on the last day before I left, I just wanted to be with my family. It had suddenly become real that I was about to fly to another country; I wouldn't be able to come home on weekends whenever I wanted.

It's just for one year, I told myself. That's all you're committing to. Then, after the year is over, you can decide if you want to stay.

As the day of my departure neared, I grew more anxious about my clothes. Everything I knew about the U.S. I'd gotten from watching television and the movies and reading on the Internet. In some ways, I felt like the young woman from *Gilmore Girls*, one of my favorite TV shows. Rory was a small-town girl like me, and she wound up going to Yale, meeting all kinds of people from backgrounds far removed from her own. Except she had very wealthy grandparents, so she never seemed to have to worry about how her sense of fashion would help her fit in with everyone else. I didn't have any clothes with fancy labels or logos, unless you counted my mountain gear from Bergans of Norway.

My mother tried to reassure me. "Oh, Monika. You'll be fine," she'd say and hug me. "Wear your new gold Nike running shoes. They're unique and will make you stand out."

Standing out wasn't what I wanted to do at all, but it was hard to explain all of that to her. Still, I packed them along with the rest of my things and hoped for the best. I was so anxious and excited the night before I left that adrenaline kept me up late. I lay in bed and flipped through a photo book that Anette had given me a few days earlier, before she and her boyfriend Jonas had returned to Trondheim. The pictures were of the two of us, from the time we were very young until just days before. In most of them we were smiling and acting goofy, huge smiles plastered on our faces. She wrote about how much she appreciated who I was and what I'd meant to her all these years. That she admired me for taking this chance meant the most to me, and I would miss Anette the most. Before I fell asleep, I tucked the book into my carry-on bag. I knew that I would want it with me on the flight over.

We all did our usual best and avoided crying as we said our good-byes at the airport. Hours later, in the air somewhere over the North Atlantic, Greenland came into view, a white expanse against all that blue. I was flying with Silje and had so many questions that I wanted to ask her, but I really couldn't bring myself to ask them. It all seemed so silly, so childlike, to wonder about clothes and food, about whether or not to raise your hand in a class, how to dial a phone number back home to someone in Norway. I sat there listening to Pink's song "Stupid Girls" and vowed that I wasn't going to let the experience change me. I was going to be myself, something that my parents had always encouraged me to do, and trust that I would be okay.

The only thing I really asked Silje to do for me was to help me pronounce the English word for the track event I was going to specialize in.

With my headphones back on and the eastern U.S. below me, I kept whispering, "I am here to run the steeplechase" over and over again.

The track coach sent along one of my new teammates to pick us up from the airport. As we drove away, I was amazed by the streams of cars traveling in both directions, the tall buildings, and the absence of ranches and cows. Our driver was dressed in shorts and a T-shirt and what seemed like winter boots—fur-lined and clunky. I thought I'd be able to fit in, though I didn't think that kind of footwear was for me. I couldn't believe that the campus was more like a city than I'd imagined, and when I saw other students climbing out of what seemed to me to be incredibly expensive cars, I was shocked to see that no one was dropping them off—those were *their* cars. They were college kids and they had cars.

When I got to my room, I took out Anette's book, put it on my desk like it was framed, hung up a Norwegian flag, and tried to make the other photos I had of family and friends cover as much of the rest of the space as possible. As more and more students arrived, I saw just how little I had been able to squeeze into that single suitcase. Students had television sets, microwaves, and they decorated their rooms to look like smaller versions of what their homes must have been like. Mine looked like what it was: a small and modest place where a young woman was staying temporarily until she figured out if she fit in and if the reality matched her expectations.

I COULDN'T HELP but think of the hospital room I was in now in connection with my first dormitory space. They were both relatively drab and confining. The language barrier prevented me from being able to communicate what I needed, and standing out as being so different from everyone else, on top of trying to figure out what they were saying to me, as well as to one another, was difficult.

At the conclusion of my exam, the doctor said I could get changed—but I had nothing to change into. My dress had been seized as evidence, and I didn't even have underwear or shoes to put on.

What am I going to do? Walk out of here in my hospital gown?

I added that to my list of unasked questions.

I couldn't be sure if I had fallen asleep during my exam, but there was another man in the room. Short and dark-skinned, he spoke with an accent that I couldn't identify. He flipped through a series of papers and looked at me, his eyes seemingly sliced in half by a pair of frameless lenses. I had the sense that he was picking up mid-sentence when he said, ". . . liver function normal."

He paused and then focused on something on his pant leg. He scowled at it and then stood and went to the basin. He ran some water and dabbed at his pants.

When he approached me again, he took a pad out of the pocket of his lab coat. "Levonorgestrel. Point seven five milligrams twice twelve hours apart. Wait no more than three days."

He went on, but the only words that I paid real attention to were "emergency" and "contraceptive."

He paused and cocked his head to one side. At that angle, the ceiling lights reflected off his glasses, the glare hiding his eyes.

"You understand?" He followed that up with something that sounded like "Marnafta."

My heart skipped a beat when he said something about a failure rate. Before I could ask him to repeat himself, he was scribbling another note, and I very clearly heard him say the letters "HIV." I vaguely recalled filling out a consent form. It seemed that the good news was that their initial test showed that I was HIV negative, but that I'd still need to take an antiviral medication for quite a while and be periodically retested. I couldn't remember if he'd said that the chances of contracting the disease were 10 to 15 percent or that I'd need to take the drugs for 10 to 15 weeks. The doctor asked me if I had any questions, and I just shook my head. He handed me the second slip of paper and left.

I lay there on the bed, my mind racing, with images of that night flashing through it. I kept seeing the gun and that other woman's shoe. The sound and the smell of the duct tape, the horrifying thought that they were going to tape my nose and mouth shut so that I wouldn't be able to breathe. I had never thought before about how I might die. I'd never had any close calls that I knew of, except for those times when a car crosses the yellow line and then gets back in place a moment before you nearly collide.

I'd heard a professor say once that in the strictest sense there was no such thing as an accident, that even if you hadn't intended to be in an intersection when another car came through a signal and hit you, you'd made all kinds of choices that day that put you in that place at that exactly wrong instant. Maybe you left something in the house before you got in your car and that delay put you there. Maybe if you'd brushed your teeth for just two seconds longer and delayed your departure, that car might have gone through without hitting you. Maybe if you'd stayed at a party longer, had decided to leave sooner, hadn't gone at all . . .

I didn't like thinking that way, about whether choices I'd made had led me to that moment when the men grabbed me. I knew that in comparison to Norway, the United States had a higher crime rate, that violence with guns was more prevalent, but that didn't happen at SMU. We lived in a nice place. We were told to be careful—Robin and I had just talked about it— but who ever thought about such a thing really happening? I can't say that I had the clichéd thought that this was all a dream and I'd wake up from it. I never had bad dreams, at least none that I remembered. Maybe there had been a time when I did dream of being alone in a hospital room, but I didn't think so. But for a class, I'd read a bit about dreams, how the brain took bits and pieces of our daily lives, things we weren't really conscious of, and put them together in ways that sometimes made clear sense and other times didn't. There was a randomness to them, and as I lay there that's what I thought about what had happened to me. This wasn't something I could have predicted or prevented, and if I played the what-if game too much, and thought that how long I brushed my teeth had such dire consequences, I'd likely become paralyzed with fear, the brush so weighted with possibilities and problems that I couldn't even lift it to my mouth.

I knew that I had to gain control of my mind; with nothing to do but lie there, I had to focus on something else besides my desire to go home. Every time someone came in, one of the policemen, or someone from the hospital staff, the good nurse who checked on me a few more times— they all said the same thing. I was so sick of being told "not yet" that I never wanted to hear those words again in my life.

The clock, a large round-faced one like the ones in some of the class-rooms at SMU, seemed frozen. Occasionally the hands would thaw and twitch ahead a few minutes. At 7 a.m. I heard loud footsteps in the hall. Those weren't the soft-soled sounds of anyone from the hospital. Those had to be high heels, and only someone who'd been out late the night before would still be wearing them. I slid off the table and ran to the door. Just as I was reaching for the handle, the door opened and Kristine, Viktoria, and George all rushed in. I only got a quick glimpse of Kristine's face before she smothered me in a hug. She looked like hell, pale and drawn, her eyeliner and mascara smeared.

Kristine squeezed me tighter and her sobs shook me. My face was pressed against her wool coat and I could feel my own hot breath steaming against my face. I began to feel faint, but I didn't care.

"I'm so sorry. I'm so sorry!" Kristine and I both said to each other. I knew that she was in agony after having the gun pointed at her and having to let go of me. I wished that I could take that pain from her.

"I didn't think I would ever see you again," she said, her voice going from a hoarse rasp to a whisper, "I didn't think I would ever see you again," over and over, looking into my eyes and holding me as if to prove to herself that I was real.

I looked at Viktoria, who had tears streaming down her face. Emotionally, she was the strongest among the three of us; this was the first time I'd ever seen her cry. How I wanted to be back at our apartment having one of our tea nights, enjoying one of her signature chai-and-soy-milk specialties, the three of us with Robin and our Spanish friend, David, all laughing and sharing jokes, telling stories about home, puzzling over the peculiarities of America and its residents. Those evenings together had made life more than simply bearable; they'd made it enjoyable.

I wanted to hear what they'd all been through, to find out if they'd been in touch with Robin, but more than anything I just wanted to get away from that place.

I looked at George and lost my composure again. I didn't have a big brother, but there'd been boys and young men like him in my life before. I knew that he prided himself on how he took care of us. I knew that he'd feel like he'd somehow failed in his duty to protect me. All that was written on his face and more. He could barely make eye contact with me. I knew it had nothing to do with shame or embarrassment or anything that had to do with the sexual nature of the assault. He was hurting because I was hurting, because he'd just spent hours with Kristine and Viktoria, all of them in a complete state of fear and panic. George was the one who wanted to make things all right, to be of assistance in some way, like he'd been for the months since we'd first met. It was as if in the few seconds we looked at each other his face dissolved and recomposed itself into a half dozen different emotional states.

Watching his Adam's apple bob up and down and his shoulders heave into a sigh was more eloquent than any words he could have managed.

"Let me get you home," he finally said, and then his tears came.

In a sense, we were all grieving in those moments, all of us wishing that there was some script that we could turn to, to tell us what to say, how to feel, how to act. I wanted to let them all know that I didn't expect anything from them but to just be there. That was enough. Their support and their signs of grieving were enough. I had no stopwatch to time it; there were no qualifying standards that they had to meet. Their compassion wasn't some emotional gymnastics exercise that they'd have to perform and I'd have to score, assigning a degree of difficulty and execution points. That they were there, that they'd been going through their own version of a painful assault, was enough. We were united in that.

Eventually, the words came easier, too easy, and we all began talking over one another's sentences. A police officer came into the room. We all stopped and looked at him. "Look over this stuff tomorrow," he told us. "It's information about where you can get help."

He held up a large manila envelope. Viktoria reached for it and peered inside. She took out a few pamphlets and brochures.

"Tomorrow," she declared, tucking the envelope under her arm.

I smiled at her gratefully, thinking of the times when I was studying and she'd taken a textbook or a notebook away from me and said that very same word. A warm feeling of appreciation spread over me. I'd so desperately wanted my friends to be there with me throughout my time at the hospital. My mind had been racing, trying to take in not just what I'd been through but all the information the medical people were throwing at me. I kept telling myself that I needed to remember this, and then the reminder to remember seemed to displace the fact that I wanted to be able to recall. I needed to slow things down, but I couldn't. I knew that there were things I needed to do; I was distracted by an overwhelming desire—to be held and comforted and cared for by Robin or one of my friends, to feel, even if just for an instant, that I was safe.

I have all the help I need now, I thought. We'd all come to rely on one another for support through all the ups and downs of our new lives in an unfamiliar environment. Though we had different backgrounds, we'd bonded in a way that felt like we'd become a little family. When tragedy struck, that's who you wanted to be with, not with professional people who were there to treat you, but with friends who wanted to comfort you.

While my friends were all there, the kindhearted nurse who had originally spotted me in the hall poked her head into the room. She was holding a folded stack of clothes on which sat a pair of shoes.

"These are extras I keep in my locker," she said. She must have realized that I didn't have any clothes to wear home.

Then she handed me a garbage bag.

"When you're home, you can change into your own clothes, and then just throw these away. You shouldn't keep anything around that reminds you of this night."

I hugged her and thanked her.

I went to the restroom next door to get dressed. I pumped handfuls of soap from the dispenser, washing my face and then gargling with pure water over and over again. When I was done, I opened the door and stepped out into the hallway.

"Hold on a minute," a different nurse said. "Come with me."

Back inside the room, she handed me a bag full of medicine and explained what I was to take, when, and for how long. And she told me about what side effects to expect. I could barely pay attention to a word she was saying. Headaches. Nausea. Sleeplessness. Dizziness. Unexpected bleeding. All I wanted to do was go home, and I finally said so.

"Please," I said. "Just let me go. I want to be home with people I know and trust."

I was partly out the door when she stopped me.

"Wait! You have to go to the pharmacy to get your medicine!"

I stared at her strangely. I was holding the big bag she had just given me. She had to be joking.

"We don't have it all here. You have to bring this prescription and they'll have the rest for you."

We all went to the hospital's pharmacy, following the green line on the floor in a maze of turns. Though I probably shouldn't have been, I was surprised when the person behind the desk handed me a mound of paperwork to fill out. It was so overwhelming that the tears began stinging in my throat.

"How are you going to pay for this today?" the woman behind the counter asked. "Cash or credit?"

"Can't you send me a bill?"

"No," she said. "You have to pay now in order to get your medication now."

I suppose I could have told her that, just a few hours earlier, I'd been kidnapped at gunpoint, gang-raped, and had everything stolen from me, including most of my clothing, but I just said, "I don't have any money to pay right now. Everything is at home."

The two of us stood there staring at each other.

"I've got this." George stepped next to me, reaching into his back pocket as he did so. I looked up at him, and he was already handing a credit card to the woman.

Over his shoulder, I could see Viktoria talking, the phone pressed to one ear, the other waving in the air like she was conducting an invisible orchestra. I had asked her to call Robin. I knew that, based on how I'd dealt with the pharmacy woman, I couldn't really trust myself to remain composed. I'd seen how George was dealing with things, and I knew that Robin would be even more devastated by what he might think of as his failure to protect me. I felt bad for putting Viktoria in that position, and I felt bad for feeling bad.

I felt George's hand take mine. "Let's go home now, Monika."

On the drive, Viktoria filled me in. Robin wanted to come to the hospital right away and asked for directions, but it was pointless for him to head out when we were so close to leaving. She told him to stay home and that I would contact him when we got back.

I sat in the front seat and George drove. I looked at the dashboard clock and it was 7:30 in the morning. The sun was fully up and I felt the way a vampire might feel: I hadn't had any water for hours; I'd cried out the rest of the fluids in my body, and each time I blinked against the painful sun, I felt like I'd dragged a dish scrubber across my eyes. My head seemed hollow, like it was a balloon on a stick.

"I can't believe that we have exams in a few days," Kristine said.

I was grateful that the conversation had turned to something other than my attack.

"We'll be all right,"Viktoria said. "We just have to promise each other we'll make the others stick to the schedule."

"That's right," I added, "We just have to focus. Losing a day like today will just make that easier. We could always come up with excuses not to before, but now—"

I let the thought hang there. Only after I'd said the words did I realize how little I really knew about what "now" might mean for me, for all of us.

We lapsed into silence. Rush-hour traffic was thick, and a couple of times I saw George catch himself just before he slammed his palm on the steering wheel. He chewed at a thumbnail, and I realized that he didn't have final exams to worry about and in comparison to everything else the traffic was a minor annoyance, but I had no idea how long it was going to take until I was truly at home again.

CHAPTER FOUR

Home

When you spend nearly nine months each year living somewhere other than the place of your birth or the country where your family and most of your friends still reside, you don't use the word "home" as casually as other people. Maybe that's true of all students who go away to college. But some people say it and just mean "I'm going back to my room," or "I'm going back to my apartment." In those cases, they're talking about a building, a location, a place, and it wasn't just my newly adopted English that had me instead saying "my place" nearly every time I referred to my housing situation. But in the hours after the attack, that no longer seemed right. In the hours since the attack, I realized, home had become Robin; home had become a state of mind, the sense of belonging I felt with him and my friends.

As George drove us along streets whose names had become familiar to me, I felt a bit of my exhaustion lifting. As each cross street passed by, it was as if my vision grew clearer, the early-morning haze outside the car and inside my head seemed to clear. As we made the final turn toward home, we headed east. The sun was still low on the horizon, and through the bug- and sap-spattered windshield of the car, everything was alternately ablaze in an aura of light and dimmed in shadow. I looked at my friends, all of them still wearing the same party clothes, and wondered if they wanted to get home as badly as I did.

I took in short, shallow breaths. I was so eager to see Robin. I felt like I did at the starting line of a race, when every second felt like forever, when my fingers and toes went numb, and my vision narrowed.

I had my hand on the door's lever as we pulled into the driveway. I eased the lever back, but the door wouldn't open. Hearing the door's lock mechanism release was like the sound of the starter's pistol firing. I was off and running. The oversized clothes made me feel like I was running in deep sand or snow. Instead of my usual running form, I ran with my hands above my head, pistoning them forward, shoving aside imaginary obstacles.

I came to a halt when I saw Robin. He was sitting on the stairs, wearing a T-shirt and a pair of jeans even though it was 28 degrees out. His chin rested on his knees and his arms hung down. When he heard me approaching, he looked up and sprang to his feet in an instant.

We each closed the distance and held on to each other fiercely. I wanted him to be as close to me as he could be, to feel as much of him against me as I possibly could. I rose up on my toes, wishing that there was a way for him to crawl inside my ridiculously billowing clothes and eliminate any remaining distance between us.

"I got into my car to drive and I didn't know where to go, so all I could do was to wait here. I wanted to be there." His voice was nearly strangled with emotion.

A rush of love filled my heart. I was so happy to see him. There was nothing to say right then; we just held each other close. He cried; I didn't. Despite everything that had happened that night, at that moment, I felt happy. It felt so right to be home and to be with Robin. It was as if all the spinning had finally stopped. Everything had been so out of control, and now I was at last grounded and safe. I was where I was meant to be.

I leaned into him as we walked up the stairs and into the apartment. It was as I'd left it. My stack of textbooks and notebooks still lay on the table along with a confetti of tiny Post-it notes and tape flags. I picked up an uncapped highlighter, thumbed its orange stump, and inspected the tiny stain.

Shrugging out of my borrowed coat, I turned and looked at Robin. He brushed away a tear and brushed his hair behind his ears as he adjusted his red ball cap.

"How do I look?" I asked, raising my hands to reveal fabric-covered fists, and then I looked down at the pool of slacks around my feet.

We both laughed, and resumed breathing again, a bit of normalcy edging some of the uncertainty into a corner of the room.

I stood on one leg and kicked with the other. I caught the clog. Robin raised his eyebrows and clapped his hands quietly and briefly.

"The circus life for you."

I wanted to keep the banter going, but my anxiety was remorseless, standing there just outside my spotlight ready to pull me back into the darkness. This wasn't my home. This wasn't my place any longer. I was certain that someone was there, in the room, lying in wait. I felt a bubble of anxiety rising out of my stomach and expanding in my chest. My breaths were short, sharp, and insufficient things that narrowed my vision and constricted my throat. I wanted so badly to brush my teeth, and the desperation to do that struggled against the fear of going into another room alone.

I was overwhelmed by the thought that someone was hiding in the apartment.

"I need to brush my teeth," I said, my voice sounding hoarse and hollow. Robin must have understood. He went with me, and we stood in the bathroom together, regarding each other in the mirror. I could see his pain and concern etched in the corners of his eyes and the sag around his mouth as he watched me quietly.

As good as it felt to finally have my mouth clean, the anxiety gripped me again. For no good reason, I fixated on the kitchen cabinets, wondering if someone was hiding in there, preparing to spring out at me. I stood there working my tongue from one inside of my cheek to the other, my eyes tracing the same arc.

"Water. I need a glass of water."

Robin made a move toward the kitchen, but I held up my hand.

I walked into the kitchen. A few glasses sat in the wooden strainer. I looked at them and then at the cabinet nearest the sink. I took a deep breath and opened that door. Just glasses. A mix of them with their mouths upturned and downturned. I took one of the downturned ones, set it on the counter, and then flipped the rest of them inside the cabinet to match the one I'd taken. I let the tap run for a few seconds before filling the glass.

I turned around and jumped. Robin stood in the doorway.

"Sorry," he said.

"It's just—I didn't hear you."

I sipped the water, and it was as if its contact reminded me that I had been desperately craving a shower for so many hours. I told Robin what I wanted and he nodded.

"That's a good idea. It will relax you."

Hiking up my pants to keep from tripping on them, I walked toward the bathroom. I got as far as the door. It was half-closed, and a panic ran through me. What if someone were in there? I put my hand on the door-knob, wondering if somehow I could pick up the vibration of another person's presence in there. The knob was cold and still. Pulling my shirt-sleeve over my hand, I used my forearm to edge the door more open. The lone window was frosted glass, and only a faint bit of light fell to the floor. I peered farther around the corner. In the vanity mirror I could see the shower curtain, a towel draped over the rod.

I was wrong . . . he must be behind the shower curtain. No, not there either. I had to get into the shower, but I couldn't stand the thought of being alone even to do such a simple thing. What if someone came in and attacked me in the shower?

"I can't do it alone," I told Robin.

His eyes narrowed in confusion. I knew he was so scared of saying or doing the wrong thing.

"Can you come and sit with me?" I felt a bit of shame coloring my cheeks and heating my earlobes. But Robin smiled, looking grateful for now having something to do.

"If you're in here with me," I said, strengthening my own will and Robin's, "I'll be able to do this. I just really need to feel clean right now."

After Robin pulled the curtain aside for me and I got in, the water thundered from the faucet into the tub. I bent to test it, then nudged the dial farther to the left before turning on the shower. Steam swirled, and

I wondered if the water could ever be hot enough to really make me feel clean. Three body scrubs hung from the rack. I picked the largest one and lathered it up while I let the spray douse my face. I lathered and scrubbed, lathered and scrubbed, until I'd worked that first bar of soap into a small wafer.

I asked Robin to bring me another bar. He handed it inside.

I am too dirty. Someone is going to have to go to the store to get more soap, I thought.

I plugged my ears and let the water thrum against my skull. I'd spent some time in the woods in cabins and tents, and I'd always loved the sound of gentle rain. This sound was more insistent, a bit of an irritant. My sense that the shower wasn't doing any good added to that irritation. I'd been asking to take one since I arrived at the hospital. I was so desperate to feel clean, to get the men off of me, but as hard as I scrubbed, they were still on me and in me.

"You don't have to answer if you don't want to." Robin's voice was tentative, rising at the end like he was asking me a question.

"Answer what?" I asked. I realized that I was so preoccupied for a moment I'd forgotten all about my fear of being alone and that Robin was there with me. I'd long since turned the knob all the way to the left to all hot. I looked at my puckered hands and wondered how long I'd been in there. Had I drifted to sleep while standing?

"I asked about your mother and father."

Robin liked my parents. They'd helped him pull off that surprise visit. My father had picked him up at the train station and my mother had managed to stay tight-lipped. I'd jokingly told her that I'd never forgive her for not, at the very least, telling me that I should have put on a nicer outfit.

My skin was red and raw in spots. The hot water had run out, and retreating from the cold water, my blood had drawn a pale blanket over the rest.

"I've been thinking about that." I shut off the water and watched as the last of it spiraled down the drain. I wondered how long it would take until the hot water tank would be full again.

Robin handed a towel past the side of the curtain. While toweling off, I said, "It's about dinnertime there, or will be soon."

I left it at that, as if it was just a matter of polite courtesy not to disturb someone's mealtime.

When I got into the living room, our head track-and-field coach, Coach Wollman, was seated on the couch. Kristine and Viktoria joined us. Coach Wollman stood, and I immediately slipped into my role as a member of his team. I tried to look him in the eyes, but I could only do so briefly. He sat back down, brushed his bangs aside, and said, "Kristine called me last night. I'm so sorry but so grateful that you're here now."

He gave me a big, warm hug. That surprised me, and I was grateful in a way that I couldn't have predicted.

Unlike me and Bo, my coach back in Norway and a man I'd known for years, Coach Wollman and I had a more formal relationship. Maybe it was because of my poor language skills when I first arrived or just my natural respect for my elders, but I wasn't comfortable opening up to him. I just didn't know him that well at that point. Part of that had to do with experiences I'd had with teachers in school back home; part of it had to do more generally with the culture I was raised in.

During my senior year in middle school, I'd sharpened my compet-itiveness to a hardened edge, both in the classroom and in my running and skiing competitions. I was shocked to learn that because I frequently earned top grades, along with my friend Ida, the other girls resented me. They accused me of breaking them down, making them feel bad about themselves because of what I was accomplishing. Worse, they spoke to their parents, and the parents spoke to the teachers, and soon I felt like I was a victim of my success. More precisely, I was a victim of *janteloven*, and the Ten Laws of Jante, a part of Norwegian/Scandinavian culture that places a greater emphasis on group conformity and harmony than it does on individual success. I'd been exposed to the Ten Laws of Jante, among them:

You're not to think you're anything special.

You're not to think you know more than we do.

You're not to think anyone cares about you.

The teachers seemed to agree that Ida and I were the culprits, that we were the ones who had created an unhealthy environment of competition. I saw it that I was competing with myself, trying only to maximize my abilities. The teachers worked hard to douse the fire inside me.

I tried to keep my mask on, appear in class as though the teacher's changed attitude toward me was having no effect. In truth, I went home and cried every day after classes were over, frustrated and blaming myself, letting my insecurities run me down. I was the one who was wrong. I should have known better. I wanted to be liked and I'd failed at being so.

Back then my parents were there to set me straight. They didn't believe in the Laws of Jante, never treated me in any way that revealed they even knew about them. Here's what they said to me:

I couldn't give up or give in.

I was a hard worker.

That was my nature.

Someday all of that would pay dividends for me.

I should trust myself and keep fighting.

I should trust myself. I should trust myself. I should trust myself.

Eventually, I had good relationships with teachers and coaches, but the idea of not standing out, not seeking preferential treatment, was hard for me to overcome.

Now, my coach was here in my apartment, and he had broken through all of those barriers. I understood that he was there to help me through it—as a father figure; not as a coach, not as someone in charge of me or making strict demands on me, but as someone caring for me the person and not just me, the runner. What had happened to me defied the natural boundaries of our relationship, so he had to treat me differently than the rest of my teammates.

"I want you to know that I, that we, all of us, want to help you in any way that we can. I know that it's only been a few hours, but there are some things we can put in place to help you get through this. Anything, and I mean anything, you need you just let me or anyone on the staff know."

"That's kind." I looked over at Robin to gauge his reaction. I couldn't tell what he was thinking.

My friends took turns filling in Coach Wollman and me on what they had been through that night. Right after I'd told Kristine to let go of me, she and Viktoria ran to George's car.

George hadn't seen a thing—he was turned in the opposite direction and listening to music. It had taken him a few seconds to understand what was happening.

Kristine yelled at him to follow the black SUV. By the time they were able to get George's car started and turned around, the vehicle was nowhere in sight. They drove around frantically until they spotted a police car parked at a 7-Eleven. All three of them ran into the store and told the officer what had happened. Several other officers showed up as they were explaining. Each car went out searching for dark SUVs, pulling over several vehicles that matched the description.

The first officer brought my friends back to the police station to take their statements, and kept them there afterward while other policemen continued searching for me. A bulletin went out to all the patrol units in the area, and the police called my cell phone over and over. Another person who'd been at our party had been standing outside and had also seen what happened, so everyone still at the party found out quickly that I had been abducted, and they, too, were frantic. While I was at the hospital, Kristine had told me that the hosts, two members of the men's soccer team, called my cell phone repeatedly and later kept in touch with her for updates. They were going to visit us in an hour or so, and I hoped that they didn't feel responsible for any of what had happened.

There were no leads for almost an hour and a half, while my friends sat at the station not knowing if I was alive or dead. Then one break came through: As the police called my phone again and again, a male with a Spanish accent answered at 3:39 a.m.

"Where is she?" the officer asked.

The man, one of my rapists, offered the address of an intersection: Munger Avenue and Military Highway. He said that's where they had just left me off, and I was fine.

Except the address was wrong. The two streets didn't intersect. No one knew whether he provided a wrong address just to throw the police off, or whether he just didn't know the area. Fortunately, one officer did know the area well and made his best guess and raced over there. That's when they found me.

As my friends talked, I began to shiver. In some ways I was glad to hear the other side of the story, but suddenly one thought consumed my mind.

I don't know why it was that I suddenly felt the urge to say exactly what was on my mind without editing it, without weighing the pros and cons and costs and benefits.

"It's my parents. They don't know yet. I haven't told them. I don't know how or if I can. At least not yet."

Coach Wollman pinched his brow. "I can't imagine how difficult that would be. I can call them if you like. Maybe if it came from someone at the university."

It was a nice offer, and it would have been so easy for me to just hand him that phone and be free of the burden, but I couldn't. How awful would it be for them to get this kind of news from a stranger who didn't even speak their language? I had to do it.

Coach Wollman left soon, repeating that he would be there to help in any way that I needed. He also took on the important role of acting as a liaison with the police or any other agency or individual that wanted or needed me to do something. I couldn't have asked for a better person to help all of us.

Once Coach Wollman was gone, I told everyone I needed a moment alone. I sat on the bed and stared at Robin's cell phone for a long time. I dialed my family's number, but couldn't hit the "call" button. I wondered if seeing his number show up instead of mine would alarm them. I was glad that he'd been in touch with them before.

I imagined a few opening words and how they might sound. There was no easy way. I just had to be as open and honest as I could. If I established the tone, then they'd follow up the same way.

I took a few more deep breaths and hit "call." While the phone rang, I stood and walked over to my dresser. I looked at a photo of my mother and father, one that had been taken at a party for my "crazy" aunt Gerd. I'm really close to my aunt, one of the craziest, and warmest, people you'll ever meet, forever making us all laugh. In the photo my parents were standing outside, the low-hanging branches of a tree like a canopy above them. Their smiles revealed a genuine happiness, and my mother rested her head on my father's shoulder. They looked so young, posing like I'd seen so many of my friends do with their heads inclined. Mentally, I tried to merge their faces, to see what parts of me I'd gotten from each of them.

I heard my father's voice and I forced good cheer into mine. "Hello, Dad. It's me."

My father sensed immediately that something was wrong. "Monika, are you okay?"

"Yes. Is Mom there? Can she get on with you?"

I heard the rustling sound of him holding the phone to his chest. I tried to picture him standing there, dressed in a favorite sweater, the dark green one with the roll collar, and his Levi's jeans. For some reason, the image of him standing there, leaning against the kitchen counter, his legs crossed casually in front of him, tore at me.

I didn't mean to, but I started crying. "Everything is okay. Don't be afraid; I'm home now with Robin and the girls, but something bad happened—"

I heard my mother's voice on the other end: "Oh no!"

I swallowed hard and said, "I was raped—"

I heard their sharp intake of breath, a gasp. Then my mother said, "*Nei, for faen!*"

I flinched. I'd never heard my mother swear before. At any other time I would have been delighted, but knowing that I'd shocked her to the point that she lost control made me wish that I'd thought all of this through better.

With no point in turning back, I rushed ahead with the story. In my mind it was as if I were two people—one me was telling them about the party, the men, the SUV, while another me itemized a list of worries: Were they afraid that they would never get back the daughter they knew and loved? Did they think I would be ruined forever by this? Were they going to regret supporting my decision to come to the U.S.?

As I continued the story, the two selves merged. I knew that if I was going to save them more anguish, I had to reassure them that I was going to be okay. I just kept talking and trying to sound confident, building my case strong syllable by strong syllable. I didn't want to pause at all, to let any sobs or shudders punctuate my testimony.

I underestimated my parents.

"Monika, we're so glad that you survived. You're going to get through this!" my mother said, enunciating each word with a precision and strength that signaled my body to stand straighter. "We can hear in your voice that you are strong."

I ran my thumb over the photograph, nearly feeling the soft give of their skin.

"No one is going to destroy you in this way. You've been fighting your whole life. We've all been tested. Look at everything you've done to this point. No one can take that from you."

My mother's words were just what I needed to hear. Both of my parents were completely clear when they spoke: They supported me; they believed that I would make it through, and they were just so happy that I was alive.

As my mother spoke, I kept saying softly, "Thank you and I know," an inadequate expression of my gratitude for what they were saying to me then and what they'd shown me my whole life. I wanted to tell them again how thankful I was that they had trusted me to come here, that they believed that I had made the right choices all along.

I asked them if they had talked to Anette lately and how she was doing. I wasn't sure what the best thing would be, for me to call her or for them to do it. We agreed that they would talk to her first, and then I would call her after some hours of sleep. I was so tired that I struggled holding the phone up to my ear.

Robin poked his head into the bedroom to check up on me; I gave him a smile and waved him in as I ended the conversation with my parents. I was so relieved that they hadn't gotten overly emotional with me. I was so physically and emotionally exhausted by that point that I lay on my bed. Robin lay down next to me, and I repeated my mom's words to him: "We are going to get through this."

He smiled and kissed me gently on my head. "But first some sleep?" he half asked, half demanded. I put the phone on my night table and turned over on my stomach with one hand on Robin's chest. We were both so tired, but we didn't seem ready to close our eyes. I kept looking at him; he kept staring out into the open. A few minutes later Robin's phone rang. It was my mom, telling me that they were looking at tickets.

"We'll be there as soon as we can." My father's tone was adamant. I knew that they both wanted to be at this place with me, but I didn't know how I might manage that. As strong and as clear-minded as they seemed now, who knew how they might respond when the shock wore off and the hours of travel weighed on them? Worse, I wasn't sure what state I was going to be in.

I stood up and began pacing the room. I was determined to face this all head-on, but the "this" I wanted to take on was my immediate future. I had exams coming up. I wasn't going to waste a semester's worth of hard work. Hosting my parents—who had never been to campus—would mean another distraction on top of a mental pile of others. It worried me also that I could control myself, that I could create a kind of necessary illusory world for myself where those events were neatly tucked away somewhere. This wasn't like it had been when I was a child and Anette and I engaged in some kind of game of pretend that my parents could inadvertently step into and end. The consequences of this game ending were too serious for me to risk letting too many other players participate. And I needed to be able to do whatever I had to do to push through exams and papers. I had to finish up the semester strong, act as if this thing was already behind me, like an assignment that I had already completed and could now forget about.

I felt as if my carefully conducted and constructed life would topple if just one new piece was added. As a habitual maker of lists and setter of goals, I couldn't see adding my parents and making sure that they were comfortable and cared for to studying, dealing with the police, following up with health care and medications, getting the necessary sleep, returning my life to normalcy. In the end, that was what I felt I needed the most—to go back to how things had been twenty-four hours earlier. Having my parents in town would only be more disruptive. Plus, I was scheduled to go home in ten days. I had to stick with that plan. While I didn't explain all of that to my mother and father, eventually they relented. I'd see them soon. I was being well cared for. If anything changed, I would let them know.

After I spoke with my parents that second time, I decided to call my sister. I knew I wouldn't be able to sleep before I talked to her. Somehow I sensed that this call wasn't going to go as well. I thought of how often my parents had trusted me, but with a sister, things would be different. She didn't have to trust me. There was something different at stake in telling her, something that I couldn't completely understand on a rational level. As well as my parents knew me and as close as we were, things were different with a sister.

When we were young, I was always the tagalong—the littlest and youngest girl who wanted to be doing whatever her sister and her sister's friends were up to. Once, Anette and her friends decided to walk to a playground in town. They ran and skipped and giggled most of the way, while I trotted along resolutely, as fast as my four-year-old legs could carry me. Once there, the older girls took all the swings, pumping and kicking furiously as they rose in the air above me. The only other equipment was a climbing apparatus—a horizontal ladder with a series of rings.

I climbed onto a metal step and jumped, my hand barely grazing the first ring. I tried again and again, squatting down until my bottom touched my heels and then springing up. No matter how hard I tried, I couldn't reach them. I stood on that small platform and looked down. Beneath each ring, a succession of kids' feet had worn away the fine gravel in a series of dark ovals. I decided that instead of trying to reach the rings, I'd just jump from dark oval to dark oval, doing a series of standing long jumps like I'd once seen somewhere.

That's when the other girls noticed me. Toril, a pigtailed blonde, squealed and pointed at me, laughing. She grunted loudly as she mocked my jumps and collapsed to the ground. She then stood and pretended that she couldn't reach the rings, though they were easily in her reach.

Anette came over to me. She hoisted me off the ground so that I could grasp the first of the rings. I hung there for a moment before working my way across.

My sister stood with her arms folded across her chest and a glint in her eye and said to Toril: "Your turn."

Toril squinted into the sun, looking first at Anette, then at the equipment, and then at me. She walked back to the swings. The other two girls got off theirs and joined Anette and me. That's how it was with Anette. She didn't have to say or do a lot, but she always let me know that she had my best interests at heart when it really mattered. Later, she'd be the one to guide me once her body and then mine began to change; she let me in on secrets involving her first innocent encounters with boys, what it was like to be in love with her Jonas.

As much as it meant to me that my parents were so proud of me getting a scholarship to SMU, it meant something different when at my farewell party Anette took advantage of a quiet moment and sat in a chair next to me. She put her hand in mine and said, "You deserve this."

"Everyone seems to be having a good time."

She laughed and playfully nudged me with her shoulder.

"Not just this. All of it. You know I admire you for being so brave. For always going forward."

I wondered as I dialed just how she'd view this setback, if that was indeed what it might seem to be to her or to me.

For a few moments after I told her, she didn't speak at all. I thought that maybe we had been disconnected. I sat and listened to the fuzzy interference, trying to picture her. She cried more easily than me, had the habit of tilting her head back when she did, as if the tears could return to their source.

To fill the void, I asked, "How are things with you? Have you been doing your shopping for the holiday?"

She started to answer my question but lapsed into silence. I heard her sigh and say, "Are you okay? You're sure?"

"Yes."

"Robin and Kristine. They have to take care of you. Let them help you."

I knew it was ripping her apart that she couldn't be there to be the one to help. I assured her that they were and that I was okay.

"I love you so much, Monika."

In my family, those were "big words," ones that we didn't always use. Anette was the lone one among us who could drop her natural reserve and shyness to open up like that. She'd been making an effort to teach the rest of us to express our feelings.

"If you need something, just ask."

She spoke the last of those words in a husky, tear-torn voice and then added through a heavy sigh, "Please."

Like my parents, Anette wanted every assurance that I was okay and also offered to come and, as she put it, "retrieve me."

I laughed at her use of that expression. "You make me sound like I'm something you left behind, the keys to your car or something."

"Don't. Not with me."

My little joke had failed, and somehow that comforted me. Even though Anette and I had been living thousands of miles apart, the bond between us was still as strong as ever. Our lives had taken different directions, but we'd promised each other that miles, men, and nothing beginning with any letter of the alphabet would come between us. I knew that if I could count on anyone in this situation, it would be Anette. Still, I wanted to look out for her as well, do what I could to lessen her anxiety.

I assured Anette that I was making an effort to get help from others. I also asked her to tell Jonas what had happened. I knew that I was asking a lot of her. She and Jonas had broken up months before. I couldn't bear to speak with him, not because I was upset with him, but because he had been like a brother to me and I hated to bring him bad news. I knew that he and Anette were still speaking intermittently, and I held out some dim hope that they would patch things up again.

Without hesitation, Anette agreed to do as I asked.

After we hung up, I decided that now I could finally sleep. I had been awake for more than thirty hours and thought the rest would do me some good. But not long afterward, I woke up gasping for breath.

I thought I could escape, but they were right there in my nightmare. My back was drenched in sweat and my heart rate felt like it was rattling my rib cage. It was so hard to breathe, and I couldn't even imagine trying to go back to sleep. So I got up out of bed to remove the chance of falling asleep again by accident. I assured Robin I was going to be okay and that he needed some rest if he was going to be able to help me. He nodded and was likely asleep by the time I settled into a chair in the living room.

I have to work on my final Sports Management paper, anyway, I thought.

I sat at my computer desk with my hands on the keyboard and tried to form coherent thoughts. About sports management.

"Electronic Arts chairman Larry Probst was elected to a four-year term as USOC chairman, taking over for Peter Ueberroth in 2008."

I spaced out for a moment and had to bring myself back to the task at hand.

"He was going to help with Chicago 2016's bid for the summer Olympics."

What if they actually know where I live, like they said in the car? What if they come here?

I pushed my chair back and went to the front door to check the lock. At odd intervals through the rest of the day I repeated the act. Then I walked over to first Kristine's and then Viktoria's room. I stood outside the door and listened to the sound of their regular breathing. I was grateful that they were able to sleep. I knew that they had to be exhausted from worry and stress. I worried about what effect all this was going to have on them.

A few hours later, just after sunset, I decided we all needed something to lift our spirits. I called George and asked him if he would mind coming by. A few minutes later, he knocked on the door.

"What's up?" he asked. "How're you doing?"

"Redbox," I said. "We all need it."

While Robin rounded up the other girls, I went back into my room. I picked up the bag with the clothes I'd been given.

"Let's go," I said when I joined the others in the living room.

Robin frowned and pointed at the bag, "What's—"

"You'll see," I told him. "This will be good."

George walked outside and over to his car, but I said, "No."

Everyone looked at me, their faces concerned.

"Sorry," I said, apologizing for having sounded so shrill. "I just feel like walking."

We headed toward a convenience store a few blocks away. A couple stood at the Redbox dispenser scanning the listings.

"Over here." I nodded toward the far side of the building, where the lights from the gas pumps cast a slanted shadow toward a Dumpster.

I pulled the T-shirt the nurse had given me to wear out of the bag. The nurse was right; it was best that I never see those clothes again. I pointed at the Dumpster and George trotted toward it and lifted its lid.

I tried to ball up the T-shirt, but it parachuted to the ground when I threw it.

"Let me try," Robin said. He wound up like he was going to hit his serve, but the shirt fell short of the mark.

For the next few minutes, we all took turns trying to throw the paper bag and the clothes into the Dumpster, oohing and aahing and laughing at our near and distant misses. Finally, I chucked the bag underhand as high as I could. I stood and watched as it arched skyward and disappeared above the lights. Then I heard a satisfying thump as it found its target.

George ran toward me, his palm in the air, and I smacked it and smiled and did a little victory dance. I ran up to the Dumpster, lifted its screeching lid, and slammed it home. The boom surprised us, and I said, "Let's run!"

We took off sprinting across the parking lot, laughing while gas pumpers stared and either shook their heads or smiled. We stopped a block away from the apartment, all of us giggling, expending whatever stress and nervous energy was still in our systems.

"The movie," Kristine said.

"We've got something," Viktoria said. "I'm not going back there. People will think I'm crazy."

WHEN WE GOT back to the apartment, we all sat in the living room and watched the movie *27 Dresses*. I wanted to see something lighthearted, and what could be better than the story of a woman who'd been a bridesmaid that many times? Besides, James Marsden wasn't bad to look at. But I had a hard time following the plot of the movie, and it was as if at times the sound faded out completely. I could see the actor's mouths moving, but I couldn't hear what they were saying.

The same was true of what was going on offscreen as well. Robin and I sat on the couch next to each other, wrapped in a blanket. Kristine and Viktoria did the same. I exchanged silly looks as bits of microwave popcorn slid down the slopes of their raised knees. The thought of eating anything made me nauseated.

Kristine scowled at us playfully. "Now I'm going to have to pay the maid extra."

I was about to tell her that we didn't have a maid, that we had never had one, when I heard everyone else laugh. Why hadn't I gotten the joke? Why was it that I had this feeling that I was walking into every conversation they had after it had started?

Robin and I sat and watched as the movie's credits scrolled along. I could sense that something was troubling him, but how could it not be? Later that night, he stayed over. We snuggled under the blankets. I was wearing a T-shirt and my underwear. I reached behind me and was surprised to feel the rough fabric of Robin's jeans. I reached up higher, and he still had on his team-issued SMU fleece jacket.

"Aren't you hot?"

He didn't answer for a moment. Then he turned his head away and said, "I'm just tired. I have to get some sleep."

"You'll be roasting and it won't be a good sleep."

Normally, Robin's body melted against mine when we slept. Tonight I could feel the tension in his body. I rolled over and propped myself up on my elbow.

His eyes brimmed with tears, and I realized what he was trying to do.

"It's all right. The thing that happened in the car has nothing to do with us. I'm not afraid of you. Nothing's changed. Not for me."

Robin nodded halfheartedly. His eyes darted around the room. A couple of times it looked as if he was going to say something, but each time he stopped.

"What is it? You can tell me. Robin, please."

His head moved to the side in a barely perceptible shake, like he was trying not to stare rudely at a couple having an argument at a table near ours.

"Like I said. I'm very tired. That's all. Tired."

I could see he had a hard time believing me, but I meant it. Not for one minute did I associate my rape with my relationship. It was a wholly separate compartment in my mind; these were bad men. They didn't care about me or even know anything about me; they just wanted to over-power a woman whom they saw as defenseless. They were vicious and cruel. Robin was kind and gentle. Some men were good. Some men were bad. I wanted to respect what Robin was feeling, so I didn't press him any further. Only later, when I woke up briefly and Robin was next to me, still fully clothed but on top of the covers, did I wonder about how things had changed for him. Glad that exhaustion prevented any further thoughts, I hugged a pillow to me, grateful for the small comfort it offered.

CHAPTER FIVE

Focus

When you're an athlete, your mind and your body exist in a kind of schizoid relationship. At times you have to be hyper-aware of every message your body is sending—whether it's hungry, tired, sore, in pain, feeling great. At other times, you have to block those messages out entirely and just gut it out, and keep asking more and more of your body even though it might not have much left to give. In training, there's a razor-thin line between overtraining—doing damage to your tissues that your body can't adequately heal from—and undertraining—not pushing yourself hard enough to tear down cells. The reason we get stronger and faster is that we tear down and repair our bodies constantly. If you don't keep pushing, your body will reach a state of homeostasis—it will adapt to that present condition and stay there. Things are a bit different for a race. You prepare and build up strength in training and then go out there and race knowing that if you push yourself as hard as you possibly can, you're going to experience pain. For me the pain of regret, for not giving it my all in a race, was far worse than any of the physical pain I experienced in the race itself. Race pain is temporary; regret lingers.

·   ·   ·

I DIDN'T REALIZE it at the time, but my first serious running-related injury, toward the end of my freshman year at SMU, would pay dividends for me down the line. I'd been used to running with slight, nagging injuries before—sore hamstrings, calves, knees—but one day while doing a workout for track, I was nearly brought to tears by a sharp and searing pain radiating from somewhere between my hip and my groin. At first I just kept running—limping was more like it—but when it became clear that something was very wrong, I dragged myself into the infield. I tried to stand on my right leg, the noninjured one, but the pain was so bad that I collapsed onto the ground. I was able to hobble into the locker room, and eventually the doctors I saw determined that I had fractured a bone in my pelvis.

I was devastated. I wasn't going to be able to run at all for the rest of the season and into the summer. Running was everything to me, and without it, would that mean that I was nothing? Worse, how was I going to occupy all the time and mental space that running filled? Without it, I knew that all kinds of negative thoughts might come rushing in.

When I went home to Norway at the end of my freshman year, my father helped put things in perspective for me. He told me that injuries were part of the process of being an athlete. They were one more obstacle you had to learn to overcome. It was a setback, yes, but how you responded to adversity was the real mark of who you were as a runner and as a person. Running wasn't just something I did in hopes of having a career as a professional, he told me; the lessons I learned from it would help me no matter what I ended up doing to make a living and to live my life. He reminded me of the truth that often the site of a fracture ends up healing and being stronger than the rest of your bones. I could come back from that injury and be better, more determined, have a better perspective about how running fit into my life.

That last part was particularly true, because with no workouts to occupy my time, I began to take advantage of the wonderful opportunities I had at SMU. And good things had come about as a result. Without track meets and training, I was able to attend the tennis match where I first saw Robin. Some good could come of bad things. I had known that was true intellectually, but when I experienced it and felt it emotionally, that lesson was imprinted on my mind in a much stronger way.

In the days after the attack, I tried to remind myself of how I'd overcome that injury—how patience and persistence and allowing other people to help me and guide me and keep me from charging too quickly
ahead and doing more damage had all worked out so well for me.

The running injury I'd suffered and the rape were very different, of
course, but I hoped that I could merge the experiences and use what I'd
learned to move on. Sometimes your body is willing to give more, but it's
your mind that talks you out of pushing on. It's a complicated relationship, to say the least. I'd always worked toward having a balance between
a healthy body and a healthy mind. Suddenly, I faced problems with both
of them. It wasn't going to be as easy as visiting doctors, checking on the
X-rays to see how the fracture was mending, and having a coach, doctor,
and athletic trainer devise a workout schedule that would get me back
to topflight physical condition. The key element for me in my recovery
from the pelvis injury had been rest. That was the one thing that evaded
me following the rape, and it was taking a toll on me.

I'd done some reading in my psychology studies about the effects
of sleeplessness on human behavior, physical condition, and cognitive
function. The effects of not sleeping are a long list ranging from irritability to overproduction of stress hormones, to less serious things like
cosmetic changes—bloodshot eyes and bags. It's no wonder that there's
debate about whether prisoners subjected to sleep interruption as part
of an interrogation are subjected to torture or not. All I knew is that as
I struggled to calm my mind and sleep each night, I felt as if I was being
tortured.

Part of my sleeplessness was self-inflicted. The first few nights after the
rape, I woke in the middle of the night hyperventilating and with my
pulse racing. I was unsure of where I was; even when I reached out and
felt Robin by my side, that feeling of dislocation didn't immediately end.
As much as I tried to block them, thoughts snuck past my defenses about
whether the Worst One, the Boss, and the Weak One, singly, in pairs, or
all together, were in the apartment. I'd lie awake, trying to summon the
courage to get out of bed. But I could almost feel someone gripping my
calf when I moved my foot tentatively toward the floor.

Eventually, I'd lower my feet and keep them on the ground. I tried not to disturb Robin and turn on the lights in the bedroom, but I'd always give in to the urge. I had to see who was there, test to see if the images I had of someone standing in the corner, or lurking just outside the closed bedroom door, were real.

I hated those nightmares. When I first came out of them, I couldn't think clearly at all, didn't know what was reality and what was a product of my dream state. I'm very much a control freak and rarely let my emotions and responses get away from me. Not being able to control my mind and those horrible images and dreams tore at me. I'd prided myself on being able to maintain my composure and hold things inside, and now they were spilling out of me in ways that frightened me as much as the nightmares did. I didn't recognize the person who was responding this way and worried that I was losing my mind. When you spend most of your life thinking that you're the cool, calm, collected one whose lists and goal statements and schedules can keep her safe and moving forward, and you're suddenly faced with something so unexpected, so not a part of your lists and schedules and vision for your life, you really do call into question whether everything that came before that incident and what's happening to you now was real or an illusion.

For his part, Robin was already on high alert. He barely slept in those first few days; he always seemed to be half-asleep in bed, fearful that one of my many nightmares would overtake me. He'd wake, hair tousled and eyes squinting as he came to my side, assuring me that I was safe. He'd trail along behind me as I inspected the rest of the apartment, opening closets, checking behind furniture, peering in cabinets.

Even though I didn't find anything, that didn't end my anxiety. I knew that I needed sleep, but I also dreaded the thought of having another nightmare, finding myself back in that SUV with those three men, the gun pointed at my head. I felt it next to my temple every time I woke up, and it was the part of the nightmare that I struggled with for a long time after. I so wanted to just lie down and sleep and have the morning sunlight filter in to wake me after uninterrupted hours. That would have been a wonderful escape, but every time I lay down, I was back in that van, seeing those horrible men, smelling their foul breath.

Someone once used the expression "between a rock and a hard place."

In learning English, I had to pay close attention, and these words made sense to me to a degree, but the phrase's subtleties were unclear. I looked it up and found out that its origins were in mythology, the story of Scylla and Charybdis. While sailing home, the hero of the story, Odysseus, had to choose between passing closer to a rocky outcropping and a whirlpool. Both were dangerous, but which to choose? That was the position I found myself in. I knew that going without sleep was no good, but were the nightmares worse? Was it my lack of sleep that was producing the nightmares and the near paranoia I experienced? Or was it the nightmares that made sleep impossible?

The strange thing was that I can't say that I felt tired. I knew I needed sleep, but an adrenaline rush like I'd seldom felt before also cascaded through my body. I felt like I was running through deep, deep snow—exerting enormous amounts of energy and gaining no ground, with little time lapsing. My worries about my classes; phone calls and e-mails to professors, to family, to friends; posting on Facebook to express how grateful I was; meetings with the investigators in the police department—all took up an enormous amount of time and energy, and the hours passed quickly. Fix this. Fix this. Fix this. Go. Go. Go. Those thoughts consumed me. So much for patience and a plan; so much for applying what I'd learned from that fracture. Intellectually I understood what I needed to do, but my emotions overwhelmed me. If I could just take care of X, Y, and Z, keep my focus on getting things done, I didn't have the time to think about what had been done to me.

I also tried hard to put on a good face for everyone else, let them all know that I was doing okay. Kristine and Robin didn't want to leave my side, and they more than anyone else sensed that I was doing a poor job of acting okay. They could see the fear and anxiety in my eyes when the rest of me was trying to say all was right. I was obsessed with my classes and making sure that I completed all my end-of-semester assignments and studied for my exams, or made arrangements to postpone those I wouldn't be able to take. A few times I felt like I was someone diagnosed with a terminal disease and had only a few days to live. I wanted to put all my affairs in order.

As well-intentioned as Kristine and Robin's efforts were, in some ways their hovering over me stressed me even more. I knew that the time they spent with me was time they weren't spending taking care of themselves and their studies. I hated the idea that they would end up paying the price academically for something that had happened to me. I pleaded with them to go to their classes and take care of themselves, but they wouldn't listen. I was grateful for what they were doing, but upset that I was harming them and becoming even more stressed myself. Nothing seemed to be clear or easy in those first few days. I so wanted some aspect of my life to be straightforward, simple, and uncomplicated.

The closest thing I got to that was having Coach Wollman on my side. When he'd come to our apartment after I was released from the hospital, he had already been in touch with a therapist, Dr. Soutter, the director of campus counseling and psychological services, and made arrangements for me to see her. Coach was caring and compassionate and very action-oriented. "Here's a step you need to take." "Here's the number of the woman you need to see. I've already filled her in a bit on what happened." That sounds a bit matter-of-fact, and to a degree he was, but he also continued to reach out to me and the others. His frequent phone calls and e-mails to check up on me made me feel as safe as I could possibly feel at that point. Just like he had in dealing with my pelvic fracture, he offered his help, but also called in experts to make sure that all of my needs were met.

I don't think I would have contacted a psychologist myself. Despite my sleeplessness and the nightmares, I thought that I was strong enough to handle this myself. I feared that I would feel weaker if I gave in and contacted a psychologist. I was used to figuring things out myself; now more than ever, I didn't want to rely on others to fix me.

I knew that Coach Wollman understood me; he got that as an athlete I was going to handle circumstances a certain way. My coaches throughout my career in various sports had eventually earned my trust. They were adults, had more experience, and always seemed to have my best interests at heart. That didn't mean that I accepted everything they did and said without question; it meant that I had an open mind about things and gave them the benefit of the doubt. Athletes are often focused on performance, on doing the best they can to excel during each race and each practice. But a good coach is there to help look at the big picture, and to help an athlete develop a plan for long-term success. Coach Wollman's role was to help me take both the long view and the short view of every race.

I was so struggling with sleep, and the sense that I was somewhat disconnected from reality, that I fell back into an accustomed role: trust the people in your life who have demonstrated their compassionate authority over you. These weren't people who craved power for power's sake—like the rapists had—these were people who genuinely wanted the best for me. Coach Wollman knew how I approached my running and my studies. He told me that with this new challenge I needed to take care of myself and not push too hard. As with a physical injury, he knew that treatment needed to begin immediately. The second day I was home, a brilliant Sunday, I found myself in the office of Cathey Soutter.

I was struck by how different her office was from the ones at the hospital. Maybe it was the absence of the clinically clean smells of the institution, the more natural lighting, but my nerves didn't completely overwhelm me as I walked into the doctor's office. It also helped that Dr. Soutter was a petite woman like me, her kind face framed by a thick bob of soft curls. She greeted me with a warm smile that eased any remaining tension out of me.

I'd never seen a therapist before; although I was studying psychology in school, I didn't really know how the sessions were going to go. Kristine came to the first appointment with me—as a support, as someone who could fill in some blanks, and because I knew that she'd had a lot to deal with as well. It was a good thing I made that choice. Dr. Soutter began the session by asking me to recount what had happened. Her voice was soft, soothing, and encouraging. I wanted to please her, but the idea of having to tell the story again seemed overwhelming. My sleep was already troubled with visions that I wanted out of my mind forever. What would talking about it, describing it, do to me?

With memories of the police interviews still fresh in my mind, I already felt talked out. Kristine did a lot of the talking on that first day, filling in most of the details about the party and what happened as I was taken away. Dr. Soutter sat and listened quietly; her empathetic expression and kind eyes helped me through. Then I had to talk about what happened in the SUV.

When I did speak, I adopted the detached tone and language that the police used with me, which was a lot like what I'd seen in movies and on television. I stuck mainly to the facts, describing the who, what, when, where, and how of the events in as dispassionate a manner as possible. We weren't getting into what I felt, just what happened.

As I spoke, I could hear myself talking, but I had that same sense of dislocation that I'd had on the night of the attack. I was looking down on me, sitting in a comfortable armchair, a coffee table in front of me with a fern overflowing a brass bucket, a few dried leaves lying on the wooden surface. When I got to the point when I was about to tell Dr. Soutter about the gun being placed at my temple, I paused. I was no longer a detached observer of myself or of the events. I felt like the barrel of a gun was being pressed against my temple. I could feel its coldness, the pressure against my skin and flesh and bone. I could even smell the faint odor of oil or grease coming from it, something that had been unfamiliar to me before that night but now seemed to contaminate everything else I smelled with nearly every waking breath I took.

I began to ramble, my face burning as I shifted uncomfortably in my chair. I placed my hands underneath my thighs, feeling their cold through the fabric of my training warm-up pants. As hard as I tried to prevent it, a thought crawled its way under my defenses.

How could having that gun against my head, something I'd only experienced once in my life, now feel so familiar, chilling but familiar, and to such a degree that I thought it might stay with me for the rest of my life?

At one point, as I described how the Worst One struggled to enter me, I was pierced by a very different sensation. I felt my flesh prickle and the hair on my arms rise. I kept speaking, but I was overwhelmed and distracted. What if I was dead now? What if all of this was a part of the afterlife? What if the reason everything felt so surreal was that the men had actually killed me that night, and this was all the afterlife? I squeezed my arm to make sure I still had feelings. Then I felt like I needed to touch other things—the chair I was sitting in, the leaves on the table, just to make sure that they were solid and real and that I was actually in the environment I could see around me.

Dr. Soutter spoke, but I had no idea what she said. I smiled and nodded politely, just trying desperately to look as if I were present and attentive. I'd had a lot of practice at that in my early days in the U.S. when the language eluded me, so muscle memory took over. Whenever she paused, my "I understand" face presented itself. Each time she kept talking, I felt a small thrill of victory; after all, I didn't want a psychologist to think I was *crazy*.

The session went by in a blur, but we made a deal to meet again the following day at the same time. That much I really did hear. Dr. Soutter said that if I wanted or needed to have someone else with me, Kristine could join us. Kristine and I exchanged glances. I got the sense that she wanted me to be the one who decided, but I wanted Kristine to decide on her own. I'd already asked so much of her and Robin.

On the way home, I began to wonder how much sense it made to try to fool a psychologist. She was there to help, and I was there trying to pretend I didn't need any help. She had told me that she had a lot of experience in particular dealing with women who had been abused and were victims of violence. She likely wasn't someone I could fool. And even if I wanted to keep up the façade, I didn't have much energy to devote to the task. I felt awful. Feverish. Sore throat. Stuffed nose. Cold hands and feet.

When I got home, I bucked the apartment door open with my shoulder and stood there wobbling in its frame. Viktoria and Robin stood up and rushed to my side.

"You're not looking so good," Robin said, his face a portrait of newly unmasked worry. This suspected physical illness was something he could respond to normally.

Kristine and Viktoria nodded in agreement.

The last thing I wanted was to have to go see another doctor and visit another health center, but I had no choice. I found myself in another waiting room, filling out another stack of papers about my health history. I didn't include anything about the rape, but sitting there reminded me of being at Parkland what seemed just hours ago. My life seemed to be measured against clipboards.

The doctor at the student health center diagnosed me with the flu. He started to write a prescription for me.

"No, thank you," I said, a little louder than I'd intended. The doctor was doing his job, but I told him that I couldn't handle another pill due to the poison I was already taking. "I hate taking any kinds of pills."

He set the pad aside and nodded. "Nothing to do then but ride it out. Come back or call if the fever doesn't drop or you feel worse."

I knew that stress depleted the immune system. So did a lack of sleep. Food was mostly an afterthought for me during those first days, something that I could barely take in until the afternoon. It was no longer the fuel that I normally looked at it as. I also realized that my body was sending me a signal. In some ways, I thought that I had broken the agreement that the two of us—my body and I—had made, that I would take care of it and it would take care of me. Who could blame it for rebelling?

Still, I couldn't bear the idea of another sign of weakness. I told myself, as I frequently did whenever I was not feeling well, that I had no time for this nonsense. I had to finish the paper I'd begun for my Sports Management class. I had to attend my Psychology class. A half-attentive and congested Monika was still a better student than a Monika who stayed home and borrowed someone else's notes, so on Monday morning, despite my roommates' and Robin's protests, I went to class. If I hadn't been kidnapped and raped just two days before, I probably would have stayed home to take care of myself so that I didn't get any sicker. But because of the rape, I felt that I had something to prove. I wanted to be someplace where I could distract myself from other thoughts. Most important of all, I wanted that day to be normal, a resumption of my life as it had been before. I also sensed that if I didn't treat myself as special or different, then no one else would, either.

I didn't know if word had spread about what happened to me, as it had about the other young woman. A number of athletes from other sports had been at the party. A few of them were in the same Sports Management class. If they did know, I had to show them that I was strong. Kristine and Viktoria were in the same class, so we met up outside the building and walked in together. It made me feel stronger to have them by my side. I didn't feel up to sitting in our customary seats in the front row; instead we sat in the very back. Whether it was the flu or the antiviral drugs I was taking, I needed to be as close to an exit and a quick route to a bathroom as possible. Vomiting had become a part of my daily routine.

I can't be sure if anyone took notice of me or connected me in any way with the crime that had been committed. I had a hard enough time just managing to stay awake, let alone observing anyone else's reaction to me. I sat in my seat, trying to stay mindful of my posture, but it was as if the floor were exerting some powerful tugging force on me. I felt as if I was watching a television show with the volume muted—I could see the professor's mouth moving, but my brain couldn't process any of the words. All nonessential functions had been terminated. I was in complete survival mode: Stay awake. Don't walk into anything or anyone. Don't operate heavy equipment or drive a car.

Within a few minutes of my first class starting, I felt that same sense of dislocation and disconnection I'd experienced the day before at Dr. Soutter's office—suddenly I wasn't sure if I was alive or dead. I intentionally locked eyes with a couple of students to test if they could see me. When they looked back at me, right in my eyes, I felt better. I was here. I was alive.

Bells tolling from the Fondren Science Building marked the end of class, and I felt like they were telling me to wake up—not just literally but figuratively. Not being able to engage in class felt like a big setback, like I'd run a couple of minutes below my personal best in the three thousand meters. I didn't like setbacks. I couldn't force myself to think clearly, and that frustrated me.

Kristine had another class immediately after our Sports Management course, so we agreed to meet at eleven fifteen at the Dedman Sports Center. We were going to work out together. As I walked along Airline Road, I was still feverish and exhausted. I knew that running had always been good therapy for me before. Even if I just went out and did a few miles at a seven- to eight-minute-per-mile pace, I would feel better just for having made the effort. Running usually provided me with a few moments of escape from what was troubling me. I sat in an isolated corner of the locker room half-awake, my mind wandering. I enjoyed the moments of solitude. At least being alone there, I didn't have to put on my act. There was no one there I had to convince that I was fine. It seemed like only minutes later that a hand was on my shoulder.

"How is it going?" Kristine narrowed her eyes and pursed her lips.

"I had no idea what he was talking about."

Kristine shrugged.

"At least you were there. At least you got through it. That's something."

I didn't respond. I'd never looked at just finishing something as much of an accomplishment.

As we stood at our lockers, my bag tumbled over. I could hear the click of my pills rattling around. I looked over my shoulder quickly, thinking that the sound was so loud that everyone was staring. There were just a few other women in the locker room, and none of them had turned my way. I knew that I needed to take my antiviral medication soon, but I didn't want to do it in public. I didn't want anyone to think that I was sick; I just wanted to appear as if everything were normal.

As we changed, Kristine and I talked about what we wanted to do.

Normally on a Monday I'd do some distance work, a minimum of ten kilometers at a relaxed pace. That usually meant leaving the confines of the track and the campus itself, either heading out into the nearby Highland Park neighborhood or driving out to White Rock Lake and the running path there. That also meant car traffic and pedestrians—people I was certain I could no longer trust.

"It's a bit cold to go outside." I felt lame saying that to another Norwegian woman, let alone someone who knew me as well as Kristine did.

"Treadmill?" Kristine stood up from lacing her shoe and smiled brightly.

"Sure." I was grateful that she hadn't called me on my transparent excuse.

For me, treadmills were a necessary evil. Running in place, staring at the same scene for minute after minute after minute, wasn't nearly as enjoyable as being outdoors and engaging with or sometimes battling the elements. With the clock and other displays flashing in front of me, I would find myself focusing too much on elapsed times—how far I'd gone and how much farther I had to go.

But it felt safer, for now. Even with Kristine alongside me, I'd still be in my own bubble. The noise of the machines, the sounds of our footfalls, would make conversation more difficult. Nearly everyone else in the long line of various cardio machines was plugged into a headset. I didn't use headphones much when I ran outdoors. On a treadmill, however, it was a needed distraction, another way to transport myself from that room and the effort that produced no tangible results.

I set my levels and stepped onto the track, then waited for it to pick up speed. I enjoyed the sensation of my feet moving and settled into the familiar rhythms of my arm swing and my gait. I was pleasantly surprised. This wasn't going to be so bad. I watched the other students at work as I moved. We were all in an enormous room, the cardio machines lined up like cars in a parking lot, the weight-training equipment spread out to cover the rest of the space, ten thousand square feet, as the university proudly stated. I watched as between sets of squats, a group of guys laughed and slapped hands with one another. They seemed so at ease.

I glanced over at Kristine. She, too, seemed lost in thought. I wondered if she was thinking about me and what had happened, or where else her mind might be. Her face was composed, and I once again admired how effortless she made running look. It was as if she barely made contact with the treadmill, as if she were somehow suspended above it and her feet only made glancing contact with it.

After just a few minutes, my legs felt wooden, the hinges of my joints from ankles to hips stiff and unyielding. I'd resisted looking down at the display to that point, but I lost the struggle. Nine minutes. That should have been just a brief warm-up period, a time when my muscles began to heat up and become supple. My heart rate and my breathing were normal, but I just couldn't seem to get loose. I was concentrating on every stride and became self-conscious about how I must look, thinking that I was one of those head-dropped, shoulders-thrusting inefficient plodders I'd sometimes see slogging along off campus. Then the light-headedness and vertigo took over. The last thing I wanted was to vomit all over the place.

I told myself that I had to keep going. I straightened my spine and tipped my chin up. I felt better for a few strides, but gradually I slumped again. Finally, at fifteen minutes, unwilling to hit the button to slow the pace, I stopped completely. I looked down at my legs, as if I could see beneath my skin and assess what was wrong. I understood something about how muscles functioned, and I decided that one of the six properties they had best explained what was affecting my muscles: irritability.

I stepped over to Kristine's treadmill and looked up at her. We each took off our headphones.

"I'm done for the day." I wiped at the sweat I'd produced all out of proportion to how much energy I'd spent. What was wrong with me? What had taken control of my body?

Kristine reached for the "stop" button on her machine.

"No, don't. Keep going. I'm just going to stretch." I inclined my head toward a series of yoga-type mats. Squares of sunlight lit the area and I thought it would be relaxing.

I spread out my towel and sat spraddle-legged on it. I bent my chest and head forward and felt a pleasant pull in my hips and lower back. I was sore and tight and wanted and needed a massage. The thought of having anyone touch me—when I still felt so unclean and anyone making contact with my body still stressed me—made that impossible. When I straightened, Kristine was seated next to me.

"Are you okay?"

"I'm fine. Just a little sick. Keep going and I'll wait for you here."

"I don't want you to sit here alone. There are more important things in life than a workout."

This was a girl who lived and breathed running, who had been among the world's elite, and here she was forgoing training just to stay with me. Muscles of steel, heart of gold.

"I never thought I'd hear you say that."

"Then I guess you don't know me as well as you think." She smiled to take any sting out of her words. "Besides, there's a reason some people call them junk miles."

I'd heard that term before—miles that you put in at a low effort just for the sake of putting in the miles. They were as much for your brain as for your body and, depending on your point view, either good or useless for your body and your mind.

"Too much thinking," I said.

"Not good sometimes." Kristine lay on her back and brought her knees to her chest and then rotated her legs to each side.

In truth I was more ready mentally than I was physically to get back to running. So much of my identity was tied up in being a runner. I had defined myself as an athlete for so long that to feel detached from that identity was profoundly disturbing. People who haven't competed at the level my teammates and I were at wouldn't understand just how fully our school life and social lives were governed by our athletic lives. Yes, we were considered student-athletes, but in reality those two words were reversed. The school was paying my tuition, and only when I got there and spoke with other students did I realize just how much money it cost to attend SMU. The school had certain expectations in return. I had to choose my academic classes based on my sports practice schedule. I didn't miss any classes by choice, but if we were out of town for a meet and the bus left at a time when I had a class, that meant I had to be on the bus and find someone whose notes I could share. When and what I ate was dictated by when and how far I would be running. Decisions about what time I went to bed, how long I was able to study each night, when I took time off to spend with friends, were all determined by my training schedule. It was like I had a full-time job.

I rose at 5:30 every morning so that I could leave by 6:10 to ride my bicycle to campus carrying the backpack I'd carefully arranged the night before. From 6:30 to 9 a.m. I'd practice, doing whatever workouts the coaches had devised. After practice I'd retreat to the locker room to shower, eat the breakfast I'd prepared the night before and brought with me, and by 10 a.m. get to my first class of the day. I'd take a break from classes by eating the lunch I'd brought along, and on those days when I had the time, I'd go to the library to read and study. By 3:15 I was back in the locker room in order to be on time for the second workout of the day at 3:30, which meant some variation in drills, weight lifting, and an easy thirty-minute run. At the end of practice, I'd hop on my bike and ride home, eating either a banana or a nutrition bar on the way. Evenings were for cooking, eating, studying, and getting to bed, not at 10:00, which I always tried for, but by at least 11:00. Repeat and repeat and repeat.

Now that I could barely run for fifteen minutes, I wondered how hard it would be not to have my teammates and friends around all the time to help lift my spirits, and to keep me from taking myself and my entire world too seriously.

My whole life was taken up with being a runner, and as great as it was to self-identify as someone who was disciplined, goal-oriented, and all the rest, I was frightened by the thought that I might have to give up the rest of it as well—the routine, the camaraderie, the sense of purpose and place and reason for being that had accumulated over time.

I was used to fighting against fatigue, distraction, temptation, and soreness to go on a run or do some other kind of workout. I used to get a great deal of satisfaction from going out in the worst of weather, when I was feeling my least capable or least motivated, and getting in a workout. The easy days were just that—easy. I had come to believe that it was the days of struggle that ultimately paid off and made the struggle worthwhile. But the medications, the lack of sleep, the nightmares—they were a different kind of obstacle. I felt as though my identity was shifting beneath my feet, and I felt powerless against the forces that were trying to reshape me.

Much of that had to do with confidence and control. I'd pushed my body through all kinds of walls before to find another burst of energy, to go longer and faster. As much as we might say a coach pushed us, in the end those achievements, those breakthroughs, were things we accomplished on our own. No one was literally pushing us. We were the ones in control; we still determined what all our boundaries were. After the rape, that loss of control, that feeling that someone else could step beyond my boundaries, push me to do things I didn't want to do at all, altered my perceptions immeasurably.

I'd had to give up control of my life in those dark moments on that night. I hated that feeling, and those first few times I tried to run and couldn't control my body, will it to do what I asked, I was seized by the possibility that I would never be able to regain control again. A crack had formed, and it seemed like that crack could lead to a larger and larger and more devastating fracture that might cause the whole world I'd built up to crumble. For the first time in a very, very long time, maybe for the first time ever, a dreaded thought took hold: What if effort didn't matter?

What if no matter how hard you worked or tried, or how meticulously you scheduled and planned, things beyond your control could happen and ruin everything you'd hoped for and dreamed and planned? What if I'd been fooling myself all along and being in control was really something freakish—something completely absurd, something I'd just imagined, something horrific and horrible and not helpful?

Kristine and I headed back into the locker room. As we got changed, I opened my backpack and pulled out a pair of warm-up pants and a hooded sweatshirt. A stack of books, my laptop, a second pair of running shoes, and a couple of magazines spilled out of it.

Kristine laughed. A joke among us had to do with how much I crammed into anything I carried. People always said that I brought a backpack larger than myself to class.

I tapped my head. "It's more crowded up here."

Kristine slid over on the bench and took my forearm. She tugged it and I sat down.

"Mine may not be as bad as yours. I can never really know what you went through, but it's on my mind. It's on all our minds. Sometimes I see those images in my head, but I chase them away."

I nodded. "I know."

"I'm not asking you to be sorry for me. I'm not even saying that I can understand what it is like for you. I just want you to give yourself a break. It's okay if you're not yourself right now. I'm amazed that you're even up and around. I'd be hiding under the covers somewhere."

"I hate being sick," I said, hoping to turn the attention away from the attack to my illness.

"I know. It's no fun." Kristine stood and shrugged into her backpack. "Just give yourself a break. Take care of yourself, but let us help take care of you."

I canceled my appointment with the therapist and spent the rest of that day in bed. Unfortunately, I wasn't alone there. Each time I was about to drift to sleep, I'd see one of the men, the strained expression on his face as he raped me, a bead of his sweat dripping onto me. I tried to think of something else, the trip I'd taken to Tønsberg, Norway's oldest city, to compete in a meet. I didn't care really about seeing the cathedral, the ruins, or even the shops. But I did enjoy the view of the North Sea. I tried to imagine that scene again, feel the warmth of the sun on my face. We were there just after Midsummer, what we call *Sankthansaften*, and I could still see the outline of the bonfire that had roared as part of that celebration. I remembered that if you put flowers under your pillow that night, you would dream of your future husband.

I woke up to the sound of unfamiliar voices. I thrashed at the bedclothes that covered my head, struggling to get up, kicking my feet to come up with some escape route. I hurled the covers aside and sat there panting, waiting. A feather from my down comforter floated in front of me. I stared at the doorknob, willing it to stay still. My fever chill gripped me, and I pulled the top sheet and blanket back over me.

I heard Robin's voice, and then I heard the front door close.

"Monika?"

I peeked out of the covers.

Thank God Robin stood in the bedroom doorway. With his hat pulled down, his eyes were in shadow. I could tell immediately that something was wrong.

"What's going on, Robin?" My voice was unsteady, and I wasn't sure I wanted to hear the answer to my question.

"Don't panic. Everything is okay, but there were some journalists at the door."

Journalists?

"I was in the other room and someone knocked. I opened the door and they were standing there. They had their cameras and recorders out, and they wanted to know if I knew the victim. I told them I didn't know what they were talking about." Robin's voice was a strained and nearly strangled murmur. He was seething but trying to stay in control. He pulled his cap off and rubbed his forehead and smiled. "Don't worry. I locked the door."

Despite Robin's assurances, I had to go to the door and check that it was locked again. Careful not to step in front of any windows, I closed all the curtains in the apartment. I wasn't going to take any chances. I returned to the bedroom and found Robin sitting on my bed, his cap still in his hands as he inspected its bill.

"This is ridiculous," he said. "How could they be here?"

"It had to have been the police. There's all kinds of rumors going around, but mostly just that I was kidnapped at gunpoint. Only you guys know the whole story."

I flushed with anger at the irresponsibility of whoever leaked my information—which must have come from the police department—and with the media themselves for being so opportunistic that they blatantly disregarded my need for safety. The men had not been caught yet and they were armed. I didn't want them to know I had spoken with the police; I didn't want them tipped off that the police were looking for them, and I definitely didn't want them to have any additional information about me. Now I was in hiding for two different reasons. I had never thought I'd have to protect myself from the people who were there to protect me.

As Robin sat there going over various possibilities—getting a lawyer involved, moving me to another location nearby, going back home earlier than planned—I remembered something. Before I was finally allowed to go home, the police had told me not to watch the news or read anything in the paper or online. I was still so shocked that I didn't think about what that might mean. Now I got it.

My identity wasn't going to be kept a secret. Back home, the media had greater respect for an individual's privacy. They would have never shown up at my door. I didn't understand how the police or the courts in the United States worked, but still this seemed incredibly wrong. Just because something horrible happened to you, did that mean that it could be on the news? Worse, how could people believe it was okay to show up on your doorstep, show images of where you lived?

Kristine and Viktoria joined Robin and me in the bedroom.

"I heard someone on campus talking about another rape today. She didn't use your name, but she did say something about the victim being an athlete."

Robin told them about the reporters outside the apartment. In an instant we were all talking over one another. I was having a hard time concentrating. There were no laws preventing Dallas media from naming sex-assault victims unless we were given a pseudonym, but I already had one: Jessica December Watkins. When I asked why that full name, I was told that when pseudonym laws came into effect, law enforcement decided to have the victim choose his or her own first name, the middle name would be the month of the offense, and the last name would be the lead detective's last name. That way, people within the department would be able to identify the case—they'd know who "Jessica December Watkins" was because they'd be able to figure out who was assigned to Detective Watkins in December.

Despite the pseudonym, though, the media had found me. Was it just a matter of time before my identity was revealed to the world? When would my attackers find out?

Finally, Kristine got all of our attention. "It doesn't matter how it happened or if it's wrong or right. What are we going to do to fix this?"

We all agreed. I had to get out of there.

Viktoria had suggested that we contact Coach Wollman. While she went to do that, the rest of us began packing our things.

"It's going to be okay," Robin said. "It's better to be safe."

"I know. I'm upset because it seems like things just won't settle down. I want things to be more normal, and they just won't."

"I'm not going to let things get bad. I promise you. This is going to end soon."

Robin held me and I felt better. I didn't like the idea of leaving the apartment and someplace familiar, but it wasn't as if I really felt safe where I was.

On top of this new worry about the media, I could see that the stress of everything was getting to Robin. He seemed pale and drawn, and his eyes had that glossy shocked look of someone who's just witnessed something terrible. I'd been checking in with him constantly, asking over and over if he was okay. As I moved around the apartment storing things in boxes, loading up my luggage and backpack, he sat on the couch staring blindly ahead.

"When was the last time you ate?" I asked him.

He shrugged and moved his limp hands slightly in his lap.

"You have to take care of yourself. If you're not strong, you won't be able to help me."

It took some time, but I convinced him to meet with our friend David to get something to eat.

I was just as worried about Kristine and Viktoria. They'd both been taking turns with Robin sitting with me, sleeping alongside me when I tried to nap. I was afraid that my nightmares had become their nightmares. I had no idea how long they were going to have to babysit me the way they were; I desperately wanted to stop feeling like a burden to my friends, but the thought of being alone still terrified me.

Just after we finished packing, the phone rang. It was a police detective, calling to tell me that we should pack up our things and leave. Somehow someone in the media had gotten word of where we lived.

Thanks for the warning, I thought ruefully.

"How did this get to the media?" I asked him. "It had to have come from the police."

"I'm sorry. We have a very large department here, and it's just not possible to know who might have said something. Reporters are around all the time."

At least the man apologized to me. I couldn't say what else I wanted or expected, but I was left with the sense that I wasn't being treated fairly or properly.

Robin had returned by the time we'd finished packing. He made several scouting trips out to the parking lot to make sure that no reporters were around. When we were sure that the coast was clear, we hustled our things into Robin's car. The women's cross-country coach, Coach Casey, had also arrived with her car. We loaded both cars up, all of us barely talking, just moving as quickly as we could.

In just a few hours, Coach Wollman had arranged the new housing for us. We headed to a dormitory building on campus that was intended for married students with children. What an odd sight we must have been, three young women arriving with our bags in the middle of December. It was an unexpected spot and not easy to find, for the media or for rapists.

The police advised us to keep a low profile and keep to ourselves for a while in this dorm. That wasn't hard for me to do, considering I was terrified of strangers and had no desire to have the world know about what had happened to me.

We weren't able to bring all of our things in one car trip, so we went back the next day to retrieve the rest of our belongings. My first priority had been to get all of my textbooks and notes. I was still studying every day, finishing up a couple of papers, still fretting over my grades.

As we neared our block, I could feel my anxiety rising. My mind and my pulse raced. By the time we pulled into the parking lot, I was having a hard time just steadying my breathing.

Kristine opened the car door, and I let out a low cry. She immediately shut the door and turned to me.

"What is it?"

"I can't."

We'd purposely come late at night, figuring that the journalists wouldn't be there.

Kristine peered through the car window.

"I don't think anybody's here."

"It's not—"

"It's okay. Viktoria and I will go. Lauren and Kylie can help, too."

We'd gotten a couple of our teammates to help us out. They were standing near the stairwell, silhouetted by a small fixture.

Somehow, the presence of the other two women helped me compose myself. I didn't want to let on that I was frightened.

"No. I'll go. Slowly. Would you mind going ahead of me?"

Kristine and Viktoria linked arms and walked ahead of me. I pulled the hood of my sweatshirt tightly around my face and walked with my head bowed. Then, as if a sudden thunderstorm had started dumping rain down on us, we all made a mad dash for the stairs. I stood at the door, running in place, trying to get the key into the lock. A few seconds later, we were in. Someone watching us would have thought that we were the criminals and not five friends trying to avoid being found by the media. We ran from room to room, putting things in boxes and bags. We ran as fast as we could, each of us with her arms loaded, or sometimes two of us carrying a box together, shuffling along as quickly as we could.

I sat in the packed interior of the car, unable to see anyone else due to all the things we'd loaded. At one point, we went over a bump and we heard something break.

"I hope it was a plate," Kristine said. "I'm so tired of washing dishes."

Silence lingered for a few seconds. "Whoever has that box, could you *please* just throw it out the window?"

Kristine's fake desperation sounded so real that we all began to laugh. Once inside our new location, we all collapsed onto the floor.

"I'm not doing another thing today," Viktoria said. "This is all just too crazy."

I understood completely. I was exhausted but too anxious to really sleep. While Kristine and Viktoria retreated to the lone bedroom, I spent a few hours organizing the kitchen. None of the plates had broken, and I considered for a moment wrapping one in a towel and smacking it against the sink as a present for Kristine. Robin was in the main room, moving boxes and bags around, trying to make space for a mattress we could sleep on. I appreciated his efforts but knew that comfort wasn't going to make much of a difference.

Between my nightmares and the unfamiliarity of the new surroundings, I barely got any sleep at all. Still, I knew that we had other business to attend to. As soon as the management office opened, I called to let them know that we had to move out of our old place. I spoke to an assistant there, and she seemed very confused. When she put our building's manager on, I said that an emergency had come up and that we'd already moved out. I could hear the suspicion in his voice. I didn't blame him— after all, we were college-aged, not from this country, and he'd likely seen and heard a lot of excuses from tenants like us over the years. He said that he needed to look at our lease to see about early termination.

Coach Wollman came to our rescue again. We let him know what had gone on, and he said that he would contact the manager on our behalf. Eventually, we got a call back. He'd arranged for us to get out of our lease with no financial penalty. "We left the place a mess, though," Viktoria pointed out. "We'll never get our security deposit back if we don't clean it up."

I sighed and shut my eyes. Robin traced small circles on my back with his fingertips, just like my mother did to soothe me. "It'll be okay. We'll work together and get it done."

Dreading my return and knowing that we wouldn't be able to do a

quick in and out of there like we had the night before, all I could manage
was a weak nod of my head and a strained smile. On top of everything
else we were dealing with, the thought of having to pay rent on two different places weighed on our minds. None of us could afford that. With
our trips home for the holiday break looming, we felt under even more
pressure to get out of the old place and into the new one.

Back we went to the old apartment, skulking inside one more time. As
we cleaned, it seemed so strange to me how as simple an act as cleaning
a sink or mopping a floor could become surreal. I found myself staring at
a bucket of water, the pine scent of the cleaner nearly bringing tears to
my eyes, and wondering, Why in the world are we doing this? Shouldn't
we be taking a break from exam preparations by watching a movie? Why
did getting out that bit of a pasta sauce stain seem like such an urgent and
essential task? Why were none of us laughing? Why weren't we listening
to music and shouting questions over it about the parents or friends who
were arriving soon and had prompted this spasm of cleanliness? Why was
it that the echoing sounds of our efforts reminded me of some horror
movie that I'd only half-watched while clinging to Robin's biceps?

When we were just about finished, another question came to me.
What had I done to deserve such loyal friends?

One more difficult task remained. We had to go from the apartment to
the on-site leasing office to sign the papers releasing us from our obligation. I didn't want to go to the office; I was afraid of who might be waiting back at the building that had obviously been identified as my home.
I was terrified of the attackers showing up, terrified of being spotted by
the media, terrified of feeling even more vulnerable. But as great as my
fear was, I was even more determined not to let anyone dictate to me
anymore where I went.

"I'll be fine. I'll get through this," I told Robin, consciously echoing
the words he'd been using with me. He looked unsure, but reluctantly
agreed to go back to the new apartment while I went to sign the papers
at the leasing office with my roommates.

The three of us walked toward the building that housed the office,
talking about how we'd miss the place, except for the upstairs neighbors
with the sound system on steroids.

"At least we got to experience what it would be like to live through a mild earthquake," Kristine said.

Keeping my eyes focused straight ahead, I said, "That's true, but—"

"Monika? Monika! My God, what's happening?" Kristine was shouting at me from across the street. I was standing on the sidewalk. A moment ago, we'd been in the parking lot, under the shade of a large oak tree near the fenced-in garbage Dumpsters. My heart was thumping wildly and my fingers were tingling. Across the road I saw someone swing open the gate and toss a garbage bag into the metal container. A moment later the sound of its lid crashing against the side reached me.

I had no recollection of how I'd gotten there. I could see Kristine's mouth moving, but it was like I was underwater and the sounds were muffled and indistinct. The thought of what had made me act that way frightened me. A few cars passed between my friends and me.

Then I saw another vehicle—a big black SUV parked right next to where Kristine and Viktoria had just been standing. It looked exactly like the rapists' car; it even had the same tinted windows. I must have run across the street on pure instinct when I saw the car, without any conscious understanding of why I was doing it.

Fear had taken control so completely that it had made me do something I wasn't even aware of doing. What else might it make me do? What if I had gotten hit by a car when I sprinted across the street like that? Would the fear have been so strong that I wouldn't have even noticed the car coming? I was already afraid of so much, and now I was afraid of the fear.

THE NEXT AFTERNOON, I was back in Dr. Soutter's office. This time, I didn't try so hard to hide what was bothering me. I told her about what had happened at the leasing office.

"It's quite common for trauma survivors to respond as you did, especially so soon after the event. Your body's fight-or-flight defense mechanism had kicked in."

I remembered telling Robin how I could outrun any potential attacker. Now I wondered just exactly how many forms attackers could take.

"But over time, that will end," she promised. "You'll learn that dangerous things don't always happen when you see a big black car, and eventually, the fear will let go."

Logically that made sense. But in the moment, to have responded like
that, without any kind of awareness of the consequences, troubled me.
I wanted that "eventually" to be now. She had said that the fear would
let go, but when? And could I let go of it? Which of us was in control? I
couldn't bear the idea that the fear dictated to me.

Dr. Soutter said that she wanted to meet with me every day before the
Winter Break. In a way, Dr. Soutter was like a professor; she didn't explic-
itly tell me that I had to continue to see her, but because of her position, I
felt that I had to. I'd never seen a therapist before, and I had thought that
it would be more like going to see an academic advisor. I'd be asked a
lot of questions, be provided with specific guidance and suggestions, and
then have the opportunity to ask any questions. That wasn't how it went
at all. I'd come in and sit down; Dr. Soutter would settle into her chair,
and after a brief introductory how-are-you-doing formality, she would
wait for me to do the talking. It seemed like everything I said, she told
me was normal. Then I wondered, If that's true, then why do I need to be
talking about these things?

I had been raised to be self-reliant, to figure out things for myself and
to trust myself. As a result, I started to resent the therapy; I didn't want to
be the kind of person who needed therapy, much less daily therapy. I was
used to coaches working with me on training plans—do this, this, and
this on these days. That produced the results that I wanted in my running;
when I followed those steps, I gradually got faster. I could see immediate
results. With Dr. Soutter, that wasn't the case. I wasn't really seeing any
results that I could tie directly to having spoken with her. I wanted to
move beyond the attack, and therapy seemed like it was anchoring me
back at that point.

None of this was Dr. Soutter's fault. She was kind and compassionate,
but I always had my guard up. I wasn't used to opening up to a stranger,
and though this was a professional relationship, I still applied some of
those restrictions on our interactions. In a way, those sessions were like
my running. I'm not a sprinter. It takes me a while to loosen up on a

run, and in those sessions, just when I'd gotten past the warm-up period and felt like "Okay, I'm ready now. I can talk more freely. I can let my emotions show," the clock told us that we were done for the day. As much as we'd both try to apply the notion of "Okay, we'll pick up from here tomorrow," it doesn't work that way. Just as you don't start a run, stop at some point, and then return to that stopping point and resume running feeling the same way, with your muscles as warm and loose as they were, the same is true with therapy. I can see now that the sessions took place too soon after the incident. It also didn't help that I woke up every morn- ing puking from the anti-HIV medication I was taking. That was on top of the flu, insomnia, and still being achy and sore from the attack. I wasn't in the best frame of mind or body when I saw Dr. Soutter. I was still too raw, too wounded—though I couldn't have said that then—to really assess or process what was going on. It was like asking someone running in the middle of a raging storm to think about what she was going to wear to a cousin's wedding in six months. My head was in a very differ- ent place. Put another way, Dr. Soutter wanted me to press the "pause" button, to freeze-frame the image, and I had my finger firmly down on fast-forward, wanting to get past the parts that I didn't like and get to the parts that I did.

Again, I was torn and nothing seemed easy and everything was con- tradictory. Even though there were many days when I didn't want to talk about it anymore, I knew this was something I needed to deal with. I wanted to deal with it right the first time so it didn't wind up cropping up in my mind years later as an unresolved trauma. Maybe if I kept going to therapy, the nightmares would stop. Maybe I wouldn't need someone to come into the bathroom with me every time I needed to go. Maybe I wouldn't worry that every single man on the way to the gym was danger- ous. Those were my goals. What specifically could I do to work out those issues the way I worked out my body?

I started thinking about how to work with my thoughts in a con- structive way. I remembered reading somewhere that it's good to write out your thoughts and feelings when you need to gain perspective, so that's what I decided to do: As soon as I felt ready, I would write about everything that had happened to me. Dr. Soutter supported the idea, but cautioned me that I should do it just a little at a time and to sit in places where I felt safe while doing it. That way I wouldn't be as likely to get overwhelmed by reliving the trauma so soon.

I didn't really know where to begin with my writing. I sat there with my headphones on, listening to Pink's song "Glitter in the Air" on repeat. I had loved that song for a long time, but the words "Have you ever looked fear in the face and said I just don't care?" took on new meaning. I'd admired Pink for daring to be different, for her bravery and toughness, for being strong and vulnerable at the same time. So on those nights when sleep wouldn't come, or when I walked to classes and wondered if people were staring at me and knew my not-so-secret secret, I listened to Pink. Maybe because I didn't let my friends and family in as much as I could have or should have, or maybe because no one can ever truly experience or fully empathize with what anyone else has gone through, listening to Pink's music made me feel less alone, like there was someone out there who knew what to say to me when others' words and my own fell short.

The psychologist was right: Keeping a journal and recounting those awful moments was hard at the beginning. It took a different type of mental courage to think through again every terrible thing that the men had done to me and to expose myself to feeling all those emotions once more. It terrified me, but because it did, I knew I had to do it. This wasn't something that I could do with someone else, like running. The memories and images that invaded my sleep and waking consciousness had overpowered me, pressed themselves into my mind against my wishes. Now, in writing my memories down, I was going to be the one in charge. I was going to take Pink's words as advice to me, to just not care, to set aside any fears about reliving those moments.

Since the attack I had scarcely been alone. I knew that writing was going to have to be something I did on my own. Kristine and Robin in particular were reluctant to leave my side. I knew that if they saw that what I was writing was making me cry, they would stop me. I didn't want to be stopped. That would be like being pulled off the track before a race was over.

I told them I needed some time alone, and they agreed, reluctantly. I wasn't going to check the lock multiple times. I wasn't going to check the cabinets or closets.

I sat down in front of my computer and I started to type.

Friday, December 4th.

That's as far as I got. I moved around the room. I needed a glass of water and then another one, and then I needed to put on another jacket because the room was cold. I was just distracting myself; I didn't want to go back to those memories. But I had to. As I put on the jacket, I remembered the book a friend of mine had dropped off a few days earlier. A woman she worked with at Lululemon had told her to give it to me when she heard about what I'd been through. On the cover of the journal was a picture of a butterfly with the word "Begin" written in gold letters on top of it. I started digging through the unpacked bags on the floor from our hasty move. There it was. Begin. I put my favorite song by Josh Groban—"You Are Loved (Don't Give Up)"—on repeat on my computer. I let the song play through several times while I sat down on the bed with the blanket wrapped around me. Then, as the music swelled at the beginning of the chorus, I started writing. Those first few words were like the start of a training run, loosening up, getting into the rhythm of it. I started off with the party, and then began to pick up the intensity, moving to that moment of terror that for the last few days had marked the before and after of my life, when Kristine and I had to let go of each other.

Then I wrote, "I felt something next to my head, on the right side of my skull. It was a gun—"

A sudden rush of random imagery and sensations flooded my mind, one after another like rapid-fire photographs—the door I first approached and its horseshoe knocker. A nut and bolt and crumpled fast-food wrapper under the seat of the SUV. My bare feet crunching across the glass- and gravel-strewn shoulder of the road, how it sparkled like fallen stars. The sour, hot breath of the Worst One as he forced himself inside me. The feel of the carpet against my face as I lay there and the muffled voices outside the vehicle argued about my fate. I felt so dirty again that I needed to take a shower.

Tears ran down my face and mixed with the water until I just collapsed there and sat in the tub and cried for a long time. The images that came to my mind were disturbing, but I didn't try to chase them away. I just let myself remember and feel whatever it was that came up. After a while, I didn't know why I was crying. Was it sadness, fear, relief? I couldn't pinpoint my emotion. Finally, I just felt empty. Empty of tears, empty of feelings. It felt strange, but it also felt good. The numbness wearing off was painful, but at least I was feeling something. I was still alive. Still breathing. I could feel the circulation returning to the parts that had shut down. I knew enough about being cold to understand that what my body had done was divert blood from the extremities to preserve the essential organs, keep my blood flowing to where it was needed in order to simply survive.

I understood while in that hot shower and flood of tears that my brain had been doing the same thing. This wasn't about survival anymore, this was about healing, about regaining strength, about letting the blood and the sensations flow through every part of my being, carrying nutrients away to do the needed work and shuttling off the debris that would only make the pain and stiffness linger.

For me no pain, no gain was going to be much more than a cliché.

CHAPTER SIX

The Station

On the fourth day following my rape, the police contacted Robin to get in touch with me.

"We need you to come down to the police station," the officer said. "Are you at the dorm?"

"Yes," I said.

"All of you?"

"You want Kristine and Viktoria to come, too?"

"Yes," he said. "It's important."

"Okay. What do you need us to do?"

He didn't want to elaborate, so I hung up and wondered what important thing they needed to talk to all of us about. I had been calling multiple times every day to remind them that I would do anything I could to help in the investigation; I was probably driving them crazy, but I just wanted to help them find these men so they couldn't do it again.

Coach Wollman, though, was furious when he found out that we were supposed to go to the station. He called up the lead detective who'd been assigned to my case, BJ Watkins, and said, "These girls aren't going anywhere until I know they're safe. There's media camped outside of their old apartment, and I just got them set up in a place where no one can find them. I'm not about to mess that up by having someone spot them coming to the police station and following them home."

"I understand," Detective Watkins told him. He knew exactly how low the media could go, having had run-ins before with one of the same reporters who were currently sitting outside my old apartment.

"What if you bring them to a meeting point with us, and we'll be there in unmarked cars? We can then take the girls to the station. We can use a restricted-access entrance and elevator. Anyone without credentials won't be around. After we're done, we'll call you and tell you when to meet us back at the drop-off location."

It felt like a presidential Secret Service escort. Coach Wollman had Coach Casey pick us up from the dorms and bring us to an arranged spot in a shopping center. We pulled in from one side, the police pulled in from another side, in a car they'd picked up from an impound lot, and we piled into their car and drove off without a word, Robin in the front and the three of us in the back.

As we drove around to the back of the police station, I could feel Kristine and Viktoria tense. We hadn't talked much on the way there, but I sensed something was different. I was seated in the backseat with one of them on each side of me, the shortest of us placed in the most cramped spot, like the youngest child. I watched as each of them sat and stared out the window, their usually animated expressions gone slack. This was my first time at the station, but I knew that it held its own bit of horror for the two of them. I reached out and rested my hands on theirs. Kristine smiled briefly and nodded. Not for the first time, I wondered what it would have been like to be either of the two of them, the panic and frustration they must have experienced in wondering what was going on with me that night, if I was dead or alive. Each of us had her own trauma from that night, and I felt terrible that they had to return to that place of fear for them.

Viktoria squeezed my hand, shut her eyes, and exhaled loudly, shaking her arms like she did in preparation for a jump. Not knowing how police investigations worked and the detective being unwilling to tell us why we had been called in added to my anxiety. As the car rolled to a stop and we stepped into the bright sunshine, my bladder suddenly burned.

What if we were there to confront in person the men who had done those things to me?

I stood rooted in place, squinting at the building and its heavily tinted windows, the grillwork that covered the bottom row of them. A door opened, and two men in suits led another man by the arms down a set of concrete steps. The held man squinted and bowed his head against the sun. The policemen, their eyes jacketed by dark glasses, nodded at the detective who'd been driving us. Robin took my hand and led me toward the entrance, his head pivoting from side to side to make sure that no one else could see us.

One of the detectives must have noted how my anxiety level had risen and read my mind. "No one you know," he said. "Besides, we're taking you guys in through the VIP entrance. Very Important Person, not Very In Trouble Prisoner."

He smiled, and Robin and I let out a brief laugh.

We stopped at a desk and were issued identification tags that hung from chains. None of us spoke. We were led to an elevator, and once we were inside, a uniformed officer who was escorting us asked, "You her boyfriend?"

Robin said yes immediately and then looked at me to see how I reacted. In all those months, we hadn't acknowledged that out loud. He'd stayed with my family and slept at my apartment, but never once had we called each other "boyfriend" and "girlfriend." We had acted very casual about things. Here of all places came the next step of our relationship. I couldn't help but laugh. Robin started laughing, too. The officer raised one eyebrow and shook his head briefly.

We went up only a single floor. I thought it was strange that we needed an elevator for that. When the doors opened, Detective Watkins was standing to one side. As we stepped out, he held his arm out indicating the way we were to go. I felt my heart rate climbing, and despite what I'd been told, I was still wondering if around the corner I'd see those three men. In a way I was going to see them. Detective Watkins explained that we were there to view photos of various men. He was going to take us into the room one at a time to view the pictures. After we came out of the room, we weren't to talk to one another at all about what we'd seen or thought. Instead of completely calming my fears, knowing what was ahead of me only heightened my anxiety. I felt like I was about to take the most important test of my life.

Detective Watkins led me to a small, sterile room where another investigator waited at a small table with a large manila envelope in his hands. I understood that inside that envelope were the images I was to look through. I stood in that doorway unable to move. I tried counting to five and told myself that I would step forward then. I couldn't. I started to shake and wondered if the detectives could see that I had. I didn't want to disappoint them, but I didn't want to do this, either. I had never in my life imagined that I would be in a room doing something like this.

"We're ready," Detective Watkins said, and it was as if his words connected some wiring in my brain that allowed me to move again.

The other investigator set the envelope of images on the table, at which I was now seated. I sat staring at the table for a moment and then looked away at how stain rings on the table's surface caught the light from the overhead. I suddenly became very aware of my body and the contact it was making with the floor, the chair, the table, the sharp flap of the envelope. I began to shake again, knowing how important it was that I get this right and angry that I had to be there at all.

I looked at Detective Watkins and the other investigator. Both of them regarded me with a neutral expression, not unkind, not bored, not angry, just looking past me like you might someone you passed by on a busy street. I suddenly felt even more alone. I was without a trusted companion for one of the first times since that night, and I hated it. As Detective Watkins left and the door clicked closed, the panic rose up in my throat. There were no windows in the room, no way for me to see my friends or signal for help if I needed it. And what if this man . . .

No. This detective is not a rapist. I forced myself to think.

In those early days I had to keep reminding myself that most people were good and the world was not full of dangerous people who would attack me at the first chance.

The detective who was assigned to the room with me finally spoke. "I don't know which of these men are the real suspects and which are not. I won't be able to bias you by anything I do or how I react. Do you understand that?"

His voice was pleasantly deep, like someone I might have heard on the radio or the television. I nodded, and for the first time he smiled a bit. "Good." He slid the envelope back toward himself and opened it. Just that little bit of encouragement seemed to ease some of my tension.

"I'm going to show you each photo one at a time. Take your time to look it over and then either say 'yes,' 'no,' or 'not sure' to each photo. No comparing one photo to the next. You can look as long as you want, but once you answer, you can't go back. You have to give an answer for each photo before looking at the next one. There will be three sets of six photos. Are you ready?"

I nodded.

As I looked at the first photo, it occurred to me what an awful responsibility this was. I might have to point at people and call them rapists. I had to figure out based on these photos who could be labeled a rapist for the rest of their lives and probably spend a lot of time in jail. It made me panic, and suddenly I became very unsure of myself.

"No," I said to the first photo.

The officer flipped to the next photo. He repeated the instructions, but this time his voice had lost its pleasant tone. I felt like I was listening to a recording that repeated the same message over and over. I looked at my hands; in the artificial light my already fair skin had taken on a chalky gray color. I felt cold, yet my palms were sweaty.

I looked hard at the person in the photograph, at the blank gaze in his eyes, and I involuntarily slapped the table. Then I jumped because of the slapping noise. I felt like someone was strangling me and I had to look away for a second.

Was he one of them? It felt like he was, but I just wasn't positive. It was a photograph—a two-dimensional thing without changing facial expressions, without voice, smell, or body language. He might have been the driver, but I couldn't say for sure. I forced myself to look at the photo again and to concentrate on each feature separately. Were those thick eyebrows the ones that I remembered? Was that mouth the one that mocked me, that laughed at me and twisted into a grimace as he forced me to the floor?

My eyes welled with tears as I said, "I think it's him."

And then I had a pang of conscience—what if I was wrong and I had just labeled someone as a "maybe" rapist? It was too hard; I looked at each photo and the faces blended together. They all appeared Hispanic, and none of them stood out as obvious picks to me. I said "no" or "not sure" to all but that one photo, feeling very nervous and anxious as I had to scan my mind for images I never wanted to see again. And always there was the gun. Had they shown me a photo of the gun, I would have recognized it immediately.

This process wasn't anywhere near as clear-cut as I would have expected it to be. I never thought I could be unsure about those three faces, and yet the panic made it difficult to be sure. There were some I was able to exclude with certainty, but none I could say a simple "yes" to.

I walked out of the room and into the hallway feeling as if I had failed the exam, that I'd barely been able to even write my name on the blue book. The feeling reminded me of nightmares I'd had throughout my school days—that pit-of-the-stomach panic that rose from opening a test booklet and realizing that I'd studied the wrong subject entirely, that instead of being a test about history, the page was filled with complex equations and notations in a language that I had only some vague sense of having seen once before.

Following the detective's instructions to the letter, I didn't even make eye contact with Viktoria as she stepped into the room next. I stood with my arms wrapped around my chest, gently rocking from side to side and toe to heel, my body barely able to keep pace with my racing thoughts. I'd seen a few courtroom scenes from movies in which lawyers reduced witnesses to crying and quaking masses of uncertainty. A part of me wanted to be like Lisbeth Salander, Stieg Larsson's heroine, someone who could be cool and calculating in exacting revenge. Except I didn't want revenge; I just wanted this to be over, to know with absolute certainty that I had identified the men who had done those horrible things to me and that they would no longer be able to do them to anyone else.

Before I was even aware of time passing, I heard the click of the door's latch and Viktoria joined me in the hallway. Our gazes brushed past each other briefly, and out of the corner of my eye I saw Kristine duck under the arm of the man who held the door open for her. Another door opened and Detective Watkins waved us toward him. Viktoria and I took seats in a kind of waiting room, sat with our hands beneath us on molded plastic chairs that wobbled as if the fasteners holding them together had all spun loose. I wasn't sure if it was the chairs or my frazzled state that produced the sensation that we were at sea, rocking over waves that upset my stomach and blurred my vision.

To steady myself, I started calculating how much longer it would be until I was on my way back home to Norway. It was December 10, 2009. I was scheduled to fly home eight days later. I struggled with the numbers for a few moments. One hundred and ninety-two hours. I looked for a clock, hoping to make the answer more precise. The room had no clock. I couldn't remember the exact time of my flight's departure or its arrival back in Norway. I normally had a good mind for details, but with those faces, I began to question just how sure I could be of anything.

I heard Viktoria clear her throat and watched her cough softly into the crook of her elbow. She sat absently tugging at a strand of her hair. The sound of the waiting room officer sliding his chair as he stood up startled me. Viktoria looked at me and rolled her eyes. I wanted to talk to her about what she'd seen, hoping that her recollection of things was better than mine. My thoughts about what it might be like to be in that room, in that building, under different circumstances, waiting to be told whether I was free to go or if I was going to prison, were interrupted by the sound of footsteps. Kristine joined us and took a seat. A minute later, Detective Watkins joined us along with Robin.

I inhaled deeply, waiting for the verdict about our performance.

Detective Watkins looked as if he was about to speak but then didn't. He rubbed at one eye and then winked it several times in a row as if to clear it of something.

"I want you to know that we've been working on your case 24/7," he said.

"Thank you. I really do appreciate it," I said.

"Several of us—we've wanted to get this riddle solved and get your attackers off the street. And now I have some information to share with you. We have the three men in custody."

For a moment I didn't believe what I'd just heard. I looked over at the other girls, and their expressions confirmed that I'd heard correctly.

"We know they're the right ones. We've had one of them in custody for several days already; we found him with your cell phone in his pocket and he has confessed. We got the other two today at their residence, along with the gun they used to threaten you. All three of them are in jail now."

I jumped up from my chair and ran across the room into Robin's arms. I cried; he cried harder.

The feeling of relief was indescribable. I hadn't fully realized just how scared I was until that moment, when this huge heaviness lifted from me. I was safe. The rapists hadn't found me. They weren't hiding outside my apartment or in my bathroom; they were in jail where they belonged. The police had done their jobs without fanfare, and had waited until now to tell me because they didn't want there to be a chance that they were wrong.

"I think this must be the best day of my life," Robin said, and his words made me feel so warm. It felt like the best day of my life, too. Better than winning any competition.

I hugged Kristine and Viktoria, so thankful that we were there together to share that moment. They'd been through so much and had been working so hard to support me. I could read the relief in their eyes as well. The three of us stood in a small circle, our heads inclined and touching, talking over one another in a nearly unintelligible language of relief and joy, about how hard it had been to look at the pictures, how we were sure that we'd somehow messed the whole thing up, how glad we were that those men couldn't come after us now.

"Oh my God, Monika," Kristine said, nearly shrieking with glee, "this is so good."

What had gone mostly unsaid among us was the fact that I wasn't the only one who was in danger all those days and nights. My two friends had also seen those men, and who knew what they might do to get rid of any witnesses? I realized the implication of what Detective Watkins had said about one of them having my phone. On it were pictures of everyone close to me. Those men wouldn't have had to try to remember what we all looked like—all they had to do was scroll through all my photos. I pushed that thought aside quickly.

Detective Watkins went on talking to us, but I could barely focus on what he was saying, words like "hearings," "arraignments," "prosecutors," and all the rest bounced around the room and were lost. I looked around the room at my friends and saw them smiling, genuinely smiling in a way that I hadn't seen since the night of the party. Once we had been escorted out to the car and returned to the drop-off point, the reality of what had just happened began to sink in. Coach Casey was ecstatic, and she phoned Coach Wollman with the news. He wanted to speak to me, but there was so much commotion in the car, I could barely hear him. I felt like I was back to square one with my beginner's English, saying over and over again, "So happy! So happy!"

A few moments later, I sat quietly while the others went on with their excitement. They had the men in custody. I almost couldn't believe it. Then, just as had happened the night the police drove me to the hospital, it was as if the scene outside the car slowed. But this was different. The lights, the buildings, all seemed haloed and frozen, like icicles reflecting holiday lights, serene and beautiful. I hadn't noticed them looking like that before, hadn't taken the time to enjoy this spectacle. I looked at my friends, their eyes bright, their voices a choir of joy. I was alive. I was with these people who mattered so much to me. My prayers had been answered.

Back at our new room, we all stood in the middle of the clutter and Viktoria asked, "So, what do you want to do to celebrate?" I could hear a tinge of teasing in her voice. They all looked at me expectantly.

I shrugged and said as dramatically as I could, "I'll have to think about that."

"Just let us know," Kristine and Viktoria said and went into their room.

Grinning from ear to ear, Robin handed me one of my equipment bags. "Let's go."

A moment later, Viktoria and Kristine returned. They'd changed into their warm-up suits, too.

"Ready?"

In the first few days after the rape, I had veered off my schedule. I wasn't a runner in the same way I had been.

A hard workout may not seem like much of a reward to most people, but for me it was. While some people might have thought, You've been through so much, you deserve to take some time off, I thought just the opposite. I *deserved* to be able to run again. I'd earned the privilege to do the thing that gave me the most satisfaction. I was determined not to let anything get in the way of me becoming an Olympian, of me reaching my most treasured goal. Unlike that first time on the treadmill, I understood that it wasn't so much my performance but my appearance that mattered. I showed up at the figurative start line for this race. The only other competitor I was running against that day after finding out the men had been arrested was the memory of those men and what they'd tried to take from me. That wasn't my body, but my spirit, my drive, my ambition, my ability to take pleasure in my body's efforts, to measure out precisely how effort and results were connected.

I suppose that in some ways it would have been no different to be working out on an ordinary December day between the track and cross-country seasons. We weren't formally meeting as a squad and adhering to a strict training regimen. If it hadn't been for the rape, I would have been running every day, balancing my schoolwork with my training schedule. The men who had attacked me changed that; I hadn't been able to maintain my discipline in the days since the rape and had been detached from everything that defined me as Monika Kørra, daughter of Kari-Ann and Tore, sister of Anette, the driven woman who had traveled halfway around the world for a chance to train with some of the best teammates in the world. Preparing for a workout was the best way I could begin reclaiming my identity, to show that being raped would not be the end of the world I had worked so hard to create. I could not erase the memories of what had happened to me, but I wanted to reduce them to just another facet of my life, another obstacle to overcome, to integrate them into the whole of my life.

My roommates and Robin understood that about me. They understood without me having to explain to them what it meant to dedicate your life to something. We'd all come from another country and made difficult adjustments to succeed in an environment that was foreign to us. I was already used to thinking of Viktoria and Kristine as teammates. Robin, who also played an individual sport in a team context, like we did, also fit naturally into that same category. We'd all experienced something horrible, in individual ways, but we all had the same goal in mind: to help me become better and to have our lives back to the way that they had been.

For the last four days, my friends had done their best to shield me from my emotions. When I started to cry, they made me laugh. When I felt fearful, they comforted and distracted me. But if I was going to conquer it, I needed to feel the pain. That was as true for my body as it was for my mind.

We went on a group run to celebrate the men being caught. I still felt a buzz of anxiety in my stomach, and I scanned the area around me nervously, but it felt good to be running. For those first four days, my fear had been real—those men were out there, they knew where I lived, and it was in their best interest that I not be around to identify them. Now my fear was all in my head. I would have to meet that fear, to look it in the face and be able to say that I just didn't care—that fear didn't have a hold on me. I wasn't there yet, but knowing that I was safe from those men, that they were in jail, gave me one less bad thing to focus on. I could cross it off my list and move on to another task on my "To Do" list.

CHAPTER SEVEN

Departure

I felt a thump against my lower back and heard the low rumble of a voice behind me cursing and then heaving a heavy sigh. I shifted in my seat, brought my legs up beneath me, and leaned against the wall of the plane. Another thump and another curse that was barely audible over the sound of the jet's engines. I knew that the man behind me was struggling to get comfortable. Kristine and I had taken our seats for the flight to London, and just before the doors were closed and we pushed back away from the gate, he'd come on board, clearly flustered. When he squeezed past the other two people in the row behind us, he leaned heavily on my seat, forcing me forward.

On airplanes I was glad that I was Little Monika; other times, I struggled with what that meant. People who didn't know me might have made the assumption that little = lesser. I'd fought that notion my whole life, that just because I was small in stature I couldn't be as good at sports as other women and girls. We all make assumptions about other people based on physical qualities. It's easy. It's convenient. But it's more often than not wrong.

Just because I was aware of the dangers of making assumptions about people didn't meant that I was immune from making them myself. I knew that even as I made the transition from Little Monika in Norway to

Monika Kørra track-and-field and cross-country runner at SMU, people were still judging me based on a limited amount of evidence they had. In some ways, I was the typical collegiate athlete. In Norway, we didn't have the same preconceived ideas about what it meant to be what Americans sometimes thought of as a dumb jock. It was also untrue that just because I was an athlete I had to be unconcerned about things like music, fashion, and other "girly" interests.

I'd never liked the idea of being labeled, and liked it even less following the attack. I felt like someone had written the word "VICTIM" across my forehead in large block letters. In my mind, I heard people talking about me, referring to me as "the raped girl, the foreign girl, you know the one." I even saw a few negative posts about me on Facebook and other places; I tried to ignore them, but it was difficult.

I was grateful to be getting away for the holidays. I was eager to get home to see my friends and family and spend Christmas with them, but I was also glad that I would be away from campus for a time. I hoped that by the time we returned, people would have forgotten about what happened to me, and would be caught up in the start of a new semester or, in the case of the team, a new season.

The police had encouraged me to leave Dallas early. With the suspects in custody, I felt a bit safer, but I was still struggling to sleep and evade the horrible dreams. I fought against the idea that I was the raped girl, the one who needed special treatment. I wanted to attend all my classes, take all my final exams, and show everyone that I was okay; eventually, though, I had to give up on that idea.

As much as our brains try to deceive us, our bodies don't lie. I knew that from running, but it took me getting sick and developing a high fever that kept me bedridden for a few days to truly understand that my efforts to keep up normal appearances were a failure and a lie. In a way, I was able to outrace the rape in the first few days after, but as I lay in bed, physically unable to get up and move around, no longer able to keep to the strict schedule that I had adhered to for so long, all kinds of questions caught up to me. Without the structure of classes, studying, and running, stressed by the rape, the drugs I was taking, and the flu, I threw myself a brief pity party. It wasn't bad enough that I had been raped, but now I was sick. And finals were on us. And I was scheduled to go home and I didn't want to be miserable on the long flight. What else could go wrong?

Losing the ability to run and to keep to my busy schedule was a blessing in disguise.

At the time, I hated the idea of being sick and stuck in bed, but I can see now that it was my body's way of doing the right thing for me. I needed to slow down. I needed to let the reality of what had happened truly sink in and make me realize that business as usual wasn't going to work, that I couldn't deny forever the reality that my life had been altered. I fought against that idea, but at least I acknowledged the fact that denial was my opponent. I've heard it said that "We lose ourselves in the things we love; we find ourselves there, too." It took me time to realize that I needed to understand the distance between who I was then and who I had been before the rape in order to start to heal.

I was both pleased and a little angry when a woman at SMU who worked with international students who had visa and travel issues was less than understanding about my request to change from leaving on the eighteenth to leaving on the thirteenth of December. It typically took a week to process international requests; when we showed up just a few days before the day we wanted to reschedule our travel to, the receptionist looked at us and shook her head. "These take a week. This isn't your first time going through the process, so I'm sure you know that."

I said that I understood but that this was an emergency. I was on the verge of tears, both because I'd failed to remember something so important and because this woman didn't understand or care how important getting away was for me. It hadn't been my idea to move up the date I left for home, but suddenly the idea of not being able to do it was quite painful.

I was tempted to say something to her about what I'd been through, but only slightly so. I tried to tell myself that she didn't know, that I was just another of the foreign students she had to deal with, all of us making requests of her. That was a good thing to remember, but simultaneous with that sentiment was the anger that she didn't understand who I was, what I needed, and how my case was different. The tension between those two desires—to be like everyone else and to be understood as somehow exceptional—tore at me.

I left the paperwork with her and fretted over her response that she would make no guarantees. It was good, in a way, that she treated me just like everyone else. I wanted that to be how everyone dealt with me, but when faced with the reality of not getting something that I felt I really needed, I saw just how fragile those feelings really were, of being okay and able to handle all of this. My stomach was in knots with worry, but someone in the Athletic Department must have intervened on my behalf. I got the approvals I needed the next day. I look back on that incident and how SMU also helped me out by paying my medical bills, with enormous gratitude. At the time, I was so wrapped up in everything that was going on, and how poorly I felt, that I don't think I expressed that gratitude fully.

I was also enormously grateful that Kristine was able to travel with me. Before the rape, we'd had different plans, but the Athletic Department had arranged for the two of us to travel together all the way home. Hoisting my SMU athletics duffel bag into the trunk of George's car, I'd felt a profound sense of relief.

Despite telling myself that I couldn't live in denial, I was glad to be leaving Dallas and heading home. I could get away from the place where the rape had happened, escape the newspaper and television coverage that was a constant reminder of it, and literally put a great deal of distance between me and the incident. I'd also be able to feel more directly the support of my family. I loved the holidays, and having something to look forward to and think about other than doctor's appointments and phone calls with police and prosecutors felt good.

Kristine and I had both talked about how excited we were to be going home, and whether it was our nervous energy burning off quickly, or the accumulated exhaustion of the last two weeks, our excitement soon turned to sleep. As soon as we'd taken our seats, we'd both put in our ear buds, and even before the plane lifted off, we both were asleep. I woke up somewhere over the Atlantic, jostled into awareness by a flight attendant and his cart rattling past. Kristine was still out, and I sat there, hoping to sleep but knowing that my mind was racing and that rest was unlikely.

As I often did when I flew, I marveled at how in a matter of hours, I could be in one world, living one life, and then be in another location, picking up that other life. Sure, there were ways in which the two lives overlapped, but I think on that trip I felt more acutely than ever before the difference between there and here. Watching that icon of a jet plane on the view screen, crossing over all that water, had me thinking about how I was in so many ways in transit.

As I sat on that flight to London, I thought about how this home-coming might be different from the ones in the past. Even without the rape, it was always an interesting circumstance to return home after being away for a few months. In the past when I'd gone home, I experienced the strange sensation of living two lives—the one in Dallas and the one at home. I'd originally left Norway determined not to change from who I was there, to remain true to my upbringing and my culture. That wasn't easy. America was a wonderful place, and I loved my life in Dallas, the relative ease and abundance it offered.

I knew that my time at SMU was changing me, just as it would have any-one. I was experiencing new things, meeting new people, being exposed to new ideas. So, of course, I was changing. Now, though, on this trip home, I felt like the focus on how I was behaving, what I believed, and how I felt emotionally would be even more intense than usual. I was going to be with my family most of the time, and it was going to be more difficult to present to them the idealized version of Monika that I wanted them to see. It wasn't so much that I was afraid of letting them see the real me, who was struggling with staying focused, who was seemingly moving in and out of conversations and interactions with no control over the direction my thoughts were taking. It was that I didn't recognize myself. I wasn't the Little Monika that everyone had grown accustomed to knowing. I wasn't the Monika Kørra who went away to America and was taking steps toward realizing her Olympic dreams. I was a new version of myself, one who was feeling both enormously grateful to be alive and still profoundly confused and angry, wondering why this had happened to me and what that said about larger questions of purpose and the remainder of my life.

I had been profoundly changed by the rape, in ways that I didn't yet understand, and I was struggling with the aftereffects. What was going to happen to me when I saw the people who cared about me the most and about whom I cared the deepest? At times, I felt like I was a little child whose identity resembled a tower of blocks. Every now and then, for no reason that I could identify, I'd knock that tower down. Either I was frustrated that it didn't look exactly like I'd wanted it to look or how I remembered it had looked, or I was just so angry at what had happened that I lashed out at the tower for being another reminder of how my life had been altered by something completely out of my control.

What was going to happen when I came face-to-face with my parents and my sister, people who would naturally and easily work their way through whatever crumbling defenses I'd built up? Would getting to know this new and struggling me be too painful for them and for me? How much was I going to have to hide from them? And what about those defenses? Was I strong enough to support them at all? How many times could I lap the track telling everyone each day that I was fine?

I decided that I had to go with my strengths, revert back to the typical Monika, the one who was strong and in control. I wasn't going to hide my feelings, but I also wasn't going to release them all and make them the focus of my return. This was Christmas after all, and I was there to celebrate it with family and friends. This was to be a time to get back to normal. More than anything else, that was what I wanted.

On the final leg home, from London to Norway, Kristine and I seemed to be the only ones awake. We sat in the darkness, not wanting to turn on our overhead lights. Something about being with so many sleeping strangers struck us as funny, and we had to fight a case of the giggles, holding our noses, snorting, tears running down our cheeks like a couple of little girls.

"Wouldn't it be funny," Kristine said at one point, "if we could get up and switch everyone's luggage?" She pointed at the overhead bin.

"It would be better if we left the luggage where it is and switched the contents."

Kristine nodded her head slowly. "You're right. That way the chaos would come when we weren't here."

"I wouldn't want anyone blocking the aisle and delaying getting off this thing."

A man a few rows ahead of us barked like a seal as he snored.

We giggled again.

After a few moments of silence Kristine turned serious. "I've been thinking about it for a while. I'm glad that I met you and I'm glad that I was there that night and that we're going through this together."

"I am, too."

"I think it all happened for a reason. From the start, I mean. Meeting. Living together."

I nodded.

"Some things are out of your control, you know. That was what was so hard about having to release my grip on you that night."

"I know. I hated the idea that you thought you'd lost or had to give up. I know you did everything you could. There was nothing either of us could do. Sometimes fighting hard won't work."

"What I've been thinking a lot about in races is that I can't control people like I thought I could. That's a wrong way to look at it. All I can do is control what I do. If someone goes into her kick earlier than I want to, I don't have to respond right away. I have to run my race, respond when I'm ready to, when it makes the most sense for me."

Even though we were talking about racing, I knew that Kristine was also talking about healing from the rape. I knew on some level that I couldn't control what those men had done to me. The only thing I could do was to take control of how I responded to it. I understood that intellectually, but I'd been so programmed for so long to keep up with where everyone else was that I knew running my own race at my own pace was going to be hard.

A silence ensued, and I could sense that something else was on Kristine's mind, that something was wrong. I asked her to tell me what was going on.

"Monika, I'm scared." Kristine took my hand. "I'm afraid of having to go back to Dallas without you."

I squeezed her hand and looked at her. I wanted to see that laughing, smiling face that I'd seen just a few minutes ago.

"I'll be back," I said.

"I mean, we're supposed to be together there, right? That's why we met. That's what all this means?"

"They're not going to win. I can't let that happen. I'll be back."

As I said the words and Kristine smiled and nodded, a distant voice, like the murmured conversation of someone rows behind us, came to me. I'd be back, but who would that I be?

As our plane approached Gardermoen airport, I reminded myself that I had so much to look forward to. I'd always loved Christmas, and this one was special for another reason. I was going to be able to see my best childhood friend, Ida, and her new baby. If anyone other than Anette knew me well and had been with me through various adolescent struggles and triumphs, it was Ida. Before the rape, I'd been so looking forward to going home to see her and her newborn son, Håkon, for the first time. I'd been thrilled when she asked me to be his godmother. I remembered how I'd thought of him the night of the attack. I thought that I'd never see him in person, that I was going to die, and now here I was, just a few hours away from actually touching and holding him.

Along with seeing Ida, I was eager to see my other friends. A group of five of us had met through our local athletic club and competed with and against one another in track. We had our own rituals and traditions that weren't related to Christmas, but they were important to me. Even though I was somewhat of an introvert when it came to public occasions, I was our little group's social director. I was always the one who planned our get-togethers. That was true before I left for the United States, and it continued after I'd started attending SMU. I was trying to prove to everyone that I hadn't changed, that I wasn't forgetting the people who'd been there for me as friends before; I loved each of them and wanted them to be a part of my life forever. I imagined that seeing them now would be a way to connect with my previous self, and I was excited to get together.

So it was with all these thoughts swirling around in my head, like the dust of snow on the ground outside the gate as the plane landed in Gardermoen, that I took a deep breath, smiled at Kristine, and rose on my tiptoes to tug at my carry-on bag. A nice man reached up to help me. I looked over at him and smiled. "Thanks," I said, "but I've got it."

CHAPTER EIGHT

Christmas

After twenty hours on a plane, I was sure I didn't look my best, so I stopped in a restroom to fix my hair and makeup. It was important to me to present myself well to my family—I didn't want them to see me looking exhausted, even though that would have been perfectly natural for anyone after an international flight. Seeing them in the terminal, I felt as though I could forget everything that had happened in the last two weeks. My mother, my father, and Anette and I all half-walked and half-ran toward one another and then formed a cluster of intertwined arms, muffled words, and tears. I'd forgotten how good it felt to be surrounded by the familiar. Even hearing the airline announcements in Norwegian gave me some comfort. Despite my resolve to present a cheerful, worry-free Monika to them, it was okay to tear up—these were tears of relief and pleasure, after all. Anette's dog, Enja, lightened the mood by squirming in her arms and trying to lick each of our faces in turn.

They got to meet and give a quick hug to Kristine before she had to run off to catch her connecting flight to Ørsta. My mom put a little paper bag in her hand and gave her a big hug.

"Gledelig Jul," my mother said, wishing her a happy Christmas. I knew that my mother and father both wanted to say more to her, but that

seemed enough at the time. I then held Kristine in an embrace for a moment. We separated and held each other's gaze. Finally, neither of us able to put into words what we both knew we were feeling, we laughed. I watched her turn and go, and get swallowed up by the crowd in the terminal, thinking about how much I'd miss her calming influence.

As we drove north on the E6, I sat in the car and felt cocooned in the warmth of the vehicle and my family's presence. Near Jessheim, my mother put our traditional Christmas CD into the player. Though none of us needed a reminder, my mother said, as the first strains of "Driving Home for Christmas" made themselves known, "This is my favorite."

I felt much calmer bathed in all that familiarity and their conversation, and then I must have drifted off. Only when we exited the highway in Løten did I wake up, but it seemed to me that only an instant and not an hour had passed by.

The first few hours at home passed quickly. I was tired from the flight and was happy just to sit and watch and listen as everyone else went about the business of getting a meal ready. Enja sat nearby, and I stroked her fur, smiling when she put her paw on my hand to guide it toward her favorite spot at the base of her throat.

My mother asked me about Ida and her baby, and I told her how eager I was to see the two of them the next day. She also asked about other plans I had for the next month, focusing very much on the present and the future, I noted gratefully. I felt like my head was stuffed with cotton or as if it were a helium-filled balloon floating tethered above my body— sounds were muffled, my vision was in soft focus, and the lights in the house cast everything in a warm glow. I even found that I had a bit of an appetite and was able to eat a few bites of the salmon and vegetables my mother had prepared. I was grateful for Enja's presence. My family and I engaged in a stuttering kind of conversation, punctuated by the sound of our silverware contacting our plates. Things picked up and evened out when Enja got under the table and tangled herself within our nest of legs, causing a pleasant commotion. More than anything, I think we were all tired, exhausted in different ways but all resulting from a central source. It was as if Enja served as a reminder of what was moving just beneath the surface, but at least the little dog was something we could all comment on without risk.

After dinner, I helped with the dishes, Anette and I insisting that my mother take a break. Anette stood with one hip leaning against the counter while she dried the fish platter. I was looking down at my hands, how red they were from the water, yet I'd had no sense at all of how hot I'd let it run.

"Are you okay?" she asked.

I nodded and showed her my hands. "An odd color."

"Your nails are bare." She frowned and twisted her mouth to the side. "Maybe we can do them later. Mine are a mess, too."

Anette held up her hands and waggled her fingers.

A feeling of dread was coming over me, and I think she sensed that something was up. I focused on the bangle bracelet she was wearing.

"Remember this?" Anette said as she worked it off her wrist and held it out to me. I examined the Turkish eye; the blue-and-white stone resembled an eye. We'd each gotten one years before when we'd visited there with our parents.

"For good luck. To ward off the evil eye." I remembered the shopkeeper telling us that. I'd kept mine tucked away in my jewelry box.

I shook my head, declining to try it on. "My hands are all soapy. It's beautiful, though."

Later that night, I lay in bed, fearful of what terrors the night might bring. I hadn't slept alone since the attack, and though being in my own room thousands of miles away from Dallas and those men was a good thing, they still roamed freely in my mind. I'd developed the habit of pulling the covers over my head, something I'd done briefly as a little girl, and the sound of my eyelashes brushing against the flannel was like a second hand ticking.

I heard a tap on the door and then it swinging open. I pulled the sheet down, and in a wedge of light from the hallway, I saw Anette, a bundle of blankets and pillows cradled to her chest, moving toward me.

"You always hog the covers, so I brought my own."

I scooted closer to the far edge of the bed, my nose prickling with the beginning of tears. I swallowed hard and said, "Just so long as you keep your cold feet off me, we'll be okay."

I felt Anette settle in and then heard the sound of Enja's paws on the carpet. I could picture her circling before I heard her settle and then sigh.

"She's a good friend for you," I said.

"It's good to have a companion now that Jonas isn't around."

I wished that Anette's tone had been more wistful, but it was matter-of-fact, though I could see through the pretense and knew that she missed him.

We talked for quite a while that night. It was as if the bed were our little sanctuary and we were floating on it surrounded on all sides by a sea that contained many creatures that might do me harm. They didn't dare show themselves as long as the two of us were together. Our conversation drifted from topic to topic and in time I could hear Anette's voice grow more faint, and her sentences became half-finished.

"It's okay," I told her. "You can let go." I thought of Kristine letting go of my hand as I was dragged away.

"There's a little shop in Trondheim, just around the corner from my flat, and the woman there—"

I waited, pleased beyond words that Anette had struggled so mightily to stay awake. When the sound of her voice was replaced by the sound of her steady breathing, I pulled my covers back over my head, thinking of good fortune and all the ways in which we try to ward off evil, and too often fail to do so, while counting the ticks of my lashes until morning.

IDA AND HER fiancé Glenn came over with their baby the following morning. It took my breath away to see Håkon's face and to think about how he had played in my mind the night of my attack. Here was my reward. My godson would know me.

I sat holding him in my arms, his tiny hand wrapped around my thumb.

"You look so tired," Ida said at one point.

"The travel . . ." I began to say more, but I didn't want to ruin the moment.

Ida nodded and shifted in her chair. She narrowed her gaze at me and then sat back as if she'd reached some conclusion.

She laughed and smiled. "You should complain. We haven't slept a decent night since he was born. Thief of sleep we should have called him."

"You must be sleepwalking."

"Feels like it a bit, but when I'm really feeling like I just can't take it and want to lie down and just forget about everything for a while, I hear him or see him do something that reminds me that it's all worth it. You'll see that yourself someday."

I knew that Ida was talking about more than just me eventually becoming a mother.

"For now, knowing that someday I'll feel that way will have to be enough." I stood and walked over to the window and pointed out an icicle that glimmered in a brief flash of sunlight. The baby smiled, squinting into the bright light.

I turned and Ida was there beside me. I handed her the baby.

"Whatever you need," she said, "I'll be here."

IN THE FIRST few days I was home, I could feel my family adjusting to me and it was easier to talk in the evenings, as if the day's energy was waning and everyone was more settled, with less on our minds. So, over the course of the next few nights, I shared my experiences with them in a way I couldn't have over the phone. They listened quietly and held me when I let them know that I'd said enough.

The odd thing was that I told the story backward; that first conversation began with me talking about the days after, finishing papers for school, dealing with coming home. On subsequent nights, I'd talk about being at the police station, the hospital, and only later could I tell them about that night. For the first time that first evening, I also admitted that I was tired.

I hadn't spoken those words before. I think it was my athlete's mentality; admitting to being tired meant that I was confessing to my body being tired, that I couldn't take any more work, that I was, in a sense, quitting.

My mother and Anette assured me that it was okay to be tired. They told me it was up to me, but I wouldn't be showing any kind of weakness if I took something to help me sleep. It would only make me feel better and help me get back on track sooner.

I gave in and took a sleeping pill I'd been prescribed. I remembered nothing until I woke the next morning. I still felt light-headed and as if a storm was raging in my belly from all the medications, but at least I had slept without being haunted. Unfortunately, when I woke up, another kind of nightmare had begun. The Norwegian media had learned of the story and I was receiving emails and phone calls. I ignored all of them at first. The phone rang, and the caller ID showed a number I didn't recognize. I felt an uncomfortable buzz in my gut. Normally I would give my name when I answered the phone, but this time I didn't.

"Who is this? What do you want?" I asked.

"I'm a media director," a man's voice said. Something about how calm he was angered me more. "I'd just like a moment of your time if I may?"

I don't know why I didn't just hang up; part of the reason was that he was being so polite, but mostly it was because I knew that if I was going to be able to have my say, I'd have to allow him his.

He proceeded to tell me that he was coordinating efforts for some of the country's news media and hoped I would consent to an interview. I was furious and not afraid to show it.

"I don't want my name or my private life written about at all!" I said. "This is nobody's business!"

He got very quiet, and we hung up quickly.

I stood there for a moment with the phone clutched in my hand, surprised by the film of moisture that had built up and how my hand ached from having grasped the handset so firmly.

I looked at my mother and my father, and they both smiled. My father said, "You have to do what's best for you and for no one else." I knew that he wanted to offer more of an opinion, say something stronger against having all our privacy invaded in that way, but also that he felt he couldn't. He didn't want to feed the fire of my anger.

My mother looked as if she was about to speak and then walked over to the refrigerator to take out some fruit she had placed on a tray. "Shameful," she said. "Don't they understand?"

It was clear that they didn't. One good thing came of that call. I was so angry, I felt like some of my old energy was coming back. In fact, I felt good enough to go to the grocery store with my mother and father to get food for dinner. It felt good to be out with them doing something completely normal.

We were standing at the checkout line, the stand of magazines and newspapers towering over me. I looked at the cover of Her og Nå (Here and Now) and a photo of the television actress Ane Dahl Torp and wondered again why some people thought I looked like her. Out of the corner of my eye the word "Texas" stabbed my attention. A copy of Norway's national newspaper, VG, had been misshelved and bowed forward. I pushed it up to read the full headline: RAPED NORWEGIAN GIRL IN THE U.S. KIDNAPPED WITH GUN. LEFT NAKED.

I suddenly felt clammy, as if I were wearing sweat-soaked clothes. I thought I might vomit. I gagged but kept scanning the article and saw photos of the three men. I couldn't get away from them, not even here, not even the place where I should have been able to feel most safe.

Brushing past my mother and father and another shopper, I ran out the door. The cold air seemed to still my swimming head. I stood just outside the entrance of the store; a few people passed me by and looked at me and then quickly away. I tried to take in great gulps of air, hoping that the oxygen would replace the anger and frustration that was swelling inside me. Was there nowhere I could go to escape what had happened?

My mother draped her arm around me and led me toward the car. My father rushed ahead to open the door for me, and I sat inside taking deep and regular breaths. I could hear my pulse pounding in my ears. My father dashed back inside the store while my mother crouched just outside the car and ran her hand in circles around my back, whispering to me to take my time.

"I just wanted to come home. I just wanted it to be Christmas. Like before," I finally said.

"I know. I know. We wanted that, too. It will still be that way."

"How did they know? How did they find out? People here aren't stupid." I looked out the window as more shoppers filed past. "They're going to know it's me. How many of us went to the U.S.? To Dallas? They'll figure it out."

I thought of how I'd come home early, before most schools let out for the holiday. I pounded my fists against my thighs. "Why did I come home early? I knew—"

My mother took my hands. "You did the right thing coming home. You can't second-guess yourself on everything. We'll figure this out."

My father had returned with the groceries and packed them in the hatch. He sat staring straight ahead. I watched him for a moment in the rearview mirror as his face transformed from angry to neutral. He chewed thoughtfully on his lower lip for a moment before he turned the key. As we made our way toward home, I watched as my parents' posture changed, as if they were wax figures slowly sagging as the car's heater roared and the wipers beat a steady rhythm. In my mind, as the wipers moved back and forth, all I could hear were the words "This sucks," over and over again in time.

After I'd had some time to cool down later that night, I called the media director I'd hung up on earlier. I didn't like the idea that someone might think I was being unreasonable. That would only compound the problem of the media being insensitive toward me. I asked him to understand that I was here to enjoy the holiday with my family and I wanted privacy. Maybe I'd be ready to talk about it later, but not now. He said he understood and thanked me. I felt much better about the situation; I didn't like the person I'd presented to him in our first conversation— someone who was too reactive, too volatile. I told myself that I needed to be in better control of myself. Factors outside my control were going to produce these kinds of ups and downs, the one-step-forward-two-steps-back dance I'd been forced to do. I had to control my reactions.

I woke up the next morning feeling groggy but determined to go for a ski workout. As I bent over to put on my socks, my vision narrowed and my head felt light and empty. No matter. I was going to do this. My parents had left the newspaper for me to see. Another headline: TOOK HER UNDERWEAR AS A TROPHY. The article went on to say that the paper had been in touch with me and that I wanted to be protected from the media. How was this headline protecting me?

I dumped my breakfast into the trash and headed out to the trails. Maybe there I'd find some relief. Starting off, my legs felt wooden, unresponsive. I told myself that was to be expected. I wasn't warmed up. I hadn't exercised for a few days. I felt as if I was taking a breath for every stride instead of every three or four. I started to get agitated, and my frustration added to me feeling like I was hyperventilating. All I wanted to do was lie down in the snow and sleep. I kept telling myself to go, to push on.

I knew, intellectually, that my body had energy stores that it could go to in order to fuel my muscles. I wasn't so depleted that I'd burned up all those resources. That meant that my tiredness, my poor performance, had more to do with my mind than anything else. I just had to push myself.

Along with those thoughts came another notion. I should just enjoy being outside. I loved being outside, and these trails were some of my favorites in the world. I'd grown up skiing and running through these woods and fields. I'd come to realize that for me, that was a kind of meditative practice—a way to empty my mind. Yet there I was, slogging along, angrily plowing at the snow with my poles, my mind filling up with more negative thoughts than I could sweep behind me.

I thought again of the statement "We lose ourselves in the things we love; we find ourselves there, too." I'd both lost and found myself in physical movement for so long that to have that freedom and that pleasure denied me was torture. I knew that I should let go of all those thoughts about how easy this used to be, how much fun it was before, and just enjoy the fact that I was alive and skiing. Somehow, that didn't seem enough.

I came back frustrated and angry. I stood just outside the door trying to gather my composure. I didn't want my family to see that I was upset, and when I stepped in the house, I saw Anette and my mother in the kitchen. I saw them smiling and heard their casual greetings, but it all seemed like we were trying too hard.

"How was your outing?" my mother asked.

"Fine," I said, then thought better of that. "Good, actually. It's always nice to be skiing."

"I wish that I could have gone with you," Anette said. "I would probably just have slowed you down."

"No," I said. "That's not true. But it was good to be alone for a bit. I could clear my head."

Though nothing that I could easily identify was troubling me at that moment, a tear slid down my cheek. I turned away from the two of them and said, "I should shower before dinner."

Later that evening, we all sat in the living room. I was on the couch next to my mother, and at one point she pulled me toward her. I snuggled against her, and she began to massage my scalp. Suddenly I was back as a little girl in the tub with my mother washing my hair for me.

"You know," my mother said, "we understand that everything is not completely fine all the time. It's okay for you to feel however you feel and let us see that. I know you don't want to worry us, but it's more of a worry to wonder than it is to know and see what's really going on in here." She tapped my head with her knuckles.

"We're going to worry anyway," Anette added. "It might as well be for the right reasons."

I reached up to still my mother's hands for a moment. I thought of what I'd told them the night before, the first part of my working back toward that night. Part of me wanted to scold them a bit, let them know that this was hard work for me. But I knew that they were right. I plunged ahead.

"I'm afraid. Of myself and how I respond to things sometimes."

"And it makes me afraid sometimes when I don't see how you are responding." My mother sighed. "You don't have to capture and hold so much in. It's okay to be angry or sad."

"But I get mad at myself when I—"

Anette came and sat down in front of me. "Please don't do that to yourself. I can see how hard you're trying. Give yourself a break. Trust us. You're not going to chase us away."

I took to heart what they were trying to tell me. I saw that getting upset with myself for being upset could just spiral and spiral. I had to accept that from moment to moment I didn't have to be in complete command of my emotions and myself. I hadn't realized just how much tension I was carrying in my whole body. Normally I was so attuned to my physical self and its state, but I'd been so preoccupied with so many thoughts that I hadn't noticed just how sore my jaw was, how I was clamping my teeth together so tightly and hunching my shoulders around my neck. It was almost as if I'd gotten to the point that I had to consciously tell myself to take in a breath.

Still, I wasn't ready to tell them about the details of the attack. I had to work my way up to that point. I continued to open up to them, reminding myself that it was okay to go at my own pace. I didn't have to match or beat anyone else's time.

For the next two days, I let my emotions dictate to me what I did, where I went, what I said or didn't say. I tried to be in the moment instead of going back to the past, or thinking ahead to the next semester, the next track season, the next steps in the investigation, and what I imagined would be a trail I'd have to pick up soon after I returned. I hadn't realized how much effort it had taken to stay in control. I don't think I was very good at the letting go maneuver; I'd still find myself feeling bad and immediately trying to figure out some way to turn that around.

From the first day I'd been home, I was hoping to see my friends and had spent a lot of time thinking about what we might do. A week into my stay, I hadn't seen any of them but Ida yet. I tried not to make too much of the texts and phone calls that went unanswered, the excuses about being too busy or too tired. "One of these days." "Soon." "Let me get back to you." I told myself that this was a good sign. They were busy with things to do at the holidays. They weren't treating me any different because of the rape. If I wanted to act as if nothing had happened or get back to normal as quickly and easily as possible, then I had to accept it when others acted that way, right?

Ida was being a really good friend, and that was what mattered most. She also told me about a chance to catch up with my graduating class. What we grow up with seems normal to us, so it wasn't until I went to SMU and talked with people from the U.S. and elsewhere that I realized it was unusual that my entire graduating class at the school of sports (the equivalent of tenth, eleventh, and twelfth grade in the States) was made up of just thirty students. As one U.S. teammate put it, that was a tiny school; she had that many fellow students in a History class. The good thing was that because our class was so small, we got to know everyone really well. I considered my former classmates friends.

Sticking to my decision to do what was as close to normal under the circumstances, I decided to attend the reunion. To make things easier for me, Ida had gone into the party to let everyone see her son and also to let those who didn't know what had happened to me. The whole evening I felt oddly off balance. At first no one came up to talk to me, and then those few who did didn't mention the attack at all or ask me how I was doing. They responded to me like I was the new girl at school, not someone they'd known well for years.

I had a lot of trouble sleeping again that night, but not because of any nightmares about that night in Dallas. I wondered if maybe I was fooling myself, that the Monika I thought I was presenting to others didn't bear any resemblance to who I'd been when I left for my second year at SMU only a few short months ago. I thought that I was dressing and acting like my old self, but maybe everyone saw through my act.

I shared those thoughts with Anette, and she shook her head. "It's not you. It's them. Don't blame yourself. They don't know how to act. A lot of them haven't been anywhere else or dealt with anything. That's not an excuse. Just because they don't know what to say doesn't mean they shouldn't say anything. That's just rude and ignorant."

How people respond in tough circumstances says a lot about who they are. I always loved Anette, but our relationship had evolved into something deeper and richer. With many of my friends from home, though, it was a much harder transition. They felt so distant. I'd bought gifts for my closest friends, and I'd thought that we'd see one another before the holiday, but we hadn't. So one morning I got in the car and drove the quiet streets toward Dania's house. As I rounded a bend, the small stack of presents slid off the seat and onto the floor, a puddle of shiny paper and ribbons reminding me of how different this year was. I grabbed Dania's from the pile and walked up the driveway, feeling an odd sense of approaching a home that was unfamiliar to me despite how many hours I'd spent there.

I briefly considered knocking on the door, being the one to make clear how strong my desire was to see her, for things to be back to the way they had been. Instead I stood there in a cloud of my own breath wondering why it was that she and the others hadn't responded to me, why it had come to this—me feeling more like a criminal creeping around than *julenissen,* the Norwegian equivalent of Santa Claus. My hope that someone would notice me and invite me in didn't come true. I left the gift on the doorstep like an abandoned child, and feeling very much like one myself, I got in the car and gave up on the idea of dropping off the other presents.

At the time I couldn't articulate this, but later on I came to better understand and put things in a different perspective. I needed to make the distinction between what happened to me and who I was. I think part of the problem was that people weren't sure what to say because they didn't want to upset me by asking the wrong thing. The rape was hard for me to talk about, and it was for other people as well. But I was not just that one thing that happened. I still existed outside of that event. I think people were struggling to know what to do because they saw me in a new way—as a rape victim. And what I wanted then, more than anything, was acknowledgment and proof that I was more Monika Kørra than Jessica December Watkins. The day after the high school event, my father asked me to go for a run with him. Since I'd been home, he'd been fairly quiet, and I knew that he was trying to be respectful, to let me take the lead in talking with him. That's how things had been between us before as well. He trusted me and was there for me when I needed him. Even though I hadn't told him how upset I was over the way the reunion had gone, I took his asking me to go along with him as a sign that he sensed I needed him.

We ran along, mostly in silence, our few comments accompanied by the sounds of our footfalls. The wind whipped around the corner of a building, inciting a tumbling riot of snow, so much like my thoughts and feelings. My throat constricted and tears fell and froze on my cheeks. I tried to stifle a sob and failed. My father wrapped his arm around my shoulder, and we both briefly staggered over a hardened clump of snow before righting ourselves.

I knew that my father was struggling with the idea that he hadn't been able to protect me from harm. When I was younger, my father and I were like best buddies. We always joke in our family that I was the son my parents never got. That I was so interested in things my father loved—skiing and running and other sports—brought us close together. In Dallas, I missed the good-luck hugs he and my mother gave me before a race. I missed seeing my father standing on the sidelines of the track with a stopwatch in his hands or at a soccer match shouting encouragement. Mostly, I missed the times when, after a race, the two of us would go home together and stop for ice cream or candy, both of us understanding that this wasn't something we would tell Mom. I couldn't keep this secret from him.

"Papa," I said, "I don't want to be here. I don't want to be here in the same world with people who do such evil things. I just don't understand—"

For a moment, my father was silent, and we both stopped and stood staring. Across the street was the Løten Idrettspark, where the track and soccer fields lay beneath a layer of snow. In the distance a large family, the half dozen or so kids filing behind the parents like ducklings, skied along the forest trail. Their peals of laughter caught the wind and took off like kites passing over our heads.

My father toed the ground with his boot and then, his tone trying to mask his own weariness and confusion, he said slowly, "So what are you going to do, then? Where else can you possibly go?"

I knew he was right, that often the act of surviving begins as no more than a kind of biological imperative. I'd spent my whole life moving, skiing, running, traveling to compete, leaving home to attend school. All of it with the idea that moving forward, not staying rooted in place, was how you lived your life and discovered what made you happy. My father and I set off again, stride for stride in silence.

Thoughts about distance had me preoccupied. The holidays were good and I enjoyed Little Christmas Eve with my parents and with my aunt and uncle. On Christmas Eve we went to church, and I sat there thinking about what it was that lay ahead for the baby Jesus, that in a few short months people would gather together in that same place and commemorate His painful death. I wasn't a particularly devout Christian, but I did believe in God, and the enormous sacrifice he asked of his Son was difficult to understand. I'd always thought that Jesus was a supreme being even though he walked the Earth and that it was somehow easier for him to deal with being hung from a cross.

This could have been my funeral, I thought.

I envisioned the casket there in front of the pulpit, my family sitting where we now sat, without me. If that gun had fired.

To keep a tear from spilling down my face, I lifted my head toward the church's ceiling. I'd been attending services there my whole life, and in that moment the ceiling's blue skies and perfectly shaped white clouds had never resonated so deeply within me. That idealized version of heaven appealed to me. I thought that if I couldn't be here alive, I wouldn't mind being in a place like that—somewhere very much like the beautiful out-doors I treasured. I would have spent time with my mom's parents, getting to know them in death in a way that wasn't possible while I was alive. My grandmother had died long before I was born, my grandfather just after. I knew that their passing had been difficult for my mother but made her strong in ways I was only beginning to fully understand. It would have been so easy for her to have gotten lost in her sorrows, drifted away. But she hadn't.

The congregation rose, and the first notes of the organ brought my attention back to the present. Anette took my hand firmly in her own, and I was once again grounded, grateful to be here instead of there, secure in the knowledge that this was where I was meant to be, where I needed to be, where I wanted to be.

Earlier that day, we'd gone to my grandparents' grave site as we always did on Christmas Eve. My mother laid a bouquet of flowers against the headstone, the blood-red roses stark against the snow, their cellophane wrapper snapping in the wind. When my mother stood back up, I saw that her eyes were tearing, whether from the wind or her emotions or some combination of both, I couldn't say. I thought then about how we as human beings weather things—storms, misfortune, and all the rest.

My father put his arm around my mom, and we all huddled together in a semicircle, sheltering one another from the wind. My mother's hands shook slightly as she raised the lighter to the memorial candle's wick; it caught and went out, then caught again as we drew our circle tighter.

"Mama. Father." My mother's strong voice cut through the blustery winds. "I just want to let you both know that we're all doing well."

She looked at me, and I felt her strength pouring into me, warming me and reassuring me.

"We all miss you, and we thank you for what you taught us. We'll see you someday, but for now, we still have a lot of living to do, and we're going to make you proud."

We lingered there in the stinging cold, our arms wrapped around one another, and I looked up into the blue sky, saw the imperfect clouds smeared across it, and thought I'd never seen anything so beautiful. I was never more grateful to be home and to be held.

I'M HUMAN, SO it was hard for me to shed other, more earthly concerns. I was struggling to let go of how much I had been looking forward to being with my friends at home. It was hard to reconcile the past with the present. When we were younger, I spent nearly every day with one or another, and often with all five, of my closest girlfriends.

Now we could barely communicate at all. We decided that the twenty-eighth would work for us all—Christmas would be over and New Year's not yet arrived, a kind of odd middle ground, a time to be filled on a calendar of days after and days before.

I had really hoped someone else would volunteer to host the get-together this time because I was so tired, but I tried to put that aside because I really just wanted to see them. The morning of the party, they were all going to go skiing, but I said that I would have to stay home to prepare. I thought maybe someone would say, "I'll help you," but no one did. My mother and sister went shopping with me to buy the food, and then I set out to prepare it.

At first I told myself that it was just the chopped onions that had me in tears, but as I stood there with the knife poised above the chopping block, I suddenly felt like I couldn't breathe. I stood there wondering why it was that I was the one doing all of this work while the rest of them were off having fun. I wanted to be having fun along with them. I wanted to be back in Portugal with them at the training camp we attended, walking the streets of Cascais and stumbling upon the best ice cream we'd ever eaten, sitting on the seawall sharing bites and moaning in ecstasy and laughing at our reactions. It was hard to believe that only a few months before we'd gone again to Gothenburg together to compete in the Världsungdomsspelen, a major track meet in Gothenburg, Sweden.

Despite all kinds of other obligations and commitments, we'd set aside four days after the competition to be together. We'd shopped together, planned and eaten an elaborate (at least for us) picnic lunch in a park, gone to clubs and danced for hours, gone back to our rooms and fretted about boys and shared our fears that we were all going to end up alone, without men in our lives, but felt glad that we'd at least have one another.

The knife clattering to the floor brought my mother running into the kitchen. She found me slumped against the cabinets, my shoulders shaking as I sobbed and sobbed, saying over and over again, "I can't do this."

My mother sank down beside me and wrapped me in her arms. "It's okay. You need this. Let it out."

We sat there for a few minutes, until I felt like every ounce of water in my body had come out of me. My mother held my face between her hands, and our foreheads touched. She looked intently at me, clearly angry. "They shouldn't have expected this of you, Monika. Someone else should have taken the lead this time."

We both knew that my reaction and her anger weren't just about the food or the preparations. It was the anxiety of seeing all of them when none of them had come over to see me or even shown much of a desire to talk to me since I'd been home. Now all five of them were supposed to be coming over together, and I felt like an outsider. I didn't know how to act or what to say. Surely they'd read the article about me, and yet no one was talking, telling me that they were sorry this had happened to me and that they'd be here to support me. *Wouldn't I have done that much for any of them?* I wondered.

Once again, Anette stepped up to defend me. She came in and saw the two of us sitting on the floor. She turned and walked away, then returned a moment later with her coat on.

"I'll be back."

She returned a half hour later. She'd talked to Dania and met with all of the girls. Anette let them know how I was feeling, both that night and about how they'd been treating me. She let them have their say about how awkward they felt and how they struggled with not knowing what to say. Anette told them that pretending like the rape didn't happen was like denying that I existed. That's all I needed, to be acknowledged, to have the truth acknowledged and then to move on. The rape wasn't all of who I was, it was just one part of who I was, but at that stage, it felt like they were denying the existence of all of me. They all cried and said that they would reach out to me. The dinner was off; I hoped the friendships wouldn't be.

After that I got a few brief phone calls from them, and we did make one more attempt at getting together, but I had to cancel because I was too exhausted. I had put so much emphasis on Christmas and making things all seem okay that I had little energy left after that. In a way, the breakdown the night of the dinner party was a good thing. It made me acknowledge that I was tired in every way it is possible to be tired—physically, mentally, emotionally, spiritually. While I had been telling myself that my ski outings and my planning for social visits and everything else were completely healthy, they were all part of an act. The facts were the facts, and to behave otherwise was hurtful. With the holidays over and that big breakdown behind me, things got better. I still felt at times as if a dark cloud was hanging over me, but I started to sense that it was, like the weather itself, subject to changes and influences that I could come to understand but likely would never be able to control entirely.

I had tried very hard that first year away from home to keep in touch with everyone. I wanted to believe that I was still the same Monika, that my success hadn't changed me just as the rape hadn't. I can see now that in some ways this break from my friends back home was inevitable. They had their new lives, some had moved to other places, and we all just walked away from our collective past. I don't know if anything would have come of us talking about that holiday, or if it was better to leave things as they lay. I'm not sure that I wanted to hear their answers, or if it was better to just remember the good parts.

Change could be good. Change could be bad. Change was inevitable, frustrating, frightening, invigorating, thrilling.

I was just beginning to understand how my relationship to that aspect of existence was going to play such a crucial role in my life.

One thing that wasn't going to change was my decision to return to Dallas. With all the ups and downs I experienced while being home, I never altered my plan to return. I had been given an opportunity to pursue a lifelong dream. Dallas and SMU were a means to achieve my goal of making my living as a runner. I couldn't let the rape end that dream. I better understood after being home that it wasn't going to be possible for things to return to normal instantly, that I couldn't just ignore my way back to a good place mentally and emotionally, and I also couldn't just wait for things to turn around in my life. I had to be assertive. I had to pursue getting better and healing from the attack. Those moments when I had to be passive and allow those men to do horrible things to me were the worst kind of necessity; I'd allowed those things to be done to me in order to survive. What would all of that suffering mean if I gave up? I'd had to surrender my body to those men on that night, but I wasn't going to give up control to them now, I wasn't going to allow them to take my dream from me.

Dallas didn't belong to those rapists. Dallas was mine.

CHAPTER NINE

My Dallas

O f course, before there was Dallas there were more tears. The tears came at the airport, but they were different somehow. I wasn't afraid of what I was going to have to face on my return. I knew that I was doing the right thing by going back, but I was going to miss my family even more than before. As my mother held me in a tight hug, I remembered what she'd said to me a few nights earlier. As we talked about some of the more painful events of that night, she'd smiled and said, "Monika, I don't know where you get your strength from."

I told her that I got it from her, from Anette, from Papa. How they'd treated me that whole winter break, how I knew that no matter whether I'd decided to return to Dallas, stay home, or take a break from school and become a beach bum in the Bahamas, they would have supported me. They'd have been concerned that I have the proper sunscreen if the islands were in my future, but that's the extent of the worry that they would have expressed. As I flew back to Dallas, alone this time, it occurred to me that they hadn't said much about my safety or their worries. That meant a lot to me. Not just that I didn't need to have the worst-case scenarios brought to my attention, but that they trusted me, and by extension, they trusted this world. We all agreed that a bad thing had been done to me, but that we had to do everything we could to move past that point.

Yes, we talked a little bit about how unfair it was that these men singled me out, but they never questioned whether or not anyone had failed to protect me—not my friends, not the school, not the police, not American culture. They treated the rape as it was—a random act, not a part of a larger pattern that reflected how rotten the world was, or how much of a mistake it had been for me to travel so far away from home. We didn't say these words exactly, but because of how they'd always welcomed opportunities for me to travel and encouraged me to experience new things, the message was clear: I had to live my life on my own terms. My parents had told me this before, and though my rape was not something any of us could have envisioned, life was going to throw obstacles in my path. How I responded to those obstacles was far more important than what I had to overcome.

I thought of my choice to become a steeplechaser in the spring of 2008, before coming to SMU. I accepted the idea that I had to run those laps knowing that with predicted regularity I was going to have to leap over that barrier and the water pit. When my coach first approached me with the idea of me taking on the challenge of running three thousand meters, jumping over a thirty-inch barrier, and trying to cross a twelve-foot-long water pit, I felt a thrill of pleasure. This was a huge challenge, especially considering my lack of height. That he trusted I had the tenacity to take it on meant a lot to me. Distance running was one thing, the steeplechase another. I'd have to master a new technique, similar to what a hurdler does in clearing those obstacles, and I was eager to get started.

The first day I worked on my steeplechase technique, I was fearless. I approached the first obstacle, carrying good speed as I'd been told, planted my left leg firmly, and led with my right leg up. The ground flashed beneath me, and then suddenly I was lying on the track, my cheek feeling the stubble of the rubberized surface. I tried to take a breath, but felt as if my chest were paralyzed.

Confused about what had happened, and with my brain receiving messages from various body outposts about damage done, I lay there. I could see other athletes staring at me, wondering what had happened to Little Monika, feeling sorry for me.

Still lying flat on my stomach, I pressed my scraped palms into the track and lifted myself into the push-up position. From there, I walked my legs toward my chest and stood. I could feel the burned flesh of my knees and elbows tingling, but I resisted the temptation to look down to assess how bad things were. I spun on my heel and trotted away from the pit, my mother's words about getting right back onto the horse in my mind.

I knew that dwelling on the fact that I'd fallen would only make room in my mind for fear. Thirty yards down the track I turned back again and set out. I measured my steps and did what I'd done before, but with every cell in my body helping me rise higher, I cleared the barrier by more than two feet. Not exactly the best technique, since it required a greater expenditure of energy, but there was no way I wasn't going to get over that steeple.

What mattered wasn't that I'd fallen, but that I'd gotten back up. Sure, I was self-conscious and hoped that no one had seen my awkward attempt at steeplechase mastery, but as I continued around the track, I thought it didn't matter that I'd been clumsy. Just because I'd fallen didn't mean I was doomed to fall every time. Look ahead, I had told myself that afternoon. Never let your past paint your future. A few months later, and after quite a few steeple workouts, of course, I qualified for the Junior World Championship in the three-thousand-meter steeplechase.

What I was dealing with now was similar to that initial experience with the steeplechase—I didn't know exactly when the next hurdle would present itself, but I had the skills to get over it. Life was unpredictable, but those surprises were more likely to be pleasant and not painful. I'd always been very optimistic, and there was no reason for that to change.

As if to confirm the view that life's surprises could be good, bad, or to be determined later, soon after I returned to Dallas, I met two women who would play significant roles in my life.

The first, I met shortly after I returned to SMU. After another frustrating workout when I felt as if my fitness level was never going to return to previous levels, Petra, another international student, from Sweden (a member of the equestrian team), came up to me and said, "This may seem a little odd, but a woman I know wants to meet you. She said she'd like to take us to lunch. She's a nice woman."

I was skeptical at first, wondering if maybe she was a reporter. I couldn't figure out why she would have an interest in meeting me.

"She's a wonderful woman," Petra explained. "I've been to her house a few times, and she's a very cool person. Her name is Kelly Green, and she heard what happened. She'd like to help out. That's how she is. She's taken an interest in other international students. She's not from here originally."

I don't know why, but after I had heard that, any suspicions I'd had went away. I'd been trying to tell myself not to be too on guard, to just let experiences come to me and remain open to them like I'd always been.

A few days later, Petra and I drove to a Thai restaurant in Highland Park. It took my eyes a moment to adjust, going from the bright sunlight into an ultra-modern room dominated by blue-and-green geometric light fixtures. I felt as if I'd gone underwater. An elegantly dressed woman stood up and waved. I followed Petra over to her table. The woman had a sleek haircut and rimless glasses. Though she was probably as tall and slight as me, she stood perched on a pair of high heels that I wouldn't have even been able to walk in. When she gave me a hug, she had to bend slightly. I heard a jangle of bracelets next to my ear as she held me and said, "I'm *so pleased* to meet you."

After we made our introductions and settled into our seats, Petra asked Kelly about her holiday trip to Canada.

"You know how much I love it up there. I know the cold and snow are nothing unusual for the two of you, but it truly is beautiful up there in the winter. I can't imagine holidays anywhere else."

Kelly explained that she'd read in the newspapers about me. She knew that I was from Norway, and she figured that I was there without a family. She just wanted to let me know how sorry she was for what had happened and that if she could help in any way, she'd be glad to. We made small talk for a while, and then she finally got around to the topic that I knew she wanted to talk about further. I appreciated her not just jumping into the attack but also not just ignoring it either.

"Enough about me, how are you doing, Monika? How have things been for you since the attack?"

There was something about her, some way in which she was able to make me feel comfortable instantly despite the circumstances that had brought us together. She seemed so at ease with who she was, and her approaching me and acknowledging immediately that she knew that I'd been raped, not talking around that fact, served as a model for how I wished everyone could have dealt with me.

"I have good days and bad days, but I'm moving ahead." I surprised myself by not choosing my usual default response, "I'm fine."

"I'm sorry about the bad days but happy about the good ones," she said, then smiled and reached across the table to lightly rub my forearm in a gesture that warmed me up to her immediately.

I was struck by how this stranger had reached out to me and treated me in a way that was so different from my girlfriends back home. Part of that was cultural. I'd noticed that Americans were more open and willing to extend to people they didn't know that well a kind of courtesy and warmth that we reserved only for those with whom we had established close relationships. Kelly had the openness and warmth that I admired about Americans, but she also carried herself with the kind of confidence and calm that reminded me of a Norwegian. In that sense, she was like my mother or my sister. At the end of lunch, she shared her phone number and e-mail address with me, and she told me that if I needed anything to be in touch. She also said that she really hoped we'd be able to get to know each other better.

I told her that I would like that, and eventually that's what happened.

As much as I missed having my mother around, I was fortunate to have other women who helped me, even before the attack. Dallas has a Norwegian Society, and two women who'd moved to the area had been in contact with me since earlier in that fall semester of 2009. I'd met with Wenche and Sidsel several times at lunches, and they'd taken Kristine, Silje, and me into their homes or on outings in Dallas, to help us get familiar with our new home away from home. They had such big hearts, and they'd reached out to me after the rape to offer whatever assistance they could. I was so fortunate to have them in my life.

I MET ANOTHER woman who had an enormous influence on me. On February 22, 2010, someone in the Dallas County District Attorney's

Office let me know that I was to report to the sixth floor of the Frank Crowley Courts Building in two days, at 1 p.m.

I had two thoughts. Why was I being called in? What about the class I had at that time?

The woman was able to answer the first question: "This is a preliminary meeting with Assistant District Attorney Erin Hendricks."

The second question basically went unanswered. This was an important meeting and I had to be there. I was a bit upset by that. I was determined to get back to being a normal student, to keep up with my classes and get good grades. With some of my finals being delayed, and classes starting for the new semester, the last thing I wanted was to fall behind in any way.

Fortunately, Coach Wollman intervened. After I told him that I'd been called in, he set things up with the DA's office. We'd meet at his office.

I had no idea what to expect from the meeting. I arrived to find two women and a man, none of whom I'd ever met before. After brief introductions, things immediately got off to a bad start. The victim's advocate gestured to the other woman, a brunette, and told me that she was the lawyer assigned to my case, and that the man was Brandon, who would be assisting her.

"What do you mean, 'assigned to my case'? I want to pick my own lawyer."

"It doesn't work like that," the lawyer said. "The District Attorney's Office represents crime victims, and they choose the prosecutor who will work with you. That's me. I'm Erin Hendricks."

"I want to choose who will represent me."

"This is how it works in America. The government gives you us, and you're stuck with us," Erin said. She offered me her hand, and I took it reluctantly. It was a firm handshake, but something about how she spoke upset me.

I had expected that I'd be given several choices for representation, and a chance to develop a personal relationship with this person so that this case would be as personal to him or her as it was to me. I saw this as my case, and I wanted it to be my lawyer's case as well. I didn't fully understand until much later that in a criminal proceeding it was the People vs. each of those men. In my mind it was Monika Kørra against those three. The way things were shaping up in those first few minutes, I felt like it was going to be Monika Kørra versus the Dallas County District Attorney's Office.

HAVING LITTLE REAL understanding of how the American criminal justice system worked wasn't helping me feel more comfortable with the process. I had a victim's advocate there with me, Coach Wollman, and now this other woman, whom I'd never met, was going to be responsible for what I considered one of the most important events in my life. I was so used to being composed in most situations and being the polite, rule-following young woman, but this whole situation was new to me. I had dozens of questions to ask, and I had no idea if they fit at all into the context of the meeting. I sat there while Erin made some initial remarks, but I wasn't really listening fully to her. I was too upset with myself for not having a better understanding of the process to fully understand what she was saying. If this was the way my trial was starting off, what else would be out of my control?

I assumed I was going to have to be at the trial. I wondered if I was going to be able to ask questions of the men who had been arrested. I had thoughts about how I was going to dress, how the process was going to affect my studies, my track meets, how I was going to be able to get back and forth from where I lived to the court. Were there going to be photographers there? Was I going to have my face plastered all over the newspapers? Were people going to know that one of them had forced me to put him in my mouth? Was I going to have to stand up in front of everyone and say, "He's one of them and he did this to me"? And what about the fact that when I'd been shown those photos I hadn't been absolutely sure? I knew that one of the men had confessed, but what did that really mean as far as the other two? Were the men going to be able to question me?

The one thing that did make its way through my tangle of thoughts also added to my frustration. Erin explained that the trial was going to most likely occur in May. She said things about preliminary motions, discovery, and a bunch of other concepts that only added to my frustration.

Five months. Another approximately 150 days. Nearly half a year to go before this part of it would even begin. I sat in that meeting room, and I had a similar sensation to the one I'd had earlier in dealing with the police. People were talking, their mouths were moving, but I had suddenly become nearly deaf. It was like I was back again in those first days in the U.S. struggling with a language and cultural norms that I had no experience with at all. I'd worked hard to overcome that the first time, and here I was back at square one.

At several points, Erin did ask if I had any questions, but I felt like I was at a lecture in a Physics class where the professor was talking about dark matter and all I could really come up with was a question about whether or not this had anything to do with why my cell phone sometimes lost reception. Finally, Erin stopped speaking.

"I have this." I reached into my bag and slid my journal across the table to her. "I wrote down everything I remember about what happened. All the details."

Erin glanced at the cover and then at me. "Okay."

She looked at the others in the room and then back at me. I sat staring at her expectantly. She opened the journal up and leafed through a few of the pages, scanning them. "This must have been difficult for you to do. Thank you, though. This will be helpful."

"I want you to know what it was like. What I went through. If some of the things aren't clear to you, please let me know. I can think about it some more and get you better answers."

"I will do that," she said, and I watched as she turned a few more pages. "If you don't mind, I'd like to take this home with me."

"Sure. I'm done with it. For now. Unless you have more that you want me to write."

"Not now, no. But thank you."

I didn't understand at that point that Erin had lots and lots of other documents to read, or that she'd already read. Charges wouldn't have been filed unless there was enough paperwork backing up the evidence they'd gathered to convince the people in charge of the courts that these men could be picked up and held awaiting trial.

I expected Erin to be so grateful to me for helping out, to make more of the fact that I was chipping in with my efforts and determination. I flashed back on dropping off the gift on my friend's doorstep, feeling like I'd done the wrong thing again by doing what I thought was the right thing.

CHAPTER TEN

My Team

I told everyone on my team, not the track team but my recovery team, about the meeting and how poorly I thought that it had gone. It wasn't Erin's or Brandon's fault that I felt like I'd been hit in the face with this part of the process, but still I was upset. I worried that I had come across as an angry and spoiled young woman who was making demands for how things should be happening even though I had no real idea of what the right versus the wrong way of handling a case was.

My team reassured me that I had every right to feel the way that I did. These people were strangers to me and they were going to have to earn my trust. No one had sat down with me at any point before that to explain fully how the legal process in this country worked. I had a general idea, but I knew nothing about the intricacies of the process.

How passionate could they be, given that scenario? I knew they were professionals and would do their job because that was what they were paid to do, but that wasn't how it was with teammates as I thought of them. Teammates should be there for you and support you because you are important to them, because you have forged a relationship that isn't based on just a roster and chance. They also know that each has a role to play. Kelly and Coach Wollman looked out for me and helped me navigate the confusing court system. They organized meetings with my lawyers (I could never get used to the idea that they weren't "mine" but belonged to the government) when I was frustrated or confused. They did everything they could to make sure that my needs and expectations were being met. Robin, Kristine, and Vicktoria monitored my emotional state and made sure that when I needed a laugh, they provided one; when I needed to cry, they held me; and when I needed to scream in frustration or anger, they took me out to run. We became even closer than we were before, and that helped enormously. I came to think of myself as a complicated case, and no one person could take on the responsibility of handling every part of me. Back home, my parents and my sister provided me with everything they always had, the kind of support that doesn't diminish through distance.

As most trusted friends would do, mine decided to try to help me get through this next phase. They saw that at least now my frustrations had a focus, whereas before they seemed all-encompassing. My team had felt helpless in the immediate aftermath of the rape because there was nothing they could do to undo it; now that my anxiety was focused on the woman who was going to represent me in the trial, they took it upon themselves to do whatever they could to eliminate whatever uncertainty I had about Erin's suitability for the task and for working with someone like me.

We learned that someone within the Dallas County prosecutor's office had some connections to SMU, and my friends began trying to get more information. They thought that if we could get some more information about Erin, about the kinds of cases she'd tried, what her conviction record was, and anything else related to her professional life, I might feel a little more at ease. In a way, it was similar to how I sometimes had to approach races and my opponents in them. For me, not knowing anything at all about another runner was more frightening than if I knew as much as possible. What was her personal best in a particular race? What kind of tactics did she use? Would she try to go out fast early and wear the rest of us down? Did she save herself for a strong finish kick and outsprint everyone to the tape? Knowing what kind of competitors my opponents were gave me a mental edge.

I'm sure that we kept Erin on edge. My friends phoned her, my coach

phoned her, all on my behalf and all with the best of intentions, but ultimately I feared that we were all proving to be a distraction. The other
thing I knew that I liked to do in preparation for a race was to clear my
own head of too many thoughts about classes, friends, and my relationship with Robin. I used headphones and my MP3 player in warm-up, just
to limit the amount of exposure I had to other people. If I had been in a
better state of mind, I might have thought that Erin deserved and needed
the same kind of space and time.

Ultimately, our undercover efforts didn't turn up anything particularly
useful. We learned that Erin was very, very good at what she did. She had
been working in the District Attorney's Office since 2002, had graduated
from SMU's law school, and had been part of the D.A. Office's Sexual
Assault Unit since 2007. We received assurances that she was very committed to my case and to me.

Looking back on it, I don't think there is any piece of information
that would have made me feel more at ease. I was still struggling with the
idea that there wasn't more that I was being asked to do on my end to
help convict these guys. I was still very much having a hard time letting
others help me. Having someone else be completely responsible for the
case made me uncomfortable, and not even having had a choice in who
that someone was to be made it even worse. I called and e-mailed Erin
all the time, asking her to fill me in on what was going on. I was sure she
thought I was a complete pest, but still I kept after her.

The first week of March, Kelly arranged a meeting for the three of
us—Erin, Kelly, and me—to have lunch. Kelly chose a quiet spot where
we could sit and talk. I was feeling anxious about the meeting and wondered if I was again going to end up disappointed.

Having Kelly there made a difference. Erin seemed to open up a bit
more; she was still her no-nonsense straight-to-the-point self, but with
Kelly there to act as a buffer, I didn't have the same sense that I'd had
during the first meeting that I was being rushed or having my concerns
set aside. The fact that this was more of a social occasion certainly helped.
Since Kelly had set it up, that meant that, for me at least, the two of us
were more in charge than I'd been at the previous meeting in Coach

Wollman's office. Then, I'd felt like, in a different sense, I was the one who was on trial. This time I got a better idea of how committed Erin was to my case. It helped that she was able to explain to me how it was coming together. She told me as much as she could about how the men had been found and arrested. I'd only known what had been written about in the newspaper and the bits and pieces that I'd been told when I was in too stressed a condition to really process the information. The three men were all Hispanic and came from Mexico. Erin told me their names, Arturo Arevalo, Alfonso Armendariz Zuniga, and Luis Fernando Zuniga. By the time our lunch was over, I'd been able to figure out that those three men were, in order, the Worst One, the Boss, and the Weak One. The Boss and the Weak One were cousins.

It turned out that my cell phone, which I'd been so worried about since the men could have used it to locate me, my friends, and many other people, had actually played a big role in the first of them being arrested.

Erin explained a bit about how cell phones could be traced to an approximate location. There were some delays that night in getting my carrier to start the process, but when they finally did, every fifteen minutes they'd ping my phone and relay the location information to a special unit within the Dallas Police Department. The police knew that even after I'd been located, someone else was using my phone, hours after I'd been released, in fact. Based on the location the pinging produced, they sent officers to try to find a black SUV with chrome wheels. They spotted one, and discovered that the person to whom the vehicle was registered was a registered child sex offender. Unfortunately, it turned out that the man driving the SUV had just purchased the car and had not yet registered it in his name. He also had an alibi for that night, said he didn't have my phone (which was true, since a few hours after he was questioned my phone was being used by someone else), and he was not my rapist.

The police were persistent. They contacted T-Mobile and got a list of all the incoming and outgoing calls since the time I was kidnapped, then researched all the addresses associated with those calls. One of them came from Red Bud Lane, so undercover police officers monitored activity on that block. When they saw two suspicious-looking men walking out of a house, they called for uniformed officers to take over. When those officers arrived, they were able to stop the two men because they'd chosen to walk down the middle of the street.

"Jaywalking." Kelly laughed and clapped her hands.

I was confused. "I've never heard of that. What does it mean?"

"In this city, it's against the law to walk in the middle of the street. That's what sidewalks are for. The point is, who knows what would have happened if they hadn't been able to stop them?" Erin shrugged.

I nodded, understanding just how much luck had played a part in all this.

One of the two men was Luis Zuniga. The men were asked to empty their pockets, and both of them had small bags of what was later confirmed to be black tar heroin. Luis also had a Nokia cell phone. When one of the officers flipped it open, a pink floral background shone on the screen. Luis explained that the phone belonged to his girlfriend.

Scanning the list of contacts, the officer saw that the first entry was listed as "BFF."

Erin sipped her water. "That was Kristine, right, your BFF?"

I don't know why, but Erin remembering who Kristine was from my journal entries pleased me. She was paying attention. Maybe I wasn't just a case or a client or a victim to her.

"In a way, we got lucky again. Having those guys on suspicion of drug possession meant we could detain them. That gave us more time to put more of the puzzle pieces together."

"It's like sitting here hearing about something on *C.S.I.*," Kelly commented thoughtfully.

Erin smiled to reduce the impact of her words. "I like a good drama as much as anybody, but those shows aren't exactly educational. They sometimes give people a very inaccurate sense of how this whole process works."

As Erin continued, I became even more aware how a combination of hard work and luck had played a part in catching the men who raped me. The same night as my attack, three Hispanic men in a black SUV had also beaten and robbed a man. They'd also stolen his phone. The police used the same pinging technology to triangulate locations of his phone that they'd used in tracking my location. Eventually, they traced one of the calls made on that stolen phone to a woman named Aracely Zuniga, who'd been pulled over on a traffic violation.

On December 8, three days after I was assaulted, Aracely Zuniga agreed to speak with police officers about Luis Zuniga, who she would eventually reveal was her nephew, as was Alfonso Zuniga.

As it turned out, her son was the man who had been arrested along with Luis on heroin charges. Her daughter, a woman named Miriam, was the common-law wife of an abusive man named Arturo Arevalo, who was the father of Miriam's two young children.

"Ms. Zuniga said she wanted nothing more than for Arturo to leave her daughter and everyone else they both knew alone. He'd just gotten out of jail and she didn't want that kind of man around her grandkids. She said that nothing good ever happened when Arturo was around."

"The Worst One," I said.

"That's the one."

"No wonder the Weak One seemed so afraid of him."

"I wish that instead of being afraid of him, he'd have knocked some sense into Arturo," Kelly said. She looked at me, stricken. "I'm sorry. I don't mean to what-if."

"It's okay," I assured her. "I know what you mean."

While being questioned, Aracely Zuniga provided police with the address of the building where both Arturo and Alfonso lived, the information that all three men hung around together, and the fact that one of them owned a black SUV.

Erin's story of the investigation and eventual arrest pleased me for lots of reasons, but the one thing that I wondered at and admired the most was how a couple of women, Aracely Zuniga and later a woman named Cynthia Frias, played key roles in helping the police. Ms. Frias was married to Alfonso Zuniga. She allowed the police to search the apartment she shared with Alfonso while he was in for questioning.

The police found a gun clip and bullets, in addition to the robbery victim's stolen cell phone.

They were unable to find a gun, but Cynthia Frias called shortly thereafter with information about where to find the gun: it was hidden under Alfonso's doghouse.

I didn't think that the women had known just how awful their husbands were, and I wondered for a long time after how they felt when they found out what the men had been arrested for. I had to believe that they had no idea that their husbands were capable of participating in a gang rape.

Again, a bit of luck had been on our side. When the other two men heard that Luis had been arrested, they had made a plan to escape to Mexico. The police showed up at the apartment complex where the two men lived three minutes before a distant cousin of theirs arrived to drive them to the bus station.

Three minutes. That was the difference between this crime being solved and me having to look over my shoulder for the rest of my life, fearing that one day those men might come back for me.

"Most cases require that we get a good break. We got one, maybe a couple, but they won't mean a whole lot if we don't take full advantage of them and get the conviction and the sentence that you want. That's not completely in my control, but to a great degree it is. I'm going to do everything in my power to make sure that everyone's hard work, your contributions, and those good breaks don't go to waste."

"Thank you. And I'm sorry if I've been—"

Erin held up her hand. "Appreciated but not needed. I admire tenacity and you've got it."

I left that lunch feeling very good about the position we were in and about Erin. She was solidly on my side, appreciated how much I wanted to help, and was passionate about the work she was doing to help women like me. I was so grateful that Kelly had found a way for us to get to know each other after all, so that I could get a real sense of Erin. It had been hard to talk to her in that first formal, awkward meeting, and I desperately needed to get to know her in order to see her as a trusted member of my team. Our lunch made me realize that she really did have all of the qualities I wanted in my legal counsel, and made me feel like I was in good hands for the next step.

I wasn't certain how to feel about the fact that Luis, having been held for three days before the other two men were arrested, confessed that he had taken part. He, of course, claimed that the other two men were the ones who had really harmed me. He had helped our case by confessing and filling in some details, but he had also done horrific things to me. Could he possibly believe that his reluctance to do such horrible things to another person was in any way an excuse? His weakness took on so many dimensions that I had a difficult time processing how I really felt about him. But it still stuck in my head that at least he had admitted what he'd done.

I was conflicted about how to make sense of Luis, but I knew how I felt about the others. When questioned, Alfonso kept spinning different tales about what had happened. Arturo had somehow snatched me as he, Alfonso, drove past us. He tried to tell Arturo not to hurt me. Arturo threatened his family if Alfonso didn't go along with the plan. Luis was trying to help me. He didn't want any part of what was going on, so he dropped me off back at the spot where I'd been grabbed.

Later, Alfonso changed his mind about what had happened. He never touched me. This wasn't the first time Arturo had done such a thing. He was frightened because Arturo had a pistol. "Arturo is bad," Alfonso kept repeating.

I knew that. That night, I'd thought of Alfonso as the Boss, since Arturo had referred to him as "my boss." Now, based on what Erin was telling me, I realized that Arturo was the one in charge, the one who had a powerful influence over the other two.

Unlike the other two, Arturo refused to admit that he had played any role at all in kidnapping and raping me. I couldn't understand how someone could lie that way, not face the horrendous truth about himself even when he was obviously cornered. At times during this whole ordeal, I may have been in denial, but I still acknowledged the truth about myself and what I'd experienced. What was it like to completely deny something so dramatic? For the first time in my life I wondered about evil people, and if they ever looked at themselves in the mirror and saw what others saw.

I didn't know how Arturo or the others could live with themselves, but I did know this. I didn't want them to live among the rest of us. Other people who were close to me didn't want those men to be allowed to live at all, but I didn't want them to be executed on my behalf. I didn't see the point in taking their lives from them—their freedom yes, but not their lives.

My priority was keeping those men away from other people—so that none of them would ever have the chance to hurt anyone else, so that no one else would have to endure what I had.

CHAPTER ELEVEN

Going Solo

Shortly following my return to Dallas after Christmas, I went for a training run with Kristine. I still wasn't feeling 100 percent, but it felt good to be back on familiar territory and running. Kristine and I started off chatting a bit, but as we picked up the pace and the distance grew longer, we lapsed into the comfortable silence that can pass between two close friends. We hadn't discussed a destination or a route beforehand, and after the first mile or so, I took the lead. I wasn't consciously aware of making this choice, but I found myself heading in the direction of where the party had been held.

As we neared the familiar apartment, Kristine reached out and put her hand on my forearm, halting our progress. Her eyes pleaded with me. With a shake of her head, she indicated that she didn't want to go back there. I slowed nearly to a stop, lingering at the crux of the intersection, feeling like it would be a good thing for me to go past the site where I was taken from, as if I could somehow transform it from a place of fear to just another stretch of road I ran along. I knew that Kristine was still struggling with putting that spot into the context of the rest of our lives, as independent women and as competitive runners. I didn't want it to become either holy ground or unholy ground. It was just a place after all, a few meters of blacktop and stones.

Still, I honored what Kristine wanted and we turned right and down another long tree-lined avenue toward White Rock Lake and the park there. As we wound our way toward the Botanical Garden and the Arboretum, I firmed up a decision I'd been toying with the whole run, concerning my return the next morning to Parkland Hospital to be tested again for HIV.

Kristine and I stopped at a mini-mart before going back to our place. We stood in the parking lot for a few minutes, sipping our vitamin waters.

I picked at the label on mine and then squinted into the sun, Kristine's image obscured by light and shadow.

"I think I'd like to go by myself tomorrow."

Kristine nodded. "You're sure?"

"I am," I said with greater conviction than I really felt. "I'm not looking forward to going back there, but I need to start doing things on my own again."

Kristine chewed at her lips for a second and seemed about to speak, but I jumped in. "I know that you're willing to go. I appreciate that, but I'm getting tired of feeling like I'm imposing on everyone's schedule. I know that's how I feel and not how you are feeling, but I hope you'll understand."

Kristine smiled and rolled her eyes. "Whatever," she said in her best American Valley Girl impersonation. She wrapped me in a hug and said, "Good luck. I'll be thinking about you."

Maybe there's something about the contrast between hospital hallways in the middle of the night and the middle of the day that makes a huge difference in perception, but Parkland wasn't as horror-show creepy as I remembered it. Instead of the awful artificial light, sunlight poured in through the windows. Instead of the hallways being empty, they bustled with activity, and instead of the emergency exit lights shining like a warning of something ominous, they simply stated a fact.

I sat in the exam room, propped my arm on the table, and watched as the needle probed beneath my skin and my blood filled the syringe. I resisted the temptation to ask how long it would take to get the results and told myself that I had nothing to worry about. I was fretting like mad inside, but I smiled and thanked the nurse who'd done the draw.

"That wasn't so bad, was it?" she said.

I immediately thought that she was speaking to me like I was a child, and realized that to her, that's exactly what I was.

I shook my head. "No. It was nothing at all really." I kept the cotton ball firmly pressed to my arm, noting the difference between the feel of my skin on my own skin and the nurse's gloves, the barrier between someone who'd gone through what I had and someone who'd not.

When the results came back negative, I felt an enormous sense of relief. I realized then just how fearful I had been. I'd have to have additional follow-ups, but knowing that it looked as if I was in the clear made me feel cleaner. I shared the news with Anette and my parents, but mentioned it casually, as if I had done well on a quiz for one of my classes, just a routine part of my day as a normal university student. The thought that I was possibly carrying a virus—one that I had gotten from *them*, had made me feel dirty and uncomfortable in my own body. I hadn't realized just how heavy the burden of maybe carrying a virus could be—it was as if I'd been dragging a car tire behind me for all those weeks.

I knew that many people lived long and productive lives with HIV, but what I had a hard time dealing with was where the microorganism had come from. Had I been infected, it would have meant that I was literally carrying in my body a part of one of those men. That would have meant that I would never be free of them, that woven into the fabric of my body would have been something of one or possibly more of the people from whom I wanted to get as great a distance as possible.

I saw passing that test as a mark of progress. Another lap to be counted off. Another runner passed, a position gained. I'd even come to terms with the fact that the trial wouldn't begin for another few months. I had a track season to focus on, and decided that I would pour myself into my training even more fully as a way of making the time pass quickly. I was a competitor, and competitors compete. They rise to a challenge and take up the fight. I took what Erin had said about good breaks and taking advantage of them to heart. I'd thought much the same thing about my having survived the attack. It was up to me to make something of this chance.

I can see now that this marked a change in the relationships I had with my friends in Dallas, most particularly with Robin. I'd always been so independent before, and then after the rape I'd needed others to help get through even the smallest things. The pendulum didn't so much swing between those two points as it did freeze at one end and then suddenly jump to the other side. I exhibited the abrupt shifts between "help me, help me" and "let me do it myself" that I'd seen in children. I became aware of that and tried to make those shifts less abrupt, hoping to strike a finer balance somewhere in the middle, but my tendency when faced with any problem was to lower my shoulders and plow forward. Keeping others at just the right distance from me wasn't easy when they perceived my actions as pushing them away and I perceived my behavior as asking politely, and maybe nudging them a bit, to give me the space I needed.

It seems strange to me even now how vulnerable I was at the beginning of the healing process, and how hard I tried later to let everyone know that this was something I could handle myself. It scared me to rely too much on others to help me with my healing. What would happen to me if they were to grow tired of me and my struggles? Unfortunately, because he was in many ways the one closest to me, Robin bore the brunt of the head-spinning alternation.

I was definitely feeling better physically. Sleep was something I began to welcome again. The nausea that had plagued me began to subside. I couldn't bring myself to eat peanut butter, something I had done regularly before. Prior to leaving for the party that night, I'd eaten a peanut butter sandwich. Memories come in strange packages.

As the first meet of the track season approached, I was starting to get some of my stamina back. Maybe that wasn't such a good thing. I was on the track, but with my renewed sense of physical strength, my determination to return to normalcy had also increased, as did my efforts to make sure I made that a reality.

During one of the sessions with Dr. Soutter, she used the term "new normal." I knew what she meant, but it wasn't until I was doing a series of four-hundred-meter repeats—one lap of the track at a fast pace followed by a brief jog and then another fast lap—that I began to really reflect on what she meant. We did those repeats as a group—all the distance runners together in a pack. I liked that, but I also knew that when we crossed the line and our times were shouted out, everyone would know where we stood in that pack. I had a kind of love/hate relationship with that idea. It was good to know where I stood compared to everyone else, but in a way this was a declaration of the state of my fitness. Runners take a large amount of pride in demonstrations and declarations of how much we are able to suffer, how much pain we can take. That's what our times in races and workouts really came down to. How much pain could we endure? Having that out there for everyone to see, when the time was fast, was a good thing.

As we passed the start/finish line for each lap, Coach Casey shouted out our times. Before the rape, I'd typically been able to run the four hundred meters in seventy-four to seventy-five seconds. During that workout, I was clocking them in seventy-nine seconds. That might not sound like much, but a ten-thousand-meter race takes about twenty-five laps, and those seconds really add up.

I couldn't accept that this slower was my new normal, not as an athlete and not as a survivor. Being "damaged" or a "victim" and having to accept that I was somehow altered by the experience wasn't something that I was willing to accept as "normal" in any way—new, old, used, abused, didn't matter. The only new I wanted to accept was better—better times on the track, better relationships with my friends and with my boyfriend.

As the last of those repeats was about to end and my legs felt numb and my lungs seared, I also thought that I wanted the world to be better. I didn't want anyone to have to go through what I had, not the initial terror or the aftermath and facing the larger question of Who am I now?

In a way I can see that, off the track, maybe I was being a bit of a narcissist, thinking that everyone was looking at me or judging me. I hated the idea that anyone would look at me with any kind of pity and think, "There's that poor girl. I bet that things are really hard for her. I feel so bad for her." That was particularly true of how I viewed my professors. I didn't want them to see me struggling in a class and think that the reason for it was because of my being raped. I still had some problems with focus, and despite people telling me in the past that I didn't have to try to write down *everything* that a professor said in class, I decided that was what I needed to do to help me improve my powers of concentration. If

I had been a bit of a fanatic about note taking before, I became absolutely maniacal about it that next semester.

Even as I write this today, I can still feel the tension in my hands as they fiercely gripped my pen and nearly gouged the words into the paper. In thinking about those days, my brow, the set of my eyes and lips, the tightness in my jaw, all come back to me. As I sat there in classes, it was as if I was engaged in a battle for position on the track, the thrashing of arms and legs, my mostly taller opposition obscuring my vision a bit. I had to push past them, get into the free and the clear. Stay focused. Stay focused.

I filled up notebooks like they were note cards; I lived in a spiral-bound world in those days. The English language was coming much easier to me, which helped, but the biggest factor was thinking of my issues with focus as an opponent to be beaten to prove to everyone, including myself, that I was undamaged by what had happened.

Of course, as is true with training and overtraining, there was the possibility that there would be some injury along the way. If I failed at anything on my return to Dallas, it was in striking the kind of balance that I'd had after I'd met Robin. He had opened my eyes to a different way of approaching being a student and an athlete. Before him, my life consisted mostly of "have to" statements and actions: I have to eat right to keep my weight down so I can perform at my best. I have to study and do all the reading because I have to get the best grades. I have to get the proper amount of sleep. The "have to" list went on and on. Robin made me realize that there was some room for "want to." He helped me see that though all my "have to"s had produced good results, I wasn't really living the life that I wanted to. He showed me how to feel more energized, more alive. I loved him and how he accepted me, how he wasn't a "have to" and I didn't have to be anyone but my true self around him.

When we first started to argue, I could blame it on the stress we'd both been under. We squabbled over the typical things: how much time I was spending studying instead of with him, what we were going to do when we did get together, how much time he was now spending with one of his guy friends. We struggled with bigger questions: Why he was comfortable sharing his feelings with his friends and not with me? Why was he trying to protect me and not let me into his world?

Things had changed because of the rape. In the end I think we both wanted things to go back to the way they were before; we tried to pretend that everything was the old normal, but the truth, no matter how much we tried to ignore it, was more insistent. I was trying to deal with it my way, he was trying to deal with it his way, and we both stubbornly clung to the idea that we wanted to do what was best for each other, but that wasn't always what the other one wanted or needed.

I didn't understand this at the time, but how I was behaving was a pretty typical response. I was taking an Exercise Physiology class, and I learned that movement was possible a lot of the time because of antagonistic pairs of muscles—one contracts and the other relaxes, and work gets done. A kind of pushing and pulling. I was pushing Robin away, and pulling close to me the things that would make it seem like I was okay, that everything was fine. Robin knew things weren't fine—he was hurting and of course knew that I was, too—but I didn't appreciate the reminders that I saw in him.

I was trying to balance, and not always succeeding at keeping so many other things in proportion—preparing for the trial, competing at track, getting my education.

I knew that I had to be selfish. I had to think of my interests and my well-being first. Though I was doing better physically, the enormous energy it took to focus on classes and keep moving forward took a toll on me. I only had so much energy and so much time. Worse, for as much progress as I seemed to be making, every two weeks, nearly as regularly as clockwork, I'd go through a down cycle that had me in torrents of tears. When we are threatened, we go into fight-or-flight mode, and I fled during those instances when I broke down. I didn't want to let anyone see me, so I'd hole up in my room, say that I was studying, tell people that I was going to the library or some other site on campus to study, and like a wounded animal retreat to some dark corner of my world. This was both an act of self-preservation and a way to spare my friends the sight of me hurting, or hurting them if I lashed out in pain, frustration, and anxiety.

I felt helpless when Robin's or my good intentions went awry and I ended up hurting him despite my efforts to spare him. I kept thinking about New Year's Eve back in Norway. Robin was still there visiting me.

Instead of the two of us having a night together, I took him to a party that my sister was hosting—a few close friends, none of whom Robin had met before. I wanted to go to prove to myself that I could handle a social situation where other people knew what had happened to me. Besides, I'd promised myself that the holiday was going to be as normal as possible, and I was going to keep that promise. I was exhausted, but I wasn't about to admit that. Robin and I had our first fight that night. He kept asking me why I was acting that way, and what was going on with me? I couldn't understand what he meant.

I was fine. Couldn't he see that? I couldn't be sad all the time.

In spite of the tension in our relationship, our physical intimacy wasn't greatly affected. I trusted Robin implicitly, and he was my first sexual partner. In hindsight I'm grateful that we had become comfortable with each other sexually before the rape occurred; it would have been far more difficult for me to trust a man if the relationship had been a new one after the attack. Not every survivor feels this way, but I never saw that what Robin and I did together sexually had anything to do with the assault. What happened in that truck was a horrible crime motivated by control and power. Robin and I were twenty-three and twenty years old respectively, enormously attracted to each other, and over the holiday, we slept together again for the first time since the attack. Robin was more hesitant than I was. He was concerned about doing something wrong, being too assertive, moving too quickly to resume what had been a wonderful part of our relationship. It was much like our first time again; I loved him and needed his companionship and support, and the kind of physical intimacy that helped reinforce all the very real and treasured aspects of our life together.

Eventually, though, our disagreements about other things became too much.

We broke up.

This was too hard.

What was the point of being together when we clearly didn't see things the same way, when no matter what I did, I ended up feeling some form of bad? It was like I was reliving those frustrating nights in bed when sleep wouldn't come, when no matter what position I shifted to I couldn't get comfortable. Eventually, I'd just get up, give up on the idea of sleeping.

After we broke up, I was devastated. I'd gone from thinking that this was the man who I was going to spend the rest of my life with to not having him in my life at all. SMU is a relatively small place, but still you could get "lost" there if you wanted or needed to. I didn't see or hear from Robin for two months. Robin had given me a white jacket as a Christmas present. The night I came back to the apartment after we'd agreed to part, I put the jacket on and lay in bed crying.

I'm fine. Why can't he see that?

Kristine was my refuge and my recovery again. As much as I was hurting, as painful as the breakup was, I gradually began to feel better, a little bit at a time. The track season being in full swing helped. I had plenty to do. My mind was full. It's just that my heart was empty.

CHAPTER TWELVE

Measuring Progress

Throwing myself into the work of recovering from the breakup, healing from the rape, and devoting myself to my classes and my training, I barely noticed the time flying by before it was spring-time. I felt torn about what I was accomplishing. I was proud of mak-ing progress—I saw that my grades on assignments, papers, and tests were pointing me toward my best performance yet at SMU—and sad that I'd let go of someone I cared about so much. While I understood that all of the emotional work was important, it was much easier to think about the progress that I could measure with a stopwatch and a grade point average. I liked that. Yet getting an A on an exam, a quiz, or a paper didn't really please me—it just made me not disappointed. I wasn't reveling in my success in the classroom; I was a grade-earning machine, relentlessly and methodi-cally churning through all the necessary work with that goal in mind.

That was true to a lesser degree on the track. I did start to enjoy run-ning again, and as my times in the four-hundred-meter repeats, for exam-ple, began to drop by a second or two, I did feel some satisfaction. That was proof that I was progressing, moving in the right direction. If those times were slower than they'd been during a previous workout, then I was angry and disappointed that I'd "proved" I wasn't making progress.

Anything that showed that I wasn't improving, wasn't making forward progress, grew all out of proportion in my mind. If I felt low energy, or if I struggled to really understand a concept that I was studying, I would be devastated. I can see now that if I looked at the big picture, the trend was definitely upward. I knew something of bell-shaped curves and incremental progress, but I was looking for straight lines and steep angles up. I'd always taken pride in being able to attack the hills and dig deep for a strong finish in my racing life, and I wanted to do the same in the rest of it.

One measure of my progress was my relationship with Dr. Soutter. On my return from Norway, we agreed that meeting once a week would be sufficient. To me, that was good news. I'd been seeing her at first nearly every day, and now I was down to once a week. Way to go, Monika.

The first session after I was back, we mostly just talked about my trip home. I didn't go into a lot of detail; mostly I emphasized how good it was to be back there with a supportive family and how much richer and deeper my relationship had become with my sister and mother especially.

Dr. Soutter told me that she could see a difference in me. At first I didn't know how to react to her statement. How could she tell there was a difference? What criteria was she using? Unlike the measure of number of sessions per week, which was a quantitative assessment, this was more qualitative and didn't offer me a whole lot of comfort. I wondered if it meant that I was becoming too good at fooling people, that even a professional like Dr. Soutter had fallen for my act. She didn't see what other times were like for me, and I didn't always volunteer what I was experiencing outside the safety of her office.

LATER THAT DAY, I decided to take a long walk after dinner. I was trying to puzzle out just what Dr. Soutter had seen in me that was so different from before. I knew that I didn't feel the same. Before the holiday break, I had sat with her wondering if I was dead, worrying about that crazy dash I'd made across the street to get away from the black SUV I saw.

I still was startled by traffic sounds every now and then, and as I walked along, my earphones in but the volume of my Pink album low enough so that I could hear what was going on around me, I jumped when I heard tires skidding. My heart raced, but when I looked around, I saw that it had been just a car that had nearly collided with another vehicle in the middle of an intersection.

One of the drivers sped off, cell phone raised out the window as a kind of explanation/apology. I remembered how frightened I had been of driving over the Christmas holiday back in Løten; at first, just being in a vehicle had brought back that night in so many ways—the odor of a car interior, a mix of stale food odors and dirt and a pine air freshener, the sense of confinement and motion. Slowly, though, as I walked along that night in late February, I recognized that I was able to handle the surprises of traffic and roadside activities without panicking. My senses still felt heightened, but the feeling wasn't anywhere near the blinding fear or panic of before. Maybe Dr. Soutter was right—something was different.

I began to look at my sessions with Dr. Soutter like visits to a professor during office hours. We talked about the specifics of how I was doing in my recovery, but we spent a lot of time discussing more general principles of mental health and recovery from trauma. Surprisingly, post-traumatic stress disorder never came up. In looking back, I realized that PTSD was responsible for those periods when my best efforts to stay positive and not let things get to me failed.

Post-traumatic stress disorder (PTSD) is a diagnosis given to people who have particular symptoms after witnessing or experiencing any kind of traumatic event.

In order for a person to be diagnosed with PTSD, certain criteria must be met. First, you must have some kind of recurrent bad thoughts associated with the event—either flashbacks, nightmares, distress when faced with something that reminds you of the event, or just an inability to stop thinking about it. I had all of the above.

You must also have symptoms of avoidance and of numbing, which can include avoiding talking or thinking about the trauma, avoiding things and people that remind you of the trauma, a loss of interest in activities you used to enjoy, a feeling of detachment from people, a dampening of your feelings, and doubts about your future. I didn't feel a dampening of emotions or lack of interest in activities, but I certainly avoided things that reminded me of the rape. A whole list of other possible symptoms fit me, too, like sleep difficulties, irritability, trouble concentrating, hyper-vigilance, and an exaggerated startle response. From the beginning, Dr. Soutter did tell me that everything I was feeling was normal. But I think it would have given me some comfort to know that there was a whole tribe of survivors like me out there who had gone through the same symptoms, that there was a name for what I had been experiencing, and that it almost always got better.

Another diagnosis, called rape trauma syndrome (RTS), a complex form of PTSD, isn't in the official diagnostic manual for psychologists, but it made a lot of sense to me when I learned about it later. Online, I read that RTS was described after researchers Dr. Ann Burgess and Lynda Holmstrom studied adult women who'd come to a Boston hospital's emergency ward reporting rape. They found that the women shared many common symptoms and patterns. The researchers divided the symptoms into four stages: attack, acute, reorganization, and resolution or integration.

During stage 1, the actual attack, lots of women freeze up like I did. Every woman thinks she would fight back and run away, but in reality, it rarely happens that way. Our bodies just freeze up on us involuntarily, and we become disoriented or disconnected. For some time soon after the rape, I was beating myself up for not fighting back physically; I kept wondering, What would have happened if I had tried kicking and screaming and jumping out of the car?

It's impossible not to wonder, but in reality I probably would have been killed if I had tried to escape. I don't think I made the wrong decision. My response was both instinctive and conscious. I told myself in the moment that the only way to get through that night alive was to not struggle against those men. When I learned about just how brutal a person Arturo was, and how much fear he instilled in family members and friends, I felt better about not having tried to run or fight. But in the immediate aftermath of trauma, that's what your mind does to you—it questions everything. It wants to go over every little detail and figure out how to "fix it" so it never happens again.

The acute stage takes place immediately after the attack, when a rape survivor might feel shock, pain, and a whole range of emotions, from shame to rage. Where I was that first semester back at school was in stage 3, the reorganization phase—the time when the survivor tries to make sense of life again and understand what happened. I just wanted to skip right ahead to stage 4, when the rape would be only a small part of my life instead of its major focus. I was trying to act as if I was in that fourth stage, but in doing so I was clearly showing that I was in an earlier phase of my recovery. That's because I was consciously making an effort to put the event behind me. I was still focused on it, so it wasn't a natural state of progress. I was very often aware of my responses and behaviors in terms of the rape. That kind of monitoring made the attack more prominent in my mind rather than less. I would eventually get to the point where I was behaving naturally, but I wasn't quite there yet.

Fortunately, one subject never entered my mind. Rape survivors often have suicidal feelings, too, but I never thought about that. I had plenty of good things in my life worth living for, and I had wonderful people surrounding me—my friends, boyfriend, family, and even my coaches and the school itself.

Having Kelly step in to provide a maternal presence in Dallas was a big help. I so looked forward to spending time with her. Lunches and teas, hanging out at her home putting golf balls on the green on their property, Kelly offered me a glimpse of another world, one far removed from what I'd grown up in and one so different from the nearly unimaginable place the Worst One, the Boss, and the Weak One came from.

Kelly didn't have any children of her own, though her husband Norman did from a previous marriage, and she treated me, Petra, and some of the other girls like family. I felt I could talk with her honestly, and she was able to put things in perspective in a way that people my own age couldn't. She talked about some of the struggles she'd had, and how she felt like every time someone did or said something that might have hurt her or made her question things, she found some way to give back to others. That was why she wanted to be in touch with me. It wasn't that she was using me to make herself feel better, but my story made her realize that whatever she was going through, there were other people who had tough times as well. Rather than just acknowledge that as a fact, she felt it was important to try to help others. She really shaped my thinking, especially when I decided that I couldn't just act as if nothing had happened to me. That wouldn't benefit me and it wouldn't benefit anyone else either.

That semester, I needed a sound structure and some stability in my life before I could make changes and truly turn the experience around. It was like getting a good base of training in before doing speed work to try to improve my time. I had to build a strong foundation first.

That was the approach that I was taking with my running, though I have to admit that at the time I wasn't quite so philosophical and understanding about the nature of recovery on the track. The SMU team had had a great cross-country season the previous fall. We won the Conference USA Championship, won our regional (with Silje finishing first overall), and then advanced to the NCAA Championship. That was all thrilling for me to participate in.

I had been very much looking forward to the indoor season, but I wasn't going to compete in those indoor meets from January to mid-March. Coach Wollman felt it was best for me to recover, regain my strength, and focus my energies on the outdoor season that began the third week of March.

I felt a mix of envy and joy when I heard the girls who did compete indoors come back and report on how things had gone. It seemed to me that before the attack my life was simpler, more black-and-white. Things were either good or bad then, but afterward everything seemed to be a kind of muddled gray. I felt a bit like Goldilocks—struggling to find anything that felt just right.

The truth was that I felt most comfortable when I was with all the other girls on the team, a place where I could retreat or be in the spotlight, depending on my mood, and no one questioned my choice. A track team is a bit different from a cross-country team. In cross-country, we all worked out together because we were involved in the same event, the same distance, etc. With track, we were more divided—the sprinters, the hurdlers, the middle- and long-distance runners, the field event participants who jumped or threw.

Because I ran the three-thousand-, five-thousand-, and ten-thousand-meter races, I spent most of my time with the distance girls, so we were

naturally a bit closer. Many of us were also part of the international con-
tingent, so we had that in common as well. So, when Silje did well, or
when Kristine, Klara Bodinson, or Sara Sjökvist ran a good race, I could
celebrate with them. The team as a whole didn't do as well as we had in
cross-country, but that was okay. We still had the outdoor season to look
forward to, and Simone du Toit, who was from South Africa, had won an
individual conference championship in the shot put. I loved the idea that
our team was made up of women from so many different places and that
we all, despite our different backgrounds, got along well and had fun. The
meets themselves, the actual competitions, were fun and stressful, but the
road trips and our antics were so much pure fun.

Maybe I shouldn't generalize, but it takes a certain kind of personality
type to be a long-distance runner, a certain level of seriousness and dedication to endure the kind of pain and effort that we do. On the long bus
rides back from track meets, the "endurance girls" and I would sit with
our headphones on, our noses in our books and notebooks, our overhead
lights shining down. We sat in the middle of the bus most often, while
behind us, the sprinters conducted a dance party / lip-synch battle / hip-
hop rhyme-off.

If I had a dollar for every time their coach had to ask them to quiet
down, I'd be a very rich Scandinavian—the term that the girls from
the U.S. affectionately used to describe a group of us. Team Scandinavia
sometimes got roped into rap contests with Team USA. Throughout the
season, the sprinters had been tutoring us in American urban slang while
we'd tried to teach them Swedish or Norwegian. The results were equally
hilarious and equally ineffective. I had no idea what I was saying half the
time, and I knew I looked a little silly, but I loved it. Kristine was a different story. I remember one time when she stood in the aisle, swaying from
side to side due to the bus's movements, and said, "Okay, everyone, listen
up now, yo. I'm gonna show you some hella Norwegian rap before I'm
outie. Then all ya'll gonna know what it like to pick up your face."

I was amazed, and so were the rest of the girls. Our laughs turned into
shouts and applause.

Kristine sat down next to me, and I had to ask, "How on earth did
you do that?"

She shrugged. "No big deal. I did that routine back in high school a few years ago."

"Kicking it old school?" I asked.

We both burst into laughter that turned to tears of joy.

Moments like that are ones that I still remember more than I do the races and the meets. I loved those girls, and being able to lose myself in those moments helped me enormously.

Even though I wasn't competing that track season, just being with the girls during practice and staying in motion were crucial to my healing.

I sensed instinctively that I had to keep running or skiing in the days and weeks after the rape. Not only was that a part of my usual routine, but I loved moving and how it made me feel. I didn't like that I wasn't moving as fast or as easily as I had in the past, but allowing my body the freedom to let loose was enormously beneficial throughout the process. Regardless of what stage I may have been in with RTS, physical activity made a huge difference in how I felt each day. I told myself that it was better to be drained of energy physically than mentally. My body was tired, but exercising gave me mental strength and energy to fight back against all the negative feelings.

I was majoring in Applied Physiology, so I was reading widely about the benefits of exercise, for classes as well as for personal reasons. I am a bit of a science nerd, so the combination of sports and science made the subject a natural for me. My interest in psychology also helped me as I worked toward feeling better and running faster.

I knew that those who'd been raped suffered in the short term and the long term. As the days passed, I focused more on what some of the possible long-term issues might be for me. With the threat of HIV/AIDS lessening, I looked at other potential threats to my well-being. I learned that people who are sexually assaulted are three times more likely to suffer from clinical depression than the average population. We are six times more likely to have to endure PTSD, thirteen times more likely to abuse alcohol, twenty-six times more likely to abuse drugs, and four times more likely to contemplate suicide.

While I think I did develop PTSD, but never received a fully confirmed diagnosis, those symptoms were relatively mild compared to what

I read about others experiencing. As for the rest of the list above, I didn't have those problems at all.

Why?

In my mind, the answer is exercise. I was traumatized by the attack, but not to the degree that I might have been if I hadn't remained active. I had a great support group, and I remained focused on the future and my education, but I'm convinced that running spared me months of the kind of agony that words like "depression," "abuse," and "suicide" convey.

It wasn't just the act of running that helped. Many people understand the benefits of yoga as a way to reduce stress. Running can do the same things; it can help reduce blood pressure, reduce cortisol levels (a hormone released when we are stressed), strengthen the lymphatic/immune system to help us fight off illnesses. The list goes on.

For me, having that knowledge helped my running. I need to understand the why and how of things, so I applied my Applied Physiology on the track. Unfortunately, I wasn't taking any classes like Applied Criminal Justice System. I think that would have helped me as I dealt with the other major competition I felt I was entered in—the trials of the three men who had brutalized me.

{ CHAPTER THIRTEEN }

Running in Circles

Today, I can see some irony in my spending the spring of 2010 running around in circles on the track. No matter how far I ran, I still got back to the same point in space. Of course, a lot changed during that spring, but the legal system made me feel like I was spinning in circles and producing nothing tangible or beneficial to my healing. I wanted those trials behind me. I wanted those men in prison for the rest of their lives. Though I was told it was going to take some time before the trials would be scheduled, and there would likely be some delays along the way, it was very, very hard to be patient. I like to attack problems head-on, but those trials were not something I'd be able to do alone, acting independently, so I had to rely heavily on others to help me get over the many anxious moments I had when thinking about what that experience was going to be like.

If I hadn't had both classes and track, that anxiety would have overwhelmed me. The trials lurked around the fringes of everything I did that academic year; they shadowed every experience I had. That's not to say that I was in a constant state of gloom, far from it, but knowing that I was going to have to testify three separate times about what had taken place that night felt like a flaw in even the most perfect of experiences.

I knew I couldn't obsess over the months and months that stood between me and the first trial. So I focused on smaller increments of time—seconds. Forty-two seconds, to be precise. On March 27, 2010, I prepared to run the five thousand at the Bobby Lane Invitational. It would be my first race of the season, my first since the rape.

I tried to tell myself that there had been good explanations for that regression.

When I toed the starting line that afternoon, I felt my usual bit of nerves gnawing at my stomach. I'd been in dozens and dozens of competitions before. My training had been decent leading up to the race. Why should this one have been any different? It was the first outdoor race of the season for me, but it wasn't like I was running cross-country, where a course might be unfamiliar to me. This was easy, right? Run straight and then turn left around the curve, run straight, turn left around the curve, then repeat that twelve and a half times.

I'm always nervous before a race. That's nervous excitement. I'm eager to get out there and test myself. That's particularly true in your first competition of the season. You've trained and trained, and you want to see how all that hard work has paid off. The thing about track and cross-country is that you're in a competition against others and against yourself. Nearly all the time, unless you're competing at a certain distance for the first time, you have some standard of your own to compete against. You want to win, but failing that, you want to go faster than you have previously.

The nerves I felt in my first race of the '10 track season were different. This was anxiety. Instead of giving me energy like nervous excitement does, this sapped me. It was like my bodily systems were in high gear and were devouring all the energy stores in my muscles. I was worried about failing, and that's a heavy weight to drag around a track. This first race meant that how the rape had affected me was going to be measured precisely, with quantitative precision. I didn't want to run slower than I had pre-rape. That would be like getting proof that I was still back there, still in that van, still hoping to get free instead of being free.

The first few laps, I felt that freedom I loved. I cruised through them, but then I faded.

After those first laps, I didn't recognize myself. This wasn't my stride.

This wasn't my energy level. Normally, I would zone in during a race. I wouldn't allow any external or extraneous stimuli in—I'd just have that vision of my desired result alone in my head. This time, my head was crowded with thoughts and impressions. How my laces felt too tight, the scratchy sensation of my hair whipping against my back and shoulders, some other competitor laughing in the infield, the clatter of the pole vault bar striking the ground—all intruded into the quiet space I normally set aside to focus on my breathing and my technique.

As I reached the halfway point, I looked ahead and saw the leaders nearly half a lap in front of me. I did something I'd never done before. I said forget it. I can't catch them. What's the point?

Those earlier physical impressions that had crowded my mind left that space and were replaced by more emotional ones. I'd been grateful since the rape that I had survived. I was grateful that I could still run, do the thing I most loved in the world. Now I was miserable doing what I'd once loved. Worse, the reason why I was doing so poorly in the race and feeling so lousy wasn't because I was injured—I'd accepted the blame for that pelvis fracture freshman year—it was because someone had done something terrible to me, something I didn't deserve. I hadn't lost the ability to do what I loved—three horrible men had taken it from me. For the first time, I questioned whether running was worth it. Was I kidding myself? Was I good enough? Was all my hard work just a way to not think about the rape? Maybe running was just an escape from the other pain I was experiencing. What was the point of that? Why suffer to avoid suffering? At least before, the pain of running was productive—I felt good about the results. But this was pointless and unproductive.

I didn't stop. But I did tell myself that even if I tried to dig deep, all I'd do is make the hole larger and not find any kind of reserve of strength or determination there. Someone else had come along and stolen it. They'd discovered that special place where I'd stored those things. What I'd relied on all my life had been taken from me.

The good thing was, my teammates understood what it was that I needed just then. As I walked off the track, Coach Wollman's expression—tight-lipped, neutral—told me everything I needed to know. He knew that I knew that things hadn't gone well. A third-place finish, out of thirty-one entrants, wasn't terrible. But I was a racer, and races were meant to be won. If you didn't beat your competition, at least you beat your own best time, gave it your all, left nothing in reserve. I wanted the ground to open up and devour me. I didn't want anyone to look at me or to say anything.

I set off on a long cool-down run, alone with my thoughts. No one had told me that it was a good try, that at least I was out there, that I shouldn't expect much of myself considering. They treated me how I wanted to be treated. Just another competitor who had fallen short. Yet whatever satisfaction I felt at being treated normally was short-lived. I was bitterly disappointed in myself. I wanted to receive a "do-over"—to get right back out there on the track and run that race again immediately. Prove to everyone, including myself, that I was better than that.

After any race, I always performed a self-assessment, an honest appraisal of how I'd done both mentally and physically. I'd question if I went out at the right speed, if I was able to stick to my plan, if I was able to stay focused and in my zone, if I was able to find energy when needed. I'd determine if I had been able to push away the negative thoughts that appear whenever it hurts the most, if I was able to finish strong. I'd review the race a few times. I'd give myself credit for the positive things and let myself be angry at myself for a few hours over the negative things. Then I'd focus on what I could do to better prepare myself for the next one. Eventually, I'd tell myself to let it go; acknowledge that I'd squeezed from it as many lessons and positive and negative strokes as I could and now it would just be deadweight that would slow me down.

This time, though, I knew that I wasn't going to be able to move past these moments so quickly. I felt the way I did as a young girl when my tongue would probe a loose tooth, sensing the coppery, salty taste of my blood and feeling the sting and the jangle of the nerve, waiting for the days to pass before that tooth would come out.

My cool-down over, I went back to the infield and slipped on my warm-up top. As I tugged it down over my head, I saw someone approaching. Kristine held her arms out to me, and I let her envelop me in a long embrace. "Screw this silly race," she said. "Let's go home. Tomorrow we're starting over."

"That sounds good to me," I said. I sensed that she understood what had happened out there, that I hadn't just not run my best, I also hadn't kept that promise I'd made to myself—to not use the rape as an excuse. I'd failed in more than one way, and that simply wasn't acceptable.

On the bus ride home I brooded about what had happened. By the time we'd made the trip from Denton to Dallas, I had come around to another way of thinking. It had been 110 days since the rape. I'd run a race. I'd done something that I loved to do, and while it hadn't gone the way I had wanted it to, it had happened. Despite all the mental agonizing I'd done, on some level I knew that Bobby Lane was a success. I was back running and competing. But still, I was counting the days until I could feel like I had before. When I could tell people that I was okay and mean it. When I wasn't just okay but better. There weren't going to be any more first races after the rape. No more counting of days since. I was thinking of days until.

The following week, I had a long talk with Coach Casey and Coach Wollman.

"Have you ever heard of Bob Beamon?" Coach Wollman asked me.

I hadn't, so Coach explained that in the 1968 Olympics in Mexico City, Beamon barely qualified for the finals and then on his first jump leaped twenty-nine feet, two and a half inches. Coach Wollman let that sink in for a moment. "He beat the world record by twenty-one and three-quarter inches. That's astounding. Since 1901, the long jump world record had been broken thirteen times and by an average of two and a half inches."

I sat there wide-eyed. How could somebody break a record by such a huge amount?

"I wish that every one of my athletes could make such a huge leap in their performance," Coach Wollman said. "It would be great to be able to run a PR every time out, but no one has ever done that. It's just not humanly possible. It was your first race of the season. You can't expect a miracle jump like Beamon's. But you can get better, which is why we measure your times in tenths and hundredths of a second. Even a fraction faster is still a PR. And you know how much work it takes to get better, even by a tenth of a second." He snapped his fingers to indicate just how short a period of time that was.

I nodded. Progress comes slowly. Once you got to our level, huge breakthroughs with seconds and seconds of improvement weren't common. The longer the race, the greater the chances you'd have a bigger improvement, but still the point was true. If you looked at the big picture and did one thing every day a little bit better, put a little bit more effort into some aspect of your training—in the weight room, on the track, while stretching in the infield, or in your mind in developing confidence or trusting your training and your race plan, you'd get better results at some point down the line.

"Think of the building blocks we always talk about. You've got a solid foundation. Let's figure out how to get progressively better, build up the rest of the structure. The Mt. Sac Relays are this weekend. I'd like to see you do the 10K. I think a thirty-eight-minute time will put you in a good place."

I walked out of that meeting both eager and anxious. I didn't know if my body was ready for a ten-thousand-meter race (6.2 miles), but I wanted to give it a go. I hadn't ever competed in the ten thousand meter on the track, just in many road races, so this all felt fresh and new to me. Running one on the road was one thing; in comparison to being on a track, a road race was relatively straight. You had a few turns and some ups and downs, but they weren't marked out as regularly and consistently as a track was. I liked road races a lot because of the variety of the course, the less predictable nature of it.

Upping my race distance was going to be a challenge. At that point, I didn't know if I'd have the energy to finish a 10K. My training had been interrupted, and I still wasn't sleeping well, but I wanted to give it a shot. My PR in a 10K road race was 35:40. Targeting two minutes and twenty seconds slower than that would have normally been unthinkable. Why set out to not do better? But this was good. Modest expectations. New experience.

For the past three weeks, I'd tried so hard to keep to my usual routine, tell myself the usual things during my mental preparation before and during the race, and tried so hard to act and think in the ways that I had in the past. This time, though, I accepted that things had changed for me.

I told myself that it was okay to repeat to myself what I'd been thinking since that run with my father: I am bigger than this. I am not my struggles.

Before we finished our conversation after that disappointing five-thousand-meter race, Coach Wollman had suggested I do something else to help relax me and energize me—yoga. I was surprised that he suggested it. Normally, he was strictly against us doing something different from staying focused on our goals and believed that all training had to be running-specific. But he understood that my mind and my body were intricately connected. There was no way my body, which was feeling much better, was going to be able to perform if my mind and my emotions were still impaired. Maybe I was able to deceive people into thinking that I was better by hiding my darker thoughts and emotions. But the stopwatch didn't lie: I wasn't doing as well as I wanted everyone to believe. As much as I tried to convince people that I was back and ready to resume my previous life on and off the track, the numbers told me and everyone else that wasn't the case at all.

That was one of the great things about having coaches. Coach Wollman and Coach Casey cared about me as an athlete, but also as a student, and a person. During my ongoing moments of crisis, they were able to coach all of me. I didn't think of this then, but it seems appropriate that Coach Wollman was our "head" coach.

The first yoga sessions I took left me more stressed than ever; my mind kept wandering to all the "have tos" and "should haves." In that hour spent stretching, I found myself thinking, I could have covered at least eight miles, or I could have read an entire chapter in my anatomy book. But something told me that I had to stick to it, keep showing up at yoga one to two times each week, and maybe I would learn how to calm my mind eventually—something I clearly needed. After a few weeks, it started to click. I felt a gradual release in my body; my muscles started to let go of the tension, my mind started to slow down, my breathing got back to its normal rhythm. It felt so good; I was mastering the positions and the breathing, and I was mastering my own stress levels.

More important than the poses and the movement in yoga is the emphasis on controlled breathing. Most of us don't think about how we

breathe. That's because the body can regulate that function automatically—or autonomically, as it's more technically known. In learning yoga,
just as in running competitively, you're taught to consciously breathe from
the diaphragm. A big part of running efficiently is breathing efficiently.
Diaphragmatic breathing is sometimes known as "belly breathing"; when
you breathe properly, as you do when you're asleep, your chest muscles
aren't really activated and your rib cage doesn't rise and fall. Instead, the
muscle just below the rib cage, your diaphragm, descends and in so doing
changes the internal pressure in your lungs and you inhale.

I realized that, since the rape, I hadn't been breathing properly. My
muscles were so tensed up because of anxiety and stress that I wasn't getting the proper amount of oxygen into my system. I had to turn off that
fight-or-flight response and get back to breathing optimally in order to
counteract some of the physical stresses on my body as well as some of
the emotional ones.

With all those hormones being secreted, my body and brain chemistry was being altered. I won't go into all the specifics of this, but mood
disorders, depression, anxiety, etc., are caused by imbalances in our bodies'
chemistry. When I ran, I breathed properly and as a result derived many of
the same benefits that someone who practices yoga would. Also, that kind
of activity released endorphins into my system. Those are chemicals your
body releases when you exercise hard. They act on neurotransmitters in
the brain to reduce the experience of pain that you have associated with
exertion. Generally, they improve your mood and produce what some
people refer to as the "runner's high," an elevated feeling of wellness.
From my science studies, I knew that exercise has been proven to reduce
stress, ward off anxiety and feelings of depression, boost self-esteem, and
improve sleep. For once, the science nerd in me had proven helpful.

I was grateful that Coach Wollman recognized how down I was mentally, how preoccupied I'd become, how my thinking needed to be slowed
in order for my body to run fast. I can't say that at the time I understood
the nuances of the scientific process. I kept doing yoga because it felt
so good, because I wanted to, because my body and mind told me to.
I found pleasure in taking on another act of using and challenging my
body. I enjoyed it so much, in fact, that I would eventually become a yoga

instructor. I want to teach others to fall in love with yoga the way I did, for its powers to calm the mind, its importance to mental health, especially in the high-speed society we live in.

In that first semester back in Dallas from Norway, I was fortunate to be surrounded by so many people who were able to form a recovery team around me. I was fortunate that my training made me so physically aware of my body, and that I had an identity that I could use to define myself as something other than a victim.

Running and exercising were a habit and how I identified myself. I was fortunate that I didn't suffer such a blow to my self-esteem that I didn't want to be around other people. I didn't always seek people out, but as was true in the case of Kelly, they sought me out. And by exercising my body, and using yoga to calm my mind, I was producing a positive effect in my brain. With Dr. Soutter's help, I came to understand that the fear I experienced, the involuntary reactions I had to sights, sounds, and other stimuli, the nightmares and images, weren't rooted in reality. They were all in my brain. She assured me that one day my brain would calm down, and those thoughts and images and responses that had me questioning my sanity would diminish. My body had been on autopilot for a while, but I would gradually regain control.

Running and yoga helped me regain control of my brain and my body, restored order where there was disorder, and I knew that I wasn't just grasping at any concept I could: solid scientific evidence supported that I was doing the right things. My logical side and my emotional side were having their different needs met at the same time.

Maybe there was some other way I could have done that, but everything I've read about exercise pointed to it as having a powerful connection to recovery from trauma. I was also learning a bit about patience, taking things as they came to me, and being grateful for the many blessings I'd received. Being able to laugh and smile, to go to the frozen yogurt shop with friends and teammates, wasn't as good as winning a gold medal might have been, but pleasures come in different flavors.

Candles

The Mt. Sac Relays are held at Mt. San Antonio College in Wal-nut, California. They were first held in 1959 and have the motto "Where the World's Best Athletes Compete." Those words are the truth, and famous Olympians like Carl Lewis, Jackie Joyner-Kersee, and Marion Jones have competed there and set meet records. Thousands and thousands of individuals and relay teams in divisions from high school students to masters (athletes older than thirty-five) all compete. Our three-day event was known as the Distance Carnival and Invitational, and it really did have a carnival-like atmosphere. For a distance runner, this was one of *the* events to participate in. I loved seeing so many other athletes there; it made me wonder what it must be like to participate in the Olympic Games.

Normally, I would have been too focused on my race to enjoy being there, but the atmosphere was so great, the crowds so large, that I told myself to have fun and just enjoy the experience. An hour before my race was to start, I left the rest of my teammates and walked around the outside of the stadium to warm up.

All that week leading up to the race, I kept thinking about that thirty-eight-minute goal. That meant that I'd have to run each mile in 6:07. That was slow compared to what I was used to. But it wasn't the pace that was worrisome. Would I be able to run more than twice as far? Could I trust that my legs would hold up?

As I walked among the various tents and busses and displays, my stomach began to feel off. I found a bathroom and discovered that my period had started. Under any other circumstances, getting my period before a race, or having to race during it, would have been a cause for worry. When your body is taxed like that, it's difficult to perform well. This time, though, I was actually happy about it. Since the attack, I'd been experiencing amenorrhea, or an interruption of my monthly cycle. That happens frequently to distance runners due to the physical stress they put their bodies under; in my case it had occurred because of the emotional and psychological stress I'd been under.

This was a sign that my body was returning to its normal rhythms. Maybe my reducing some of my expectations for myself was a good thing. When I joined the pack of runners at the start line—there were fifty of us crowded there—I took a quick glance up in the stands. Coach Wollman was there with his stopwatch and clipboard. He gave me a big smile and a wink. I smiled back. In the past, we would have both had our game faces on—all serious business. But he was reinforcing that this was supposed to be fun—it warranted hard work and dedication, but it was also something to give us pleasure, make our lives more enjoyable. His being there, and his gesture, also reminded me that I was part of his team. He'd pulled me back from the brink when I'd thought about quitting, when I had all those doubts about whether the struggle was worth it.

After the gun went off, I tried to avoid getting caught up in the tangle of limbs as we all fought to gain our normal stride as quickly as possible. I knew the pace that I had to keep, and I was determined to stick with that. As we came around to complete the first of twenty-five laps, Coach Casey was on the inside of the track and told me what my time was. I was pleased that I was right on target, and I remained on that pace through the first ten laps.

"Right there, Monika. Just like that. Stay right there," I heard Coach Casey say again. This time, there was something in her voice; it was now higher pitched, more excited than it had been. I wasn't even at the half-way point, and for her to be expressing that kind of emotion clued me in. She must have seen something about me, about my stride, about my facial expression, how I was carrying my body, that she liked. I was feeling strong, and even though I'd just completed a little more than four thousand meters, or slightly less than 2.5 miles, I wasn't feeling any kind of strain at all. My shoulders and arms were relaxed, my spine straight, and my legs seemed to be moving easily.

I was on the inside lane, but there was a mass of other runners in front of me. I couldn't stay behind them all. My body was feeling too good to be hemmed in by all these other women. I took a quick glance over my shoulder and edged to the outside. I'd be covering slightly more distance, but the path was clearer. One by one runners fell away behind me. With each lap, I heard and saw Coach Casey's growing excitement. At one point, with five laps to go, I heard Kristine yell, "Monika, you're flying!"

It felt that way. The week before, my legs and the rest of my body had felt so heavy, as if with every stride I took I was sinking into the track's surface. This time, I felt like I was gliding along on the slick surface of the track, barely making contact with it, feeling its rubbery surface propelling me forward.

As I came around on the final lap, I heard Kristine's voice again, and I felt lifted by her words. I went into a furious kick and sprinted toward the finish, passing a few more girls. As I crossed the line, I threw my hands in the air and shouted, "YES!" as loud as I could. I slowed a bit and then stopped. Instead of sagging to my knees or collapsing on the ground, I walked along with my hands on top of my head, gasping for air, but absolutely elated. I didn't care that I had finished in twenty-first place or that my little victory celebration seemed out of place given where I'd finished in the order.

I had set out to run a thirty-eight-minute race, and I had finished in 36:50.34! One minute and ten seconds faster than my goal; one minute and ten seconds behind my PR. To me, that was as if I'd set a world record, won the world championship, done a Bob Beamon. I felt like myself again. I'd loved every second of the race. I'd dug deep late in the race to find something extra to give and I'd found it. That night, when I called my parents to let them know how the race had gone, I could barely contain my excitement.

"Congratulations! I'm so happy for you," my mother said.

My father echoed her words with praise of his own.

I hung up and realized that for the first time in many months, I wasn't just pretending that I was myself again; I truly did feel like myself again. I knew my parents felt a huge relief receiving that phone call, too. It was such a big contrast from when I had called them in December. Then we had all tried to convince one another I would be okay; now for the first time we saw signs of my progress in black-and-white. Being able to reassure them, as they had me, made me feel so good.

WHILE MY TIMES on the track occupied much of my thinking, at least I felt like I had some control over them. There was another event on the horizon, and its time was completely out of my hands. In our first meeting, Erin had told me that the trial was going to take place in May. I placed that on my mental calendar and prepared for it emotionally. But not long after that, the trial got delayed because the DA's office needed more time to prepare the case. That was better than going into it underprepared, so I recalibrated my expectations. A month's to six weeks' delay wouldn't be ideal—that would put it into June or early July, when I'd be back home in Norway—but I was prepared to do anything asked of me, and at least this way it wouldn't interfere with final exams.

With everything else going on—my breakup with Robin, the mixed bag of results in training and in races—I was balancing a lot of hope and hurt that entire semester. I was back to living the "have to" life: I have to get good grades. I have to get back on the track and do well. I have to graduate on time. I have to stay strong and independent. I have to be ready for the trial.

The "have tos" did make the time pass quickly, and before I knew it the semester was almost over. A couple of weeks before final exams, in early May, I received a text message from Robin's sister asking if I wanted to get together for coffee. She was in town to visit Robin. I'd known that the two of them were very close—he described her as his best friend—but I'd never met her in person. Seeing Anna made it even more clear to me how much a part of my life he was and what a void his absence had created. She reminded me so much of him. She had so much of the same upbeat energetic personality and way of making me feel comfortable that I opened up to her immediately.

I told her how much time I'd spent listening to heartbreaking love songs, and about the pleasant/painful tears I'd shed in thinking about the brief time we spent together. As we talked, I thought about how I'd felt about Anette's ex-boyfriend Jonas. Right after I'd called Anette to let her know about the attack, she'd gotten in touch with Jonas. They'd been apart for six months, but she realized how much she missed him and needed and wanted him in her life. They resumed dating, and I gained back the big brother I'd missed so much.

So when Robin's sister told me, "I just want to see Robin smile again," I knew how she felt and what I had to do.

I contacted Robin and we arranged to meet. Waiting for him to show up, I was more anxious than I'd ever been in my life. I talked myself into and out of a half dozen or so outfits, rehearsed conversations, and imagined what it would be like to have him wrap me in his arms again to tell me that everything was going to be okay.

Reality met my expectations. Robin and I shared how miserable we'd been being apart, how much time we spent thinking and wondering about the other person, and how much we missed being able to talk with each other. Robin wasn't naturally as shy as I was, and he'd had other girlfriends before, but he told me that he'd never felt as comfortable being himself around another person as he had with me. I told him that I felt the same way, and tried again to explain to him that I'd had to do what I thought was best. He told me that he understood, that he couldn't *really* understand all that I'd been through, but that the only thing that made any sense to him was being with me.

In an instant, all of the pain our breakup had caused was wiped away. I was amazed by how a simple touch and a simple word could so alter how I felt and what I thought. When I was with Robin, I felt like I did after a great yoga session. I was relaxed and at ease. The tension I seemed to carry around with me the rest of the time, the pressure I put on myself to succeed, to get the best grades, to set a PR, all seemed to just dissipate. I'd been doing well in classes and sometimes on the track, but it all felt hollow. Not being able to share it with someone I loved and cared about deeply made all those efforts seem like empty gestures, a shout of joy swallowed up in a vacuum. With Robin back by my side, things made sense. I was able to put my priorities in better order and see that all of the other worries I had were just preoccupations, not something I could really build a happy and satisfying life around.

ROBIN AND I picked up from where we'd left off. We spent as much time as we could manage together. I still wanted to study and complete the mission that I'd started at the beginning of the semester. Robin respected that, and my efforts in the classroom paid off: I earned straight A's for the semester.

Still, the ups and downs continued. I focused on the ten thousand meters for the rest of the season, leading up to the conference championship meet from May 13 to 16 in Orlando. We were leading the competition after the first day, but days two and three saw us slipping down the leader board. I had to be realistic. The previous year, the winner in the ten thousand had set the meet record, running a 34:41.14. That was more than two minutes faster than I'd run at Mt. Sac. Instead of thinking of winning the race outright, I focused on bettering my time. Running in April in Walnut, California, is a lot different from running in mid-May in Orlando, Florida. Everyone has to compete under the same conditions, but the heat and humidity really drained me. After five laps I felt just like I did that first race back. I wanted to walk off that track. I had no energy left in my body. But I refused to stop, and I pushed through to the end, feeling like I had raced at least a marathon as I crossed the finish line. I hung in there to finish in 37:44.49, for twelfth place. I didn't beat my PR and I didn't earn us any points. We wound up finishing fifth in the conference. It was hard to think of the seniors on the team ending their collegiate careers on such a down note, but for the underclassmen like Silje, Kristine, Viktoria, and me, the proverbial "you'll get them next year" still applied.

· · ·

JUST BEFORE I was ready to head home to Norway for the summer, I received another phone call from Erin. The trial had been postponed again. Something about the docket being full, not enough courtrooms, a busy schedule for the judge, a big city, and a lot of cases to be tried. "Sorry. Don't be discouraged. We'll make this happen."

I tried to focus on the good things those last few days before I left to return home. Just before I left, Robin and I spent the day together. The campus was strangely quiet, the carillon sounding almost plaintive, as if it were asking where everyone had gone. We were in the between time—the spring semester over, graduation done, the summer session not yet going—and that seemed to match my mood. Some things done, others still on the horizon. Maybe I was getting some of that good balance back that I'd had with Robin before. Maybe I could define a little bit differently what it meant to succeed. When I was back with Robin, I was able to see that when we were separated, I had become like a little grade-earning, time-counting machine. I'd recognized that fact before we were back in touch, and I was frightened. But I didn't know how else to respond at the time. At least being that way meant that people wouldn't see me as broken. They'd see me succeeding, but they wouldn't see me as happy—at least not as most of the people I knew thought of it.

Robin and I walked holding hands through campus. We'd spent the day playing tennis, then eating frozen yogurt. We had no particular destination in mind, but as if drawn by gravity, we wound up outside the Dedman Center, a place where we'd both spent so much of our time working out. We sat on the steps of one of the monuments outside it. From there, I could see the tennis courts where I'd first seen Robin playing tennis, the place where we first met. I'd been too shy to say hello to him that first time, but things had worked out.

In the last dying rays of the evening, we both lay down and stared into the soon-to-be-night sky. Robin slipped his hand into mine, and I felt really at peace for the first time since the attack, no other thoughts than that I was exactly where I wanted to be at that moment, and that I simply had to trust that time and distance wouldn't matter. Though many things were out of my control, they were going to work out; the effort I'd put in was going to pay off.

. . .

I CAN SEE now that I made some mistakes in how I approached things in the immediate aftermath of the rape. I went out too hard, too soon, and I "blew up" at the most crucial part of the contest. I had no finishing kick the last four hundred or so yards of the three thousand when you try to go into a higher gear. I had to stay relaxed while running, keep my thoughts quiet and few. Tensing up depleted too much of my energy. Rushing and pressure and focusing only on the goals and times and not the experiences themselves took me out of the moment. I was thinking too much about the ends of things, the results—my time in a race, the trials and the men being sentenced, getting past the effects of the rape. When you spend that much time worrying about putting things behind you—other runners, bad experiences, and the rest—you don't have time for the present or the future.

A few days after that peaceful day with Robin, I flew home alone for summer break. I was exhausted by the trip, and as soon as I got home and chatted briefly with my mom and dad, I staggered up the stairs. When I flipped on the light switch, I let out a squeal of joy. My mom and dad had completely redecorated my room for me. My favorite color combination is black-and-white, and the new comforter, the curtains, the nightstand and dressers were all in that scheme. I ran back down the stairs and threw my arms around the both of them and told them how much I loved what they'd done and loved them. When I saw their faces and realized how happy it had made them to make me so happy, I nearly started crying.

My mom sensed that a fresh start with a different look would help erase some of the bad memories I had of the sleepless nights and the horrible nightmares I'd had in that room the last time I was home. So many times when someone has to deal with a bad occurrence in life, and I can remember doing this myself with other friends and family, people will say to the person who is in need of help, "Let me know if there is anything that I can do." We all have good intentions when we say that, but it puts the burden of making an active choice on the person who is already most likely feeling like a burden, has little energy, and is struggling to get by. My mom and dad took the initiative to do something for me. They knew me well enough to know what would please me, but honestly, even if I had come home and they'd decorated my room in plaid and polka dots, I would have been happy that they'd done something for me to show how much they cared.

I was resolved to pace myself better that summer, and I was grateful that Robin was going to join me in Norway. He was the one who preached the importance of relaxing and pacing myself, and with him around most of the summer, I think I passed his class in the fine art of chilling. I still ran, did some competitions. I kept to cross-country races and road races where I didn't really have any times to compare to. I didn't want that kind of pressure over the summer, so I wasn't completely obsessed with my results. I loved running back in Europe, seeing women I'd competed against before and simply enjoying the fact that I could run, that I could move, and that I was very far away from Dallas and the impending trial.

I was still kept apprised of any developments and delays, either via phone or e-mail, and having an ocean between the courthouse—and the jail where the suspects were being held—and me definitely helped me keep things in a better perspective.

It helped that Robin was there, but he was going to stay in Norway to pursue a job opportunity after I returned to Dallas in August. I had mixed feelings about that. His remaining in Norway gave me hope that the two of us might have a future together. But I wanted him in Dallas with me. I still had two years to go before I would graduate. I wanted him there, but not for the same reasons as before—not so that I could feel safe. Those men didn't pose a danger to me anymore, but whenever I was sad, angry, frustrated, or whatever, Robin seemed to know what to do or to say to help ease my mind. I was nervous that I would return to being the machine I had become the spring semester of 2010—the too focused, too intent, too preoccupied woman too in a hurry to put everything behind her. I'd have to keep that "Robin balance" on my own. Worse, the first trial had been postponed again, until October. How would I handle that without Robin there with me?

That summer at home made me feel like even without Robin there with me, I'd do well in facing the trials. I had been able to rest and store up a lot of energy. Even with Robin around, I spent as much time with

Anette as I could. She had been practicing yoga for a while before I started, and we took classes together. For me, at first, yoga was about stretching my muscles and breathing. I didn't have her full sense of it as a philosophy, a way to work with your mind and your emotions to get to a better place. As the summer went on, and Anette talked to me about that element, I became convinced that yoga was going to be one of my keys to surviving what lay ahead. For the most part, though, I tried to stay focused on the present and enjoy the time I had with the people I loved.

The change-in-scenery effect also came into play when I returned to Dallas. For the fall of 2010, Kristine, Silje, and I got an apartment together off campus. I don't think I realized until we were in the new place how bad the energy had been in that previous apartment, the cramped married student housing that we'd escaped into.

Anette had accompanied me back to Dallas, and that meant everything to me. I'd come to rely on Robin to supplement my sense of security. Without him there, Anette stepped into that role. Having her with me the first week back was wonderful. Each day, we attended yoga classes, where we practiced staying in the moment, and I found that focusing even more intently on what my body was doing, in a way that was different from running, proved very relaxing. We went shopping, took long walks, tanned by the pool, and simply enjoyed life. We didn't talk much about what was to come—the trial—and treated the week like we were on holiday.

Watching Anette be driven off in a taxi to the airport, I felt that all-too-familiar sensation of glad/sad. We'd had such a great time together, but her leaving meant that summer break was truly over. It also meant that I had to focus anew on the trial. Whatever lessons I had learned about breathing, staying in the moment, relaxing, and all the rest got stowed away like summer outfits giving way to sweaters and coats.

I switched into machine mode again, in workouts and in classes, and I felt the stress and tension of what I was going to have to face working its way through my body, conquering it.

I trusted Erin and Brandon, but the whole legal system seemed so complicated to me. I wanted those men to stay in jail for the rest of their lives, and I worried about whether a jury would be willing to sentence them to that. I figured that anyone would understand that what they had done was completely awful, that was clear, but could the jury put themselves in my shoes? Would they understand just how horrific those moments were and how much my life had been altered by the actions of those men, despite my best efforts to establish a new normal?

I tried so hard not to think about the trial and my attackers, yet it felt like my efforts had the opposite effect. I remember reading for a class an article about the pink elephant phenomenon. If someone tells you, "For the next minute, I want you to think of anything but pink elephants carrying polka-dot umbrellas," you will have a difficult time not thinking of them. If that same person had mentioned pink elephants but then said, "Observe your thoughts and note where they go," chances are you would still think about the elephants briefly, but then your mind would naturally wander on to other things. In a way, my efforts to not think about the crime were making it almost impossible for me to think about anything else.

I was usually a very healthy person, but that semester it seemed as if I was attracting not only elephants, but germs, too. Fighting off colds, the flu, and other infections beat up my already weakened immune system. I'd taken the strong antiviral drugs for the first four weeks after the attack, and the side effects were brutal. I wondered if there had been some long-term effect that lingered, or if it was just that all the stress had finally caught up with me. If I wasn't a runner, it might not have been so bad, but when you're an athlete, you're so attuned to how your body is doing that any alteration from prime operating condition sets off alarm bells.

I tried to center my attention around my performance on the cross-country course. As a team, we'd finished the 2009 season ranked twenty-fifth in the nation. In the 2010 preseason, a track and cross-country coaches association had us ranked twenty-second nationally and number one in our region. I felt added pressure to lead the team as one of a few upperclassmen on the team. Neither Kristine nor Silje was competing that season. It seemed as if the injury and illness bug had gotten them. They both were unable to train well in the off-season and at the start of the regular season, so Coach Wollman decided it was best that they red-shirt—be withheld from competition for the season and preserve that time of NCAA eligibility until later. For cross-country season we traveled a lot, and the bus rides, flights, and hotel room stays were real opportunities to enjoy being with teammates. Without our two leaders, and with a lot of underclassmen on the team, I became a source of information for the other girls. I knew the courses; I knew the opposition. The night before meets we always had a team meeting. One night before a meet at the University of Texas at Arlington, Coach Casey asked if anyone had anything to say. I looked around the room and saw many of the girls looking my way. I never liked speaking publicly, but I knew that I had to say something. So I started talking about something that had been on my mind for a while. Track and cross-country are odd sports, I observed, because you are both competing with and against your teammates. In order for us to do well as a team we had to keep that in mind. Encouraging one another, helping one another, was hugely important. I told them, "We have to take responsibility for ourselves while still looking out for one another. Trust and support will make the difference." I didn't say this to them, but I was thinking about how so many people were contributing to my recovery, how much of the work was mine to do, but I wouldn't have been able to do any of it without the advice and encouragement of others.

A few weeks later, at a meet in South Bend, Indiana, hosted by the University of Notre Dame, we endured one of those miserably wet and rainy days that make cross-country a real test. The wind was blowing sideways, we were shivering and mud-covered, and we struggled as a team, finishing in twenty-third place, with our top runner coming in seventieth overall. Not a good day at all. After the race, we got together as a group for a long cool-down, laughing at the irony of the term, and I noticed that one of the girls, Caitlin, was crying as we ran. I got alongside her and asked what was wrong.

"I don't want to do this anymore. This is no fun."

I knew that she wasn't talking about just that day and running in those conditions. We'd all underperformed, and Coach Casey had let us know that she wasn't happy about it. I also saw some of myself in her, putting so much pressure on herself to always be the best and run her best every time out. She worked so hard, she didn't deserve to feel bad.

"Sometimes, you just have to not give a shit."

The rain eventually eroded the shocked look on Caitlin's face. She started to smile and tilted her head up like a little girl and drank it in.

She later told me how much that meant to her and how she'd learned a lot from me. I just wish that I had done a better job of taking my own advice.

In October, SMU hosted a Take Back the Night event. I'd heard about the foundation that organizes these events, and has since the 1970s, but I'd never attended one before. Take Back the Night is a campaign to encourage women to be careful when they go out at night, to empower women to combat violence. The point of the rallies is to raise awareness about all kinds of sexual violence that occurs. Originally, the events were a way for women to show support for one another, but over the years the events have evolved to be more inclusive.

I'd seen fliers announcing the candlelight vigil and parade posted around campus for a few weeks prior and planned to attend. At first I thought that I would go alone, but Kristine and Silje had also seen the announcements, and they wanted to go as a sign of support for me and for others who had suffered some form of sexual violence. As we walked on campus that night to the meeting place, I was surprised to see at least a hundred and maybe two hundred people there. The marchers were predominately women, but a few men were there as well. I had expected it to be a very somber event, but it actually felt more like a social occasion. The three of us stood and talked while we waited for a few of the organizers to hand out candles.

I'm not a completely sappy romantic, but I'd always associated candlelight with romance or church. When I took the candle offered me, and a few moments later when the participants began to pass the flame from person to person, my eyes welled with tears. When Kristine helped to light my candle, my hand was unsteady, so she held it still. The three of us linked arms and joined the others in the walk from the quad to the Student Center. It seemed appropriate that the two of them were with me. Though Silje hadn't been at the party or with me in the weeks after the assault, she had become a big part of my life that semester.

Every time I felt down because of a bad performance on the course or when a phone call with Robin didn't happen or didn't go well, they were both there to lift me up. Our training runs together always ended up with us saying this: "We won't give up no matter what." Giving up wasn't a part of our nature, but we all had moments when we were tempted; in a way, that Take Back the Night event was an extension of what my friends and family had been doing for me the last ten months. Bit by bit, I was taking back my life from the fears and the anger and the frustration.

When we gathered outside the Student Center, a man I didn't know, who didn't introduce himself, stepped in front of the marchers. We gathered around him in a semicircle. He made a few remarks thanking us for attending and said, "Have you heard of anyone who has been sexually assaulted? If so, then blow out your candle."

We did.

I looked around, and almost without exception everyone's candle was out; wisps of smoke trailed into the night sky. Before the candles had been extinguished, I'd noticed how their glow illuminated everyone's face, how cheery the atmosphere seemed, like we were all sitting around a campfire. In the near dark, people still talked, but there was more of a hush than when we'd been walking.

Everyone relit his or her candle from someone whose hadn't been extinguished or had already been lighted again. The beauty was that despite the ugly truth of how many people were affected by sexual assault, there was always someone there to offer you help. No matter how dark it got there was always going to be some light. Those lights were out there to help us and guide us; we just had to turn toward them and be open to the experience of getting help.

As the ceremony continued, the leader asked if we had an acquaintance who'd been victimized, then if we knew a family member or friend. Each time the number of candles being snuffed was fewer and fewer and the communal glow remained brighter. Each time my candle was relit, I thought to myself, "Thank you, family and friends."

I anticipated what was coming next, and I felt an unsettling sensation in the pit of my stomach. I looked at my candle. It was a white taper that had lost about half of its length. A coated paper cone kept the dripping wax off my hands, and it was nearly full with the melted wax. I could see across the way from me a woman I thought I recognized from one of my classes. She stood with her candle raised, almost like I'd seen our pastor do when conducting the Eucharist. The light from her candle reflected off her glasses, making it impossible to see her eyes, just the flame fluttering in the wind, and to each side of that other pinpricks of light.

A gust of wind came up and my light flickered but didn't go out. The rape had strengthened my faith and my belief that all things happen for a reason. It sometimes takes us time to figure out that reason, and this event was helping me make better sense of the attack. I think that image of my flame nearly going out was symbolic. It reminded me how grateful I was that I'd survived that night. I'd felt that way in the beginning, but as time passed, I had spent more time thinking about what had been taken from me than thinking about how glad I was to still be alive. In that moment, I felt a profound gratitude that I could be there, holding that candle and standing between my good friends. I felt myself release something; perhaps it was anger, or frustration, or simply the question of why this had happened to me.

When I heard the speaker ask us to blow out our candle if we ourselves had been a victim of a sexual assault, I hesitated. In my meetings with Erin and Brandon, they'd told me that it wasn't a good idea for me to go public with my story before the trial began. That would generate more publicity and could possibly give the defense an advantage. Blowing out my candle wasn't the same thing as going to the media, but I was still publicly acknowledging the fact that I was one of the ones for whom we were gathered to take back the night. I hesitated and then took a deep breath before blowing out my candle.

Tears balanced on my eyelids when I looked around at all the other people who stood with their candles still aflame. I blinked to try to clear my sight, and a young man I didn't know stepped forward to relight my candle. My throat was so tight I couldn't even get the words out. I shut my eyes and another tear leaked down my cheeks. Silje and Kristine each put an arm around me and hugged me. I took another deep breath and looked up into the night sky and the stars, more light.

I wished that I could have said something to the man who lit my candle that last time, but he had resumed his place in the circle. I whispered the words "Thank you" to the stars, to everyone there, to my friends and family.

People started to file into the Student Center for the next phase of the evening. I told Silje and Kristine that I would join them in a minute. I needed a moment alone. I wanted nothing more at that point than to be able to share my story. I knew that I couldn't, but I promised myself that when I had the first opportunity to do so after the trial I would. I wanted to relight candles. I wanted to let people know, no matter what happened to them, that they could get back to the place they wanted to be. I didn't just want to be the one whom other people gathered together to support. I wanted to be the one who did the supporting.

Inside the Student Center, an open microphone session had begun. People were encouraged to share their stories. At first no one stepped forward. I fought the urge to do so. Finally a young man stood in front of us. At first he didn't speak. He wore a ball cap, and he stood alternately tugging at it and then thrusting his hands in his pockets. The room was silent. We could hear his stuttering breaths through the microphone. When he began, it was as if I was watching someone pull back his bandages to reveal a horrific wound. I felt so bad for him, and yet I so admired him for his courage to speak about how he'd been sexually abused as a child. When it was clear that his story was coming to an end, I wanted to rush up there and thank him for being so brave.

I don't know what came over me, but even before he was done, I quietly slipped out of the Student Center unnoticed. I think that I was frustrated by not being able to speak at that moment, but also frightened by the thought that someone might come up to me after, or even just look at me and know that I was one of the few that night who had blown out that final candle. I wasn't strong enough to deal with that kind of attention yet, and I was overwhelmed.

Instead, I hustled home and changed into running clothes. I ran through the streets, taking back the night in my own way, my tears taking me back to all those months ago when on another night I'd wondered if I would ever see a star again, if the constellation of broken glass and dirt on that carpet and on that roadside was the last image I'd ever see.

CHAPTER FIFTEEN

Beyond a Reasonable Doubt

After numerous postponements, the first of the three men's individual trials was scheduled to begin on December 13—just past a year after the attack. I spent a lot of time talking with Erin and Brandon about how the trial process would go. In Norway, a trial like the one Arturo Arevalo was facing would be conducted by a panel of judges and what we call "lay judges"—citizens who essentially act in the same capacity as the professional judges. There would be only five people total who decided the defendant's guilt or innocence. If someone wanted to appeal a guilty verdict, then they would face a jury of their peers—five men and five women—who didn't have to agree unanimously on a verdict. Seven out of the ten voting in one direction would uphold or overturn a lower court's verdict. In the U.S., in most states, the verdict has to be unanimous. I thought of my experiences with people generally and how hard it was to get everyone to agree on what pizza toppings to order or what movie to watch. Unanimous scared me.

Erin and Brandon explained to me a concept that they wanted to make sure the jury also understood, a principle that the whole American system of criminal justice was founded on. A person was considered innocent until proven guilty beyond a reasonable doubt, which meant that the state (or, as I thought of them, "my lawyers") was going to have to prove their case. The defense didn't have to do anything if they didn't want to or, more accurately, if they felt that the prosecution hadn't done their job. Erin and Brandon explained to me that the defense not putting on a case was nearly impossible to imagine. They'd have to show the jury the ways in which the state had failed to prove that Arturo Arevalo was guilty of the charges made against him.

The tricky part for me, and the two district attorneys assured me this was the case for everyone, was what "beyond a reasonable doubt" meant. Everyone had a different interpretation of that concept, so there was likely to be some doubt in every case. I thought of it this way: If you placed the facts of the case that you were sure about on a scale and weighed them, and then you placed the things you were unsure of on that same scale later, depending on which weighed more—certainties or doubts—you'd vote for guilt or innocence. I have since learned that my understanding was incorrect and that the burden to prove guilt beyond a reasonable doubt was much more difficult than I thought. I'm glad I didn't know this at the time.

The DAs also reviewed with me some of the other things specific to my case. I assumed it was a good thing that Luis Zuniga had told police that Arevalo was the one who came up with the idea and had forced his cousin and him to take part. Brandon explained that it was, but there were certain limitations. There was something called the Accomplice Witness Rule. That had to do with cases like this one where one person charged with the same crimes was going to testify against someone who participated in the illegal activity. Because accused people are sometimes given a break on their sentences, some jury members might look at that testimony and dismiss it. They might think that one person turned on another because that person was getting a good deal from the state, or that one person had just made something up in order to incriminate another. On the other hand, for a different juror an accomplice saying that someone else committed the crimes would be enough to convince him or her beyond a reasonable doubt of the accused man's guilt.

As a result, the Accomplice Witness Rule instructed the jurors that they couldn't vote guilty if the *only* evidence that convinced them was the accomplice's testimony against the accused. They could factor it in, but if that was the only testimony they believed, then they had to vote not guilty, that the state hadn't proved its case. I had a bit of trouble with that idea, but Brandon and Erin urged me not to get too concerned about it. They felt like they had a strong case that they would prove, and having Luis's testimony would only make the case even stronger. They reminded me of the scale: The DNA evidence would be one piece that weighed a small or large amount depending on the juror and the juror's beliefs about DNA and scientific evidence. Another piece of evidence was Kristine's testimony, and of course my own. And my lawyers told me that they were going to do their best to make sure that anyone with a bias that might hurt our case wouldn't be on the jury.

All the references to potentially, possibly, bias, and all the rest made it hard for me to feel confident about how the case would go. I knew in my heart and in my mind that Arturo Arevalo was the Worst One, but would twelve people's hearts and minds agree?

I can see now that, for me then, the idea of hearts and minds potentially not being in agreement was a real possibility. I was living that out in another part of my life. Robin and I had continued our long-distance relationship for about three months when he came to see me in October. Seeing him again made me feel wonderful and it made me feel sad. Those three months had been filled with ups and downs, times when I could see that things would work out between us, that the distance wasn't too great, and other times when I felt like I was running a very hilly course, struggling to rally enough resources of energy to get up that next incline. When I was being honest with myself, even from the crest of one of the hills when things were going well, I could see another series of hills and valleys stretched out toward the horizon. Did I have what it took to continue on that course?

We knew what it was like when we were together and things were so good, and this new version of how we interacted wasn't even close to what that had been. In running terms, we set a PR together when we were both in Dallas, and now it felt as if we were struggling to even come within minutes and hours of that time. After a few months of trying to make it work, we agreed that we both had too many obstacles ahead on our own paths to be able to support each other the way we should, and we ended things again.

We'd been through so much together, and now for it to end so badly made me incredibly sad. I held on to the hope that once things were better in his world and in mine, we'd be able to get back together. I had opened up to him in a way that I had never revealed myself to anyone else, but I didn't look at our breaking up as any kind of rejection.

My focus was now entirely on school and the trial, which was finally almost ready to start. I also knew what I needed to do for myself to power through my days leading up to it, when my anxiety was climbing. I got up at six in the morning and went for a run to clear my head of the clutter that accumulated overnight. Something about getting my body moving, that constant race between thoughts and legs, gave me the energy I needed. I wasn't happy that the trial would take place while I was still focused on classes and final exams. In mid-November, I once again found myself facing the prospect of talking to or e-mailing professors to let them know that I'd be missing classes and would need to reschedule some finals.

One of the strangest parts of my experience at SMU was the disconnect in perception I had about those who knew who I was and what had happened to me and those who didn't. The attack had dominated the news back then, and even though I'd never been directly identified by name, I still walked around thinking that everyone knew that I was the one. I was shocked when a couple of my professors admitted they had no idea that I was involved in that case. I'd been assuming that everyone knew, but clearly I was wrong. I guess it made it easier for me to think that, but at the same time, I felt like I had been walking around carrying an ugly secret. The effort to hide from people who knew had been sapping my energy. Now I wondered if that had been a wasted effort.

I wondered about other potential wastes of energy and the effects they had had on me. I had worked every day to get rid of those terrible images from that night, but I couldn't do that completely because I had to testify about them in court. I knew that I was going to be asked about those events, and as much as Erin and Brandon tried to assure me that the case didn't rest solely on what I said in my testimony, at times it felt that way to me. And on top of all that, I wasn't sure how I was going to react when I saw that man in the same room with me.

Fortunately, I had plenty of reinforcements to help back me up. My mother and father were together with me in Dallas. It hurt me to know that the first place they were going to see of my new hometown was a courtroom. But they wanted to be there and support me if things got tough. Silje, who had been together with Kristine and me, supporting us every day, never hesitated to go with us to court that day. My Norwegian friend Wenche, who had been living in Dallas for more than twenty years, immediately offered to be there taking care of my parents. It was so good for me to know that they had someone whom they could speak Norwegian to and who could answer their questions. Two of the loveliest women in Dallas, Kelly and Sidsel, who had taken on a mother's care of me after the incident, also wanted to be in the courtroom to support us. I felt so grateful that everybody wanted to be there for me. It made everything so much easier, and I was able to appreciate all the nice things surrounding the trial. I couldn't believe that so many people cared so much that they wanted to get together in this way just for me.

The night before the trial, I lay in bed feeling like I was pinned in one uncomfortable position by all my concerns, large and small. Would I be able to remember that in court I was Jessica Watkins? Would I accidentally state my real name? Would I break down completely and not be able to tell my story? Would I go blank? Would I appear too cold and unemotional?

I drifted into brief moments of sleep and then woke up thinking that hours had passed. My clock told me a different story. When the first gray light of the morning of Tuesday, December 13, leaked across the ceiling, I got out of bed and pulled on my running clothes. It seemed appropriate that a light rain was falling; low clouds and fog haloed the lights of the passing cars, and the streetlights and the rainbows on the wet pavement signaled a promise that better days could be ahead. My thoughts slowed and quieted while I ran on in the rain, my effort warming me, the sound of my steps soothing.

Once back at the apartment, I felt sodden and chilled. As I let the shower stream bring warmth back into my body, I couldn't help but think of that first shower after the attack, Robin outside the curtain, when I felt so sure that I'd never feel clean again. How might I feel if Arturo Arevalo, the Worst One, wasn't convicted? Would I ever feel safe again? Would I go back to feeling like the attack was meaningless, that everything I'd been through that night and after in order to put my life back together had been without purpose? Would I go back to being that girl on the side of the road, naked and blinded, wondering whether the next step would bring me salvation or more pain?

The water turned cooler, but I stayed where I was, letting the shower's spray cool my fevered thoughts.

My parents, Kristine, and I drove along in Kelly's car, the only sound the beating of windshield wipers. I sat there staring straight ahead, focusing on my breathing. At one point, Sidsel's car pulled alongside us at a stoplight. Silje waved and smiled at me, and I raised my hand to acknowledge her.

Erin greeted us outside the Frank Crowley Courts Building. After all the introductions were completed, made awkward by the jousting of umbrellas, she escorted us to a waiting room. Just outside the door, she stopped me and asked to speak to me.

"I just want you to be sure that you want your parents in the courtroom. I don't want this to be more difficult for you than it has to be."

I thought about that for a long time. I wanted to honor my parents' wishes and their efforts to support me. In some ways it would be good to have them there, but I also wanted to protect them, to keep them from having to hear the worst parts of what happened that night. I decided it was best to listen to Erin's concern, and I explained to my mother and father that it would be best if they weren't in the room during my testimony.

"Just knowing that you're here is enough," I said.

"We'll do what you and the lawyers think is best," my mother said.

"We know you'll be strong," my father added.

Both Kristine and I wanted to go in there as soon as possible to get it over with; we had had enough of waiting at this point. Several policemen were going to testify before we were called, and Erin told us that it could be a long time before it was our turn to speak. So we all settled into the waiting room. Kristine and I looked at the bright blue walls, the low tables and chairs, and the toys, games, and puzzles stacked on a bookcase.

Kristine raised an eyebrow and smiled crookedly. "So, we're in the kids' section?"

"It looks that way," Silje said. Kristine and I were both glad to have her there for support.

I picked up a can of Play-Doh, opened it, and smelled the familiar scent that immediately took me back to my own childhood.

Even though we were anything but kids and were there to do anything but what you'd want a child to have to do, the setting relaxed me. We settled into full-sized seats. Through the open door we saw others who were waiting to testify in other trials, their expressions ranging from bored to angry. The three of us talked about anything but what we were about to face.

As the hours ticked by, the atmosphere in the waiting room became more relaxed. We talked a lot of nonsense, and it almost felt like Silje, Kristine, and I were back home in our apartment on a normal day.

At around 1 p.m., a bailiff came into the room, interrupting a silly conversation we were having about a celebrity news story. He looked right at me. We all fell silent. The plan had been for Kristine to testify first. My heart started racing. Had something gone wrong?

"Ready?" Oh my God, that question was directed at me. My heart jumped again. I nodded; I really couldn't say anything about if I was ready or not. I gave my mother, my father, and the girls a hug to take in their support before I followed the policeman down to court. In a few minutes I would see *him* again, the Worst One. My parents had agreed to stay in the waiting room and Kristine couldn't come in before it was her turn to speak, but Silje came down with me. It felt so comforting to have her with me.

We stopped at a passage that separated the court with doors that had glass windows. I could see him right away, only from behind, but that was enough.

The thin hair, the short neck, the bad posture; my skin began to crawl. I could feel my legs shaking. I had thought that I was ready, but then I started shivering and my breathing became irregular. I knew that all this was a physiological response to the adrenaline I was producing, but still . . .

I told myself that it was now or never; this was my opportunity to prevent him from getting the opportunity to do this to another innocent person. Okay, Monika, be strong, you can do this. Look at him, do what

you have to do to make sure that he won't get out of the hellhole that
he has been spending his time in the last year. I was used to doing this,
talking directly to myself, a habit I'd developed after the attack. I took
three deep breaths all the way down to my stomach, just like I practiced
in my yoga classes that felt so far away from this moment. I could hear the
humming in my midriff when I exhaled, but that made me feel better.

Okay, I was ready; ready to end this chapter of my life; ready to do
what I could to get him locked up.

The minutes grew longer when I stood there watching him through
the window.

"Jessica, let's wait in this office for a while."

I had to bite my tongue and not correct him. I understood the need
to protect my identity, but I hated the idea that I had to pretend to be
someone else. I couldn't be someone else. I am Monika Kørra, a normal
girl who had a horrible thing done to her. Jessica was the name given to a
victim; I was determined to step out of that role. I was never going to live
my life as a victim, and each time I heard that name, I felt like someone
was trying to label me and, worse, to box me in with a set of expectations.
I had to agree to using that pseudonym in court, but mentally I never
accepted the idea.

"Why? What are we waiting for?" I followed the policeman into an
office that was connected to the courtroom.

"It will just be another minute. The court has to take care of some
other business."

Another delay! Silje held my hand and looked at me in a way that told
me that everything was going to be fine.

I sat down in an office chair and didn't know exactly what to do. There
was a Post-it notebook on the desk in front of me. Normally I would
never touch other people's things, but I found a pencil and started to draw
hearts in different sizes and shapes.

The police officer came back and explained that there had been a
mistake.

"Kristine is on her way down. She is going to testify first. You may go
back to the waiting room. It will take a while."

I felt like asking if he was kidding me, but fortunately the words got stuck in my mouth. I continued to draw hearts on the yellow papers.

Kristine came down just minutes later. We were able to give each other a big hug, promising that nothing was going to break us as long as we stood together. She was taken into the courtroom. I watched as the door shut and saw a sliver of Kristine when she raised her right hand and swore to tell the truth and nothing but the truth. I felt a hand lightly touch my elbow. The bailiff shook his head. I'd also seen Silje in the courtroom and found a seat beside my two American mothers.

It was so hard not to be able to be there with Kristine and support her. She chose to go through with this so that the man who had hurt me that night should get his punishment, and I wasn't even allowed to support her. But I thought about how strong Kristine was and that the other members of my support team were with her, and I realized that she was going to be all right.

She was just as determined as I was to get this man locked up, out of the society we live in. Now I just had to wait and send good thoughts and strength to Kristine. I continued drawing hearts, exchanging a few words with my mother and father about Anette's expected arrival time, how the bad weather in Germany might affect her flight.

My heart fell when I saw Kristine back in the waiting room. Tears streamed down her face, and she stood for a moment slump-shouldered and looking like she might collapse. I hugged her and I could feel her straightening up. When we separated, she wiped away her tears and began to smile.

The court was adjourned for lunch, and we wanted to get out of that room, so we stepped into the hallway.

Kelly came up to us, accompanied by Sidsel. "Kristine was awesome," Kelly said. "She was so strong."

"It was so emotional," Sidsel added. "I don't see how anyone on the jury couldn't have been moved."

Kristine and I exchanged a smile, and when Silje joined us, the three of us held on to one another for a long while.

With the adjournment, we had over an hour of waiting before it was time for me to get started. I didn't feel like eating. The image of the back of that man's head earlier had made me lose my appetite. Then I remembered that my mom had slid a box of snacks and a thermos of coffee into my bag. How could I not enjoy that sign of love and care?

We'd all been instructed that we couldn't discuss any details of what had gone on in the courtroom. A couple of people munched on snacks and sipped coffee and soft drinks. The hour passed slowly.

They weren't quite finished with Kristine's testimony, so she had to go back in after the break. The police officer asked me to go with them downstairs and wait in the small office again.

"This won't take long, and you're up next."

I hugged my parents, and they told me they were proud of me and loved me.

The bailiff was true to his word. I only sat in the small office for a few minutes before I heard a tap on the door. As I stood up and walked through the door of the courtroom, I felt my pulse quickening again, just as it did when I approached the starting line to begin a race. I was ready to fight; ready to let justice win once and for all. I stared at the back of that man's head as I entered the room. Now it was his turn to feel the fear of not being able to live a life in freedom. I had to take my eyes off him and walk over to the judge. Erin had shown me photos of the courtroom, including pictures of Judge Jennifer Balido, so that nothing would overwhelm me as new. The woman I saw sitting there seemed younger in person. Though her expression was neutral, her round cheeks and brown hair reminded me of many women from back home.

"Do you swear that you will tell the truth and nothing but the truth?" I raised my right hand and gave my promise, thinking that the next time I was going to make a promise in public the situation should be completely different—I'd use my real name.

Erin asked me to present myself to the jury. I had gone through this part carefully in my head time after time; to pretend to be someone else was not something I was used to. I managed to give my name as Jessica Watkins, even though it felt so wrong.

Erin started her questioning. She was good; she was leading me through her examination in a safe way, so that we would look strong in our case. I tried to describe the evening with as many details as possible. Many people had told me that the defense was likely to challenge me on this point: How could I remember everything in such detail when so much time had passed? To remember has never been a problem; forgetting was difficult. I had never tried to get this episode out of my memory, because that was a fight that I didn't believe I could win. But I had won the struggle to take control over my thoughts and feelings, and that is a victory that I can celebrate for the rest of my life. So I just had to think that the memories would help me do my best in the courtroom.

At one point, Erin picked up the cell phone I had that evening, as evidence. She showed the messages and phone calls between my friend and me about what was going to happen that night. She proved how the time on the messages matched my description of the events, with unknown numbers there as well, calls that were made by others besides me.

Again, I experienced the sensation of both being inside myself and watching myself. I had expected to be overwhelmed with emotions, even tears, at this point in the hearing. But I just didn't feel like it, didn't feel like I had more tears to give. I must have emptied myself in the months before.

It felt safe to realize that the feelings were well processed: You can look him in the eyes now, you are strong enough! I summoned the courage to look him straight in the eyes—those eyes that I had feared would be the last thing that I was going to see in my life. I wanted him to see that I was a human being—a human being with dignity.

What I saw back was a void. He seemed completely empty—totally dead. He looked in my direction, but really his eyes were somewhere else. It was like he saw straight through me, or was looking at something that just he could see. I had to give up; he was never going to realize that I was a human being.

I continued to answer Erin's questions. A picture of a girl who looked really sick was shown on a big screen to my right, straight in front of the jury.

"Can you describe what you see in this picture?"

I froze.

My God, it was me.

I didn't know what to say; the girl in the picture looked completely gone, like she was living in another world, like him. Her eyes didn't focus on anything; she just stared straight out into space. Her eyes were blank and intense at the same time. Duct tape was still glued on her hair. Her lips were the blue of cold, the blue of fear. She sat with her hands tightly knit, balled into fists beneath the blanket, pressed close to her chest. It had been hours since the attack; I was safe at the hospital, but I was still defensive, still in hyperprotective mode, still looking wary, like a wounded animal, feeling cornered and wanting to flee even though those around me only wanted to help and not harm.

I took a couple of deep breaths before I could go on.

"It's me. In the hospital. After the worst night of my life."

Erin kept the picture on the screen during the entire trial. The eyes of the girl looking at the jury with an empty expression.

I kept composed throughout Erin's direct examination, and it seemed as if it was over in an instant. Among many things asked of me, I confirmed that he had been there that night, that he had been the Worst One. There was no doubt.

Then it was time for what I had anticipated would be the most difficult part. One of the two lawyers representing Arturo stood up and looked my way. I had envisioned this moment for a long time. I stared back at him, giving him what I thought was my most hardened glare. I thought that I would make it as difficult as possible for him to defend a person who had raped this girl, a girl he now had to look straight in the eyes. I looked at the picture, then back at him.

He smiled at me. I could read genuine kindness in his expression. I immediately sensed that he was one of us, he was not an enemy. I smiled back just to confirm that it was okay. He started by asking about the different tests that had been done to me at the hospital. Questions about how they had been done, how many tests had been done, and so on. I had to look at Erin when I heard her heave a sigh. She just rolled her eyes.

I felt relieved that she was thinking the same thing I was. How could I know how many tests had been done from the upper arm and from the lower arm? "I don't know" was my best answer. He then got into the actual incident and was trying to ascertain exactly who had done what.

He sat down after just a few questions; the papers he was holding in his hand were shaking.

I looked from him to the judge, wondering if he was all right. Erin had more time to continue questioning. I hoped that Mr. Mazek understood that I knew that he was only doing his job.

Erin only had a few more questions for me; she looked happy with what she'd gotten. The judge said in my direction, "You may step down, but please remain in the court building." I had to look at her twice to make sure that it was actually over, that I had done my part to get him out of society. I got up from the chair, said good-bye to the girl on the screen, straightened my back, and began to walk out of the courtroom with my eyes turned to the Worst One, cold as ice.

I smiled at Erin and Brandon to thank them. They nodded confidently at me. No point in lingering. I then focused my eyes on the door. That was my way out; that was my exit; that was the way that would lead me to my family and my friends.

As I walked along the corridor, I thought about how surreal this had been. I had thought about testifying for so long, and now, in seemingly an instant and a blur, it was over. I felt like I did at the end of a cross-country ski race with interval starts, when the competitors all start at different times. I'd crossed the finish line, but I wouldn't know the final results until later, after others had done their job. I felt a mixture of relief, pride, and emptiness that my part of the race was over.

When I got back to the waiting room, everyone rushed toward me, and we all embraced in a wonderful group hug, all of us talking over one another, all of us essentially saying that it was finally over for me, for all of us. After a few seconds, we all burst into laughter, a communal expression of all of our relief, a sentiment we could all express and understand despite our language differences.

For more than a year, I'd been thinking about what I would have to say, what it would be like to face Arturo Arevalo again, and now those doubts and wonderings that at times crowded my head or lurked in the shadows at the back of my mind were gone. I felt free.

Kelly and Sidsel, who'd been in the courtroom, came in.

"The judge adjourned the proceedings. That's it for the day," Kelly said.

Erin and Brandon had told me that they didn't expect the trial to last more than three days. As much as I had hated all the delays, once I was called to testify and sat there in the courtroom, it was like someone had pressed the fast-forward button on my life. I wanted things to slow down a bit. I was grateful for that. Anette was scheduled to come in, and I wanted her to be there for the verdict. Despite the circumstances, I was grateful that the two parts of my life—Løten and Dallas—were joined. I'd never had my two families together before, and I wanted to savor every minute of that I could.

Talk quickly turned from my testimony to plans for the evening and the next days. We all agreed that our being in the waiting room wouldn't have any effect on the outcome of the trial. Why put ourselves through that? Why be in this place where none of us wanted to be?

The next two days we all stayed at home. It was so nice to have Mom and Dad with me. We just enjoyed ourselves, went to Starbucks and sat outside in the sun, went out in the evening to see the beautiful Christmas lights, ate with my good friends, who quickly became their friends, went shopping like all the other crazy people just before Christmas.

Friday came before we knew it. Erin had called the night before to let us know again that we should be in court that morning.

I slept better than I had the night before I testified, but still not particularly well. I felt pretty confident that Erin and Brandon had enough evidence, but it is strange how our nerves can get us to doubt. When I got out of bed Friday morning, I stuck to my routine and went for a run. Oddly, changing into my courthouse clothes, I felt like I was putting on my uniform. I was in race mode, focused and nervous, telling myself that the result didn't really matter. Guilty or innocent, I was going to be okay. I had that same inner conversation the rest of the morning: It's going to be okay. Just believe.

My parents sensed that I was in that runner race day zone, and they didn't say much to me. I was too nervous to eat, but sat at the table with them as they drank and ate and asked a few questions about what Erin had told me.

I repeated what I'd said the night before. Erin said it was always difficult to estimate exactly when a trial and a jury's deliberations would end.

The proceedings were to resume at nine o'clock, and she wanted us there just before then.

I was nervous, but I was also eager that morning. Not just because I hoped the trial was going to be over, but because I was going to get a chance to see Erin and Brandon in action. They expected to deliver their closing arguments that morning. I felt like I'd been kept in the locker room for so long. Now I was going to be along the sidelines watching the two of them do their work.

Erin and Brandon met us just inside the courthouse doors. Instead of being escorted to the waiting room, we stood in the hallway and then, just before nine, walked into the courtroom. Just setting foot inside there elevated my heart rate. I felt my body tense. It was strange to sit looking at the judge and her bench and not out at the audience. I remembered how odd it felt for me to sit with the judge over my shoulder. I could vaguely remember what she looked like, but sitting facing her, I was left with the impression that she wasn't as no-nonsense as she at first seemed; there was something kind about the set of her eyes.

It was important to me that I sat between Mom and Dad; they were my guardians, after all, the people who had cared and protected me from the time I was born and would still feel that responsibility and act in that regard for as long as they lived. We sat holding hands, my mother brushing her thumb across mine. I felt a bit of the tension easing out of me.

A few moments in, Mr. Mazek, Arevalo's attorney, said to Judge Balido, "I would just ask the Court for a directed verdict that the state hasn't proven the case beyond a reasonable doubt." My heart leaped and my throat tightened. I didn't really know what a directed verdict was, but I remembered what Erin and Brandon had said about reasonable doubt. Mr. Mazek was saying that my lawyers hadn't done their job.

Judge Balido paused for a moment, then said, "Okay." I felt tears welling, and my parents gripped my hands tighter, sensing my emotional response. "Your motion for direct verdict is denied. Okay. Anything else?"

I had to remind myself to breathe again. I felt so relieved, and I expected the opposition's lawyer to protest somehow. Instead, Brandon said, "Nothing else from the State, Your Honor."

As the jurors filed in, I tried to quickly explain to my parents what had happened. My mother rolled her eyes and shook her head while my father nodded and put his hand on my mother's shoulder to help calm her.

I turned my attention to the jury. I hoped to read their faces to see if their expressions revealed anything to me. Mostly, they looked distant, detached, not really bored but weary.

The State had the burden of proof, so they went first. Brandon rose, and I was surprised by how he began. He kept referring to the jurors as "you guys," and that seemed really informal to me. After a while, I figured out what he was doing. He was telling them he wasn't "unmindful" of what they'd been through. They'd been forced to sit and listen, and they'd done a great job of that, he pointed out, and he thanked them for their patience, especially for how the Court had "dragged you in and out of here," and apologized for sometimes being late.

Then he finally said that he knew that the thirteen of them had a job to do, "to ensure that Arturo Arevalo never has a chance to do this again. There are thirteen people on this earth who can be heroes and saviors for Jessica." I put myself in the jury's position and thought I'd like to be able to think of myself as a hero and a savior.

Brandon led them through the trial and the things he had addressed with them as far back as when the jury was selected. He spent a lot of time talking about DNA and how all that evidence was handled. He also mentioned that some of it was found on that "little, little dress." I smiled briefly at that remark, thinking of how I'd always been known as Little Monika, but shuddering when I thought about the dress, how much I'd liked it, how hard those men had struggled to get it off of me, and how I never wanted to see it again.

I felt my concentration drifting in and out, and I wondered if the jurors were having the same trouble. This wasn't easy to listen to or to follow closely. Brandon did get my attention firmly back in place when he said, "You would expect to find the perpetrator's DNA on the inside of the dress. Every single genetic marker, folks, 397 million to one."

He went on about the DNA on the duct tape and then Judge Balido said, "You've used nine minutes." I don't know why, but hearing a time announced like that made me feel better about the whole thing, put me back on the track or the course. I wondered how much time Brandon was going to be given, if he had some kind of PR of his own to beat. Was this just the first lap?

He next talked about the Accomplice Witness Rule and put it in simple terms. "Did what Luis say about the crime that was committed match what Jessica said? Did it? Think about it in your own mind." I liked how Brandon asked those questions. Even though he said "Did it?" he said it so gently that the jurors couldn't have thought that he was challenging them, just reinforcing the idea that what the Weak One had said about the Worst One was the same as what I had said. How could he be biased if he was telling the truth, especially since he and I had never spoken after that night, could have never linked up our stories? We both spoke the truth. Brandon also reminded the jury how I'd seen that man's face because he was the one who wanted to kiss me. How that was the worst thing of all because I couldn't distance myself from what was being done to my face.

He also accounted for the difficulty I had in identifying Arevalo in the photos or remembering his heavily tattooed arms: "It was poorly lit, her head was down, she did not want to look, and she told you it was the worst part." He emphasized that point about it being dark when he talked about Arevalo not being able to identify that the dress I was wearing was full of patterns and bright colors. If the accused and his victim both had trouble seeing, then that proved that it was too dark to see clearly. He appealed to their common sense and ability to reason clearly.

I thought Brandon did a good job of accounting for the things that I might have had questions about if I was a juror. He wrapped up his time by saying, and I agreed, "The only just verdict in this case is guilty, and we would ask that you do so swiftly." Amen to both those thoughts.

I sat back in my chair and sighed, feeling like there was no doubt that the jury had to see things Brandon's and my way. My mother and father both looked pleased to see me smiling. My father pulled me toward him and kissed the top of my head. I could almost feel him transferring his faith and his confidence to me.

Mr. Boncek, the second of Arevalo's lawyers, then took over for Mr. Mazek. I didn't want to listen to him. I knew he was doing his job, but it was hard to accept that someone was trying to allow that man to go

free and to think that others were praying for him to escape punishment for what he had done to me. His wife and his children were in the
courtroom, but I couldn't bring myself to look at them. I held on to my
mother and father's hands extra hard. I was a bit afraid of how they might
react to what was being said. I've always been told that I have a look that
could kill, and as we sat there listening to the defense attorney I realized
where I'd got it from.

I wanted Mr. Boncek to look at me when he spoke, when he was
defending this man. He did not. He did not look at my mom or dad. I
thought for a second that he was too cowardly to look at us, but then I
realized that this was a sign of his compassion. He did not want to harm
any of us. Then the worst thing in the trial of the Worst One happened.

Mr. Boncek attacked Luis Zuniga, the man who'd turned on the other
two, and let the jurors know that he was likely to get a pretty good deal
for himself. The defense attorney stressed that Luis was a drug user, that
the day after the rape, though he was unemployed at the time, he'd had
enough money to go and purchase drugs. Where did he get the money?
Could it have come from selling the watch they'd taken from me? How
trustworthy was a rapist and a thief?

My mouth went dry as I sat there, imagining what it would be like
to be a juror and hear those words. Would I be able to trust what someone like Zuniga had said? Mr. Boncek hammered away at that point,
asking jurors, of the three men, Arturo Arevalo, Luis Zuniga, and Alfonso
Zuniga, which of them wasn't related by blood? Blood will tell. Blood
is thicker than water. Didn't it make sense that Luis would try to save
himself, save his relative, and sacrifice the one man to whom he had no
real connection?

The emotional side of me said no, but the logical side of me said that
there was some doubt. Was it reasonable doubt? Had Mr. Boncek planted
enough seeds in the minds of the jurors to make it less than clear-cut?
How much doubt was enough to make them vote for not guilty? By the
time Mr. Boncek finished up his look at the DNA evidence, why none
of his client's was found on my cell phone that everyone said he had been
talking on—because the police hadn't bothered to have it tested—he
had opened up the door to many other questions about how the police

and the prosecutors had handled my case. By the time his nearly twenty minutes were up, when he finally said, "You'll see the gaps in the proof, the doubt that exists in this case based on reason and common sense. I'm going to ask you to do the right thing, the just thing. I know it's difficult because of the nature of the crime, but this isn't a decision based on sympathy or what the public might think, because you were the only thirteen people that sat in here every day and listened to this evidence, and I'm going to ask you to go back there and find Mr. Arevalo not guilty, because that's what he is. Thank you."

My mind was swimming. How could both lawyers say that based on reason and common sense two completely different conclusions could be arrived at? Did people have good common sense? Could they really reason?

I thought of my own struggles since the trial, how reason and emotion had been locked in a battle, how at one time I could believe one thing to be true and in another moment I could believe its opposite. After all, I'd always believed that running gave my life meaning, and then at another thought I believed that I should quit doing it because it was completely pointless and meaningless. What did that say about the truth?

I didn't have a long time to contemplate that, because next it was Erin's turn to speak.

"You have eighteen minutes and thirty seconds," Judge Balido told her.

Erin stood and stepped to the front of the courtroom.

Eighteen minutes and thirty seconds. One thousand, one hundred and ten seconds. I thought about how many laps of the four-hundred-meter track I could do, how much ground I could cover, in that time; I could easily do five thousand meters and more.

The picture of the shocked girl with the blank gaze flashed on the screen again.

Erin began by reminding the jurors what their job was, and she then said, "And I would suggest to you that what you need is right there." She pointed at the photo and then at me. "All you need is her testimony. Through her strength and bravery, she told you what she suffered that night. She came before you, and in great detail she told you what happened. And she said, they did everything to me. And she told you that the man sitting right there, those eyes, that face, he was the worst. And that is all you need."

I was thrilled to hear that. I'd thought for so long that the fate of this trial was out of my hands, but Erin told me that it wasn't. This proved it. I did have some control, some contribution to make, and Erin had said that it was the most important one.

Erin went on to show that there were other reasons to convict Arevalo beyond what I'd said. I heard the words, but they didn't carry the same emotional weight, until she mentioned Kristine and her bravery. I thought again of how fortunate I was to have her as a friend, along with all the others in the courtroom and elsewhere who were so supportive of me.

As Erin went on, I saw better the prosecution team's strategy. Brandon had been very factual in his arguments. Erin hit on the emotional side, using heavily freighted language. She left the best of the worst for last: "And it has been our burden and our misfortune to have to talk about these awful, nasty, terrible things that happened to that perfectly innocent victim, that has been our misfortune and our burden, but that's what we have done and we have given you exactly what you need to do your job."

She paused and looked back at the photo of me.

"And I am confident that the thirteen of you—the twelve of you"— she corrected herself to account for the one alternate juror who'd also sat in—"will do just that. And when you return a verdict of guilty, of which you can be proud and never look back, you will tell this man, Arturo Arevalo, you will tell him that there is no place in civilized society for you."

As she sat down, she looked at me and smiled confidently. The last word had been spoken. Now it was up to the jury.

CHAPTER SIXTEEN

Release

We all settled into the larger of the two waiting rooms. I thought about going into the kids' room since I'd done so well after Kristine and I had spent our time there before testifying, but I didn't want to give in to superstition. Besides, I was so nervous that I needed my mother and father and everyone else's good energy to offset my own doubts.

I could see my mother struggling with what to say, but my father stepped in.

"So, I don't know if I told you this, but I did forty kilometers on my roller trainer last Saturday. My legs felt strong."

"How long is the race?" I asked.

"Birkebeinerrittet, my main goal is 92K, but I'll do some smaller races leading up to it."

My father had recently become interested, borderline obsessed, with cycling. Many of our conversations centered on his training, a subject I really enjoyed. He was a veteran runner and skier, but cycling was relatively new to him.

The conversations in the room seemed to ebb and flow. I took a lot of comfort in hearing my native language being spoken.

I tried not to look at the clock and calculate how long some event was taking. Brandon and Erin had prepared me with the knowledge that juries can take a long time to make up their minds and arrive at a verdict or they can sometimes take a very short time—time seldom had anything to do with their decision about guilty or not guilty. When Brandon stuck his head in the room to let us know that the jury was in, I felt my heart skip a beat. I immediately glanced at the clock—twenty-five minutes. More than a minute faster than the quickest 10K a man had ever run and nearly four minutes faster than a woman had covered that distance. It felt like it took us that long and that far to walk down the corridor to the courtroom. My mother and father held my hands. Neither the judge nor the jury was in the room as we entered.

I had to take two extra deep breaths before I took my seat behind the district attorneys. I had to make sure that I had enough air. We were told to rise just as I'd sat down. I felt my parents' firm grip. I looked at each in turn, and their expressions said the same thing: we will manage this together no matter what. The judge received the document on which the jury verdict was written, black on white. She looked like she was reading it over and over.

I started to get worried. Was she reading something that was so shocking she had to take time to compose herself? Judge Balido asked the foreperson of the jury if the paper she had was the verdict she had signed.

"Yes it is, Your Honor."

Judge Balido nodded and then continued, "We, the jury, find the defendant guilty of aggravated sexual assault as charged in the indictment."

My whole body shuddered. I shut my eyes and whispered a thank-you.

There was one thing left. Judge Balido then said, "I would like a show of hands of everyone if this was your individual verdict."

Twelve hands went up. They had all agreed: guilty, guilty, guilty, guilty, guilty, guilty, guilty, guilty, guilty, guilty, guilty, and guilty.

I could let go of the air I had held inside me.

"Thank you very much," Judge Balido said.

The judge then announced that the penalty phase, when she would hand down her sentence, would be held on Monday. We'd have the weekend away from this, and as much as I wanted everything to be over with, I was glad that snowbound Anette would be able to be there. She'd be sure to add to our colorful celebration.

On that day, Monday, December 20, 2010, Justice Day, I wanted to wear colors. Colors with a lot of life. I would dress myself as if I were going to a party. I asked the others to select happy colors, too. That morning, I stood before the mirror. I had put on a pair of black dress pants, a part of what I came to think of as my court uniform, but I had opted for a tomato-red blouse. I stood there tidying up a scarf I wore around my neck—its bright swirls of primary colors adding to my party mentality. Kelly came to pick us up in the morning, and Sidsel and Wenche, my Norwegian friends from the Dallas area, were already in court as usual. Once they slipped out of their overcoats and folded them neatly in their laps, I saw that they had done as I asked—bright block prints, vibrant reds and greens—and it looked like we were going to a Christmas party and not a courthouse.

Several of my good friends from school were also there that day. I wished that Kristine and Silje could be with us to celebrate, too, but they had gone home to be with their families for Christmas. They'd offered to stay, but I wanted them to enjoy as much time as possible back home. I wished Robin had been there to hear the sentence, too; he deserved to see that justice would win, for a girl he had helped to see that love conquers hate.

On my birthday in September, right before we decided not to be together in the same way anymore, he had given me a card that I picked up to read before I got dressed in red that morning. It said: "Together Monika we can fix everything!" We had done that, so far, but now it was time that I did it myself.

Brandon and Erin called two witnesses to testify before the sentence would be given. They were there to provide additional evidence that this man was a danger to society. As they were sworn in, I watched their eyes go to the Worst One. I saw a mixture of fear, hate, and vindication there. Arevalo stared ahead blankly, seemingly in his own world. How appropriate, I thought; he wasn't fit to move about freely in ours.

Both of the men told a variation of the same story. That night they'd been out minding their own business when they'd been assaulted and robbed. Both of them spoke of having a gun pressed to their head; each man raised his right hand, formed it into a gun, and held it against his temple. I could see the gesture, but for the first time in a long while I couldn't feel the cold metal against my temple. Knowing that Arevalo had been found guilty and was about to be sentenced had freed me from that.

At the conclusion of the men's testimony, Judge Balido stated that she would take some time to consider her decision. We all rose as she walked out of the courtroom, and I wondered what she wore beneath her black robe. I knew she had a serious job to do and that required her to wear that dark robe, but what was she really thinking and feeling? Throughout the trial, she had seldom revealed any kind of emotion. I wondered if she wore her impartiality like a robe, something she put on when she stepped into the courtroom, while in private she was as disgusted by Arturo Arevalo as everyone else seemed to be.

Brandon came over to us and said, "I can't give y'all any sense of how long this will take. Don't take this into account, too much to heart. It's all part of the process. I've got to ask you to be patient one more time."

We walked out of the courtroom. I saw the two men who had testified and walked up to them. I nearly let it slip, but I recovered at the last moment and said, "I'm Jessica Watkins. I wanted to thank you for being brave and saying what you did."

I held out my hand.

The first man nodded, and a brief smile moved across his face before his expression went blank. He didn't meet my eyes, and that unnerved me a bit. The other was more gracious, less nervous, and he gave my hand a firm shake and told me how sorry he was for what had happened to me. "I can only imagine what you've been through. This was tough for me and my family, but for you—" He took a deep breath and shrugged his shoulders.

As I walked back to my team, all of them clustered together in the fluorescent light like a bouquet in a florist's refrigerator, I saw a smaller group clustered beyond them. Arevalo's wife and other family members sat somberly waiting. I thought of what it was like in cross-country when I saw the opposing teams clustered together. Arevalo's family members

were, in a way, the enemy, the ones I had to beat, but I felt a kind of kin-
ship with them. Just like opposing runners, we were engaged in the same
struggle, and would feel similar kinds of pain. I didn't like wanting to beat
these people, to take a father away from his children, but I knew, deep
in my heart, that they would be better off without that kind of negative
presence, that lurking violence, in their lives. I wanted to be able to walk
up to them and tell them that I was sorry, but just as in a race I wouldn't
say anything like that until we'd all crossed the finish line; we still hadn't
broken the tape, we still had more race to run.

I was so nervous and sad then. My thoughts that this would be a
celebration and my party outfit suddenly felt ill-fitting, inappropriate. I
needed a moment to compose myself, and I walked into the bathroom.
I stood in the ghastly artificial light, leaning forward against the sink. One
of the taps was leaking, and water dripped into the basin with a plink that
echoed in the tiled room. The girl in the mirror didn't match the girl in
my mind. She didn't look ready to celebrate. She looked about to faint.
The pallor of her drawn skin was exaggerated by the chewed lipstick slash
of her frown.

"Just believe," I said, surprised by the sound of my voice. I repeated the
words in English and again in Norwegian.

I splashed water on my face and twisted the knob as tightly as I could,
but the drip continued, marking the seconds until this race was over.

I've always been a big believer that the image you project into the
world produces results. If you look and act like a winner, you will be one.
I reached into my purse and pulled out my red lipstick. I couldn't control
what happened to Arevalo's family. All I could do was hope and pray that
they would be well. I had to look out for me and my interests. And that
day, a celebration was what I both wanted and needed.

I rejoined my team, and was startled when Brandon interrupted my
mom and Kelly's hugs by saying, "Court's back in session."

Judge Balido took her seat, and for a moment I thought she was looking at me. Then I watched her eyes as they darted around briefly, following a fly. She shook her head and then said, "Mr. Foreman, has the jury
reached a verdict on the punishment?"

The head juror stood and said, "Yes, we have, Your Honor."

I wished that I had a water bottle with me. I felt like every bit of moisture had been taken from my body.

"If you would, please, tender it to the bailiff."

Just believe, I told myself. *Just believe.*

Judge Balido took the paper from the bailiff and read it silently for a moment. I could feel my pulse throbbing in my neck.

"We the jury, having found the defendant guilty of the offense of aggravated sexual assault as charged in the indictment, assess his punishment at confinement in the Institutional Division of the Texas Department of Criminal Justice for life."

All I really heard was that last word. We all knew better than to shout for joy, but it took as much discipline as I had not to do so.

Judge Balido continued, "Counsel, do you believe your client is mentally competent?"

After his attorney said yes, Judge Balido asked Arevalo to stand and asked his attorney if there was any reason in law whether or not his client should be sentenced.

Without pause Mr. Mazek said, "No reason in law."

Judge Balido nodded. Then she addressed Arevalo directly, telling him how horrible the crime he committed was. I knew that the judge had been fair and impartial throughout, and I was pleased that she finally got a chance to offer her opinion. Her words seemed to have little effect on Arevalo. Maybe it was because he didn't speak English and the words had to be translated, but he stood there like someone standing in the middle of a rainstorm being pelted by drops but not flinching at all.

As her last official act, Judge Balido asked the bailiffs to take Mr. Arevalo away. I sat riveted, watching him to see if he would look over at his family, whisper some words, offer them some kind of reassurance.

He didn't.

Everyone rose, and the judge left the courtroom.

I just sat back down and stayed there. Did not move. My tears came flooding out. "Oh my God," I gasped. I didn't expect this—the verdict yes, the punishment yes, but not all the tears. I hated whenever someone saw me crying, but they poured out of me. I was crying with joy, crying in relief, crying with so many emotions overwhelming me that I couldn't think straight. So much was being released, as if Judge Balido had freed me and not just imprisoned someone else. I was free to live a life without fear. I know that you should not show that much emotion in court, but for just one minute in my life I had to give myself permission to let go of control.

We had won.

Erin and Brandon joined us in the hallway. I congratulated and thanked them both. Erin took me by the crook of the arm and led me to the side.

"I know you want to be with your family right now. I'll be quick about this. I have a good feeling about the next trial. Alfonso Zuniga's attorney will let him know that his buddy just got a life sentence. That should put the fear of God in him. I wouldn't be surprised, and I hope that this is the case, but I wouldn't be surprised if he changes his plea to guilty like Luis Zuniga did. That means you won't have to go through this again. I thought that would make you feel pretty good—a little icing on the celebration cake."

I put my arms around Erin and thanked her again.

"That would be so good." With the verdict and now this news, I felt that some of the extra weight I'd been dragging around for more than a year had now lifted. I remembered watching Arevalo walk out of the court in chains and thinking that the weight of what he had done was now on him. If Alfonso Zuniga pled guilty, that would be more weight off me. Erin's words had given me even more reason to hope that my life would be back on track soon.

All of us went out to have a lovely lunch in the West Village. The baby blue chicken salad tasted better than anything I'd eaten. I had not had any appetite before then, but now food tasted so good. Then, after lunch, it was time to get home and put on my running shoes. I just had to go out and run, to clear my mind and feel that I still was alive as Monika, running Monika Kørra. I just flew; my legs were so light, I felt that I was the stone man from the Norse myth of Per, Pål, and Askeladden when he gets to take the weights off of his legs. Now the Worst One had weights put on his legs instead, and I, on the other hand, had been released.

{ CHAPTER SEVENTEEN }

Asking Why

One of the most important principles of training as a runner is mixing in easy days or rest days to give your body time to recover and rebuild stronger. Admittedly, I wasn't as good about doing that as I should have been, but post-trial with my family and friends gathered around and Christmas just four days away, I did get a chance to relax. Not that I didn't run, but with Erin's words about the possibility of a guilty plea coming down the line, I was able to forget about legal matters and remain hopeful that another season—in this case *seasons*, with indoor and outdoor track on the horizon—wouldn't find me having my attention split among competing factions. Unity was very much on my mind.

For so long, I'd felt like there were two of me. Maybe that had to do with living with the reality that I was both Jessica Watkins and Monika Kørra. I waited until two days after the sentencing to have a conversation with my family. Ever since the attack, I'd felt like I needed to do something to help make sense of what happened, to unite those two selves—the Monika from before and after. If I was going to have to live with being raped, then I could justify that better if my horrible experience could benefit someone else.

I sat my parents and Anette down and presented to them the logical case that I'd been preparing for a while.

"I know that last year when I saw that newspaper article in Norway that hinted at my identity, I freaked out. I was angry. I was scared. I wanted to have control of what got said and when."

My family all nodded.

Anders Giæver from our national newspaper in Norway, *VG*, had been in touch with me. He wanted to do an article about my experience. I had agreed to be interviewed. He was going to call me on Christmas Eve morning. I wanted my family to support my decision. I reminded them of how I felt about contributing to others, to turning this into a positive experience somehow.

My parents eyed each other warily. "You know, Monika," my father began, "that we respect your decisions. But I have to remind you that what you went through was a very private matter. You have nothing to be ashamed of. You say you want to have control, but you can't control what other people are going to think or say or do. I just want you to under-stand that there are consequences to every choice. I trust you've thought all of this through."

"I have. And I have a life in both places now. Home in Norway is where I feel most accepted. I don't want to have to hide there. What I'll do later about here, we'll see."

My parents didn't think this was a good idea. We were very private people, and we lived in a relatively small place; was it fair that because I wanted to come forward they'd all find themselves in the public eye? They also felt that I was still in the early stages of recovering, and anything I might do that caused a setback just wasn't worth it.

I think my dad sensed that a reasoned approach wasn't working. He normally chose his words so carefully and revealed little emotion in these discussions. So when he said, "Monika, I'm frightened for you. My job is to protect you, and I couldn't do that on that night. But I can do that now. I'm asking you to not do this. We can't control what other people might say or do. But you can control this."

But I was stubborn.

It was my life. What had happened had happened to me. I had to deal with this my way. I needed people to see *me* again, not the rape victim. I needed others to talk to me like before, without being afraid that I would be shattered to pieces if they said or did something "wrong." I needed to tell everyone that what happens to us does not define who we are; we can overcome it and gain strength from it. I needed to feel the relief that comes with not having to drag a heavy secret around. I had also started toying with the idea of writing a book about my experience.

I also knew that I had been accepting help from so many people that I wanted to help others in return. It was a blessing that I'd survived, and I believed I was given a second chance because I was supposed to do something about the issue of rape in the world.

I spoke openly and at length with Mr. Giæver, and on December 27, his interview article ran in *VG* with the headline I REFUSE TO LET IT RUIN MY LIFE. I meant that, and this was another important step to make that statement true. I read the piece online and was really happy that he concluded it with this line: "Don't call me a victim, there's so many things I rather want to be." That was true as well. Maybe this Jessica Watkins identity issue could work in my favor. Maybe she could be the victim, and I could be all of the other things that I wanted of and for me.

I didn't get to gauge the reaction to the article in Norway. The article did exactly what I'd hoped it would do, but it would be a long time before I learned that. We were spending the holidays in the U.S. and then just a few days in Norway before I had to return. But when I came home that following summer it was as if people saw me in a new light. They treated me like they had before. They even came up to me to tell me how sorry they were about what had happened to me and that they admired me for speaking out. Some people even shared with me their own challenges.

I spent New Year's Eve day 2010 packing. I was standing holding on to two dresses, deciding which of them I should take back with me, when my cell jumped and my ringtone sounded. I picked up the phone, still clutching the two dresses, and said hello.

"Hi, Monika, it's Erin."

I could tell immediately that something was wrong. I mentally spun my wheel of misfortune, wondering what had happened. What was going on with the trial dates? Had Arevalo escaped, been set free by some mistake?

Instead, Erin told me something that I had never considered.

"I'm sorry to have to tell you this, but I'm no longer employed by the

Dallas County prosecutor's office. I got fired. It's complicated, and I don't have a lot of time to explain, Monika. I have to be out of this office in a few hours; they're shutting down my e-mail, but I wanted you to know that I'm not fired from your life."

I set the dresses on my bed, their dry cleaning bags heaving a sigh to match my own.

"What—" I stopped myself. This was a hard thing for Erin personally. How it impacted me could wait.

Erin must have read my mind.

"Brandon will still be working with you. Don't worry. You're in good hands. I want to make sure you have my cell number, my home phone. I'll also send you my personal e-mail address. I'm not letting go of you, you hear me?"

We spoke briefly before hanging up. I didn't like the idea that our team was being split up, but I had no choice. This wasn't like when one of the seniors on the team graduated. You knew that was coming, and you prepared for losing a part of yourself. And it wasn't like losing one of the girls to an injury. You knew that she'd be back, she'd still be around the training facilities, still in daily contact. Erin was gone from my legal team.

I wanted to know why this had happened, but Erin could only say that the reasons were political and complicated. I'd eventually find out it had to do with her boss being a Democrat. The team that had been so successful was losing a valuable member. We'd all have to work that much harder in her absence. So much for a rest and recovery period.

I walked into the living room, and my parents looked at me and immediately rushed over.

"What's wrong?" my mother asked.

"Erin. She got fired."

"What? She did wonderful." My mother's scowl matched my own.

"Listen," my father said, "that's not good. But in a day or so we'll be in the mountains skiing. We'll deal with this after. Now's the time to relax and enjoy. The mountains, Monika, remember them?"

I hugged him. "I remember."

My father knew exactly what to say. Even on the long flight home, I didn't fixate on Erin's news and the upcoming trial—not completely, anyway. And my father had been right. Being back in the mountains was exactly what my soul needed. Even though I was more active in Norway than I would have been back in Dallas, I felt more rested. Being on cross-country skis felt right to me. This was the environment I'd grown up in and thrived in.

The plane ride back reminded me of when I flew home for the first time after the attack. I was switching identities again. The more miles I put between me and Norway, the more I settled back into Dallas Monika. I used some of the time to write, some of it to puzzle out just how my desire to be a help to others would fit into all my other plans, how they would mesh with the rest of my American life. Shortly after I arrived in Dallas, I let Kristine and Silje know about the book project and my desire to turn the experience into something beneficial to others.

"Whatever we can do, let us know," Silje said.

"That's great!" Kristine smiled and then her eyebrows went up. "I wonder who'll play me in the movie."

We all laughed. It was great to be back, back in the arms and minds and hearts of my team within a team within a team.

I didn't have to wait a long time to turn my attention to all the things that were next. Track practices and classes got me back in a good groove. Erin was true to her word and e-mailed her personal contact information, and we shared our feelings with each other. I was so incredibly grateful for what she had done and hoped that she was doing okay. She assured me that she was, and was taking a little bit of time to think about the next steps for herself. Life would go on, she reminded me.

As soon as I returned to campus, I met with Brandon. He had told me that he had some news for me. As much as I told myself not to antic-ipate too much about what he might have to tell me, I walked into the Starbucks thinking that he was going to share with me news that he and Alfonso Zuniga's attorney had reached an agreement. They hadn't. In fact, Zuniga's attorney had taken an outrageous position.

"Five years?"

Brandon sipped his coffee and nodded slowly, his eyes large and disbe-lieving. "Yes. Can you believe it?"

"No."

"He claims that he didn't know what was going on, that he was there driving and the other two told him to pull over and that was as much as he was involved. He's willing to plead guilty if he gets five years at the most."

"No way!" I slammed my hand down on the table. I quickly looked down when I saw a few people glancing our way. Even in Norway, with our liberal court system, he would not have gotten that light a sentence if he'd gone to trial.

Brandon remained his usual calm self. He had a way of always staying cool, and that helped me settle down.

"You're right. There's no way that we can make that kind of plea agreement. At first I thought his lawyer was trying some kind of negotiation tactic, but he's stuck to that."

"Well, I went through one trial, I can do another."

Brandon smiled. "I thought you might say that. We're going to get him, don't you worry."

As well as Brandon knew me, and as much as I knew that I had to be flexible and adjust, worry began to take over. The night after my meeting with Brandon, I couldn't sleep at all. Maybe it was silly of me, but after the first trial, I had felt such a sense of success and really believed that I was on to the next phase in my life. I'd focused so much on that first trial and how it would signal the end. It was as if I had been in a race, counting down the laps to the last one, the bell lap, and had gotten to the finish line, expending all my energy in a last kick and winning the race, with everyone coming up to congratulate me, but then a few hours later, I'd been told that I hadn't run the right number of laps, I needed to drop everything, get back in my running clothes, and go and finish the race.

As upset as I was, I knew that I couldn't let Zuniga and his lawyers get away with five years. When I came back from Brandon's meeting, Kristine and Silje could sense immediately that I was upset. They joined me on a run, and we talked about what had happened. They told me that they knew that Coach Wollman would understand, as he had before, that I wasn't going to be like the rest of the girls on the team whose time was more or less their own.

"I just want to be normal again," I shouted as we weaved our way through campus.

Kristine laughed and said, "When were you ever normal?" She picked up the pace and I sprinted to catch her.

"What's so special about being normal?" Silje said. We resumed running side by side, and Kristine and I both laughed. This was a common topic among us. The life of an athlete set us apart and we liked that. Fitting in wasn't as high on our list of priorities as it had been when we first came to campus as foreign students and foreign student athletes. We'd stayed true to ourselves, but we'd found a place in the campus community and outside of it. We had our quirks, and though we were three girls from Norway, eventually everyone got to know us as individuals. Silje was the dutiful one, the one who was most dedicated to her running and her studies. Kristine was the entertainer. Wherever Kristine was, you'd hear laughter. I existed somewhere in the middle ground, in some ways more like Silje, in others wishing that I could be more like Kristine. There were times when those identities merged, and I thought once again of the sometimes-you-just-have-to-not-give-a-shit advice that I'd given to a teammate.

I decided this was one of those times.

"Last one there has to pay!" I said, reversing direction and heading toward the frozen yogurt store.

I had months to prepare for the trial. Brandon let me know that one of the challenges I faced was having gone on record in the first trial with my account of the events. I had to make sure that I didn't deviate from what I'd said the first time around. I read and reread those transcripts, reviewed with Brandon the key points in my testimony, and went back through the journal I had been keeping.

I noticed that from the first days after I was raped, I had been trying to make sense of the "why?" At first, there was the inevitable "Why did this have to happen to me?" but even in the earliest entries, I could see that there was something deeper than that.

I've always understood, on some level, that running was a very selfish endeavor. *I* benefited from it physically, mentally, and spiritually. But there was a kind of halo effect: when I felt good about my running and myself, then I treated other people better and they may then have treated other people better as well. For a long time, that was enough. I felt good about being a positive person and that I had generally a very good and strong relationship with most everyone else I came in contact with.

I worried sometimes that the inverse of that could be true as well, that a kind of devil's horns effect might exist. If I was crushed by this experience and allowed it to drag me down, I might negatively impact other people. I was fairly close to being obsessive about preventing that from happening. I found that I frequently exhausted myself, and most likely everyone else, in my efforts to, as I'd said while running with Kristine and Silje, be "normal."

Even though I'd laughed and joked with them about it being okay to not be normal, the fact was that when I was really honest with myself, I knew the rape had altered me. I wanted to be a normal girl who didn't have to wonder when she met some guy at what point in the relationship she would have to tell him about her secret past. I wanted to be a girl who wondered if a guy liked me or not only because of some part of my personality or looks and not because of something that happened to me in the past.

But I also wanted to help people. And if I was really going to do that, I had to let them see some of my weakness and vulnerability. Ironically, in a way, that would be showing them my strength. I was hurting, I was exhausted, I was confused, but I'd come back from that and won. I'd be lying, and doing people a disservice, if I came across as if none of this was a big deal, if I let people believe that I was unaffected, that it hadn't been a struggle for me to figure out the best way forward. I'd come to see that my recovery was littered with missteps. I was also starting to better see how I'd been making similar mistakes in my life and in my recovery. If I learned from my mistakes in my running, I could do the same in the rest of my life.

I still wasn't sure exactly what that plan would look like, or how it would fit into my schedule. Before, that would have driven me crazy, but I was learning to give myself a break. As that Take Back the Night event had shown me, sexual crimes affected the lives of a lot of people. I could help them and, in doing so, help myself. It was now a question of knowing which was the lead leg and which was the follow. Funny that I had to learn how to put one foot in front of the other in the correct order after all these years.

I've always been a believer that nothing good ever comes about from things being easy. Having to testify again was going to be hard and take a lot of preparation. There would likely be some ups and downs in the trial. That's how things went for me in other parts of my life—especially on the track. One step forward, one step back. That proved to be the case on April 2, 2011, when I ran the three-thousand-meter steeplechase at the Bobby Lane Invitational in Arlington, Texas. I came in second, but my time was slow, almost a minute behind my PR. That was one of the down moments. I hoped that on April 11, when I was scheduled to testify, I'd have one of those up moments.

The worst thing about that race wasn't my overall time; I had come in second place by just a second. What bothered me was that I hadn't dug deep and fought at the finish to overtake the other woman. My focus was so split by the trial that I had no mental energy at all that day. I wondered if I could have won if I had kept my head in the game. As I cooled down, I beat myself up about how I'd come to Dallas as a runner on a scholarship, and that was my job, and I owed it to these people to devote myself wholeheartedly to training and racing. That was all true, but I realized that I also had to understand what everyone else seemed to: that I had to put it all in perspective.

I didn't have time to dwell for long on my poor performance. Wenche picked me up in Arlington right after my race so we would make it to the airport in time to pick up my mother. Something about having my home-and-away mothers with me made it a bit easier to get over how poorly I'd done in that race. The race that really mattered was the trial. This was the last one. I'd have another season of cross-country and track to run once this trial was over. I would be able to work as hard as I could in training and racing then, but I had to keep in mind how divided my time was now.

The second day of the trial, I found myself with my focus split again. I had an Applied Physiology exam scheduled for the afternoon. Meanwhile, at the same time Brandon was involved in jury selection. He didn't think I'd have to testify that day, but I was to keep my cell phone with me in case I needed to rush over to the courthouse.

I had told my professor, Scott Davis, about the trial. He'd had no idea

I was the rape victim, and that surprised me. He said that I could bring my phone with me to class—something normally prohibited. I thanked him, but prayed that I would be able to finish the exam in peace. No luck, though; in the middle of the exam, Brandon called. Dr. Davis met my gaze and nodded. I got up and went out into the hallway, not caring that everyone else in the exam room had looked up to follow me. My heart racing with anticipation and thinking that I was going to have to rush out of there, I answered the call.

"Hate to tell you this," Brandon began, and my heart sank. "The judge is sick. Postponed for today."

Brandon called again later that day and asked me to meet him the next morning. At the time I didn't think it was odd that he wouldn't be in court, but when he showed up he told me that the judge had postponed the trial for another week. He offered to make alternate flight arrangements for my mother, who had come into town to support me during the trial but was now scheduled to leave before it even started. I tried to turn this news into a positive—the delay meant that my mom would be with me for a few more days. Fortunately, her very understanding boss let her extend the time away. But as my mother put it, even if she hadn't gotten permission, she would have stayed. "Some things are more important than work," she told me. We'd been having a good time together, and I wanted to focus on that and not on any disappointments.

The delay also meant that I wouldn't be able to race at the Mt. Sac Relays. This was the best meet of the spring season, one I'd really been looking forward to, especially since I'd done so well in the 10K the year before. Now, instead of returning to the scene of a major milestone in my training and my recovery, and being able to measure my progress, I was going to be stuck back in Dallas.

I'd been mentally pointing toward this race all season, and now it was being taken from me. Sure, having my mom there in Dallas was great, but I really, really wanted to be on the starting line with fifty or more other runners, to bring to life all the mental images and sensations I'd been carrying around in my head the whole spring as I worked out.

I'd also miss out on the bonding time on the plane, hearing the teasing the scared flyers got, the laughs the snorers wouldn't hear, the paper wads being tossed into their slack mouths. Staying in a hotel packed with other student athletes, and just hanging out with people my own age and with a similar interest, was the payoff for all the hard work we put in. A meet like Mt. Sac was spread over several days. You got away from campus and classes, and your workouts only took a small portion of your time; since you were competing, once your race was over, you could just enjoy the experience.

I wasn't just disappointed. I was pissed off. I *loved* that race. No matter how positively I tried to spin things, it felt like every time things seemed to be progressing, I had to take another step back. I wasn't looking to party or to hook up with anyone; I just wanted to be a regular college kid—someone who could get away and have some fun. To add to it all, the new timing meant that Kristine was going to have to miss Mt. Sac, too. I laughed the first time I heard someone described as a Debbie Downer (and had the term explained to me). But was that what I was? Not only did I mess things up for me, but I put other people's fun in jeopardy or took it away from them altogether. I could live with having all my race preparation go for nothing. I could live with not being able to get out and have fun. But I couldn't live with denying Kristine that same opportunity.

I told Brandon, "I know you want to save Kristine's testimony until later in the trial, but she has to go first. She's put up with enough. If I have to miss the race, then I have to miss the race, but I'm not making her miss it, too."

"I appreciate what you're saying," he said, "but I can't do that. You leading off and her taking the baton at the end? That works. You don't mess with success."

I appreciated the track reference, but I wasn't going to be thrown off that easily. We argued about it for a bit, but he finally agreed. "Okay, okay." Then he took a breath. "I think you should know this: Zuniga's wife and kids are going to be in the courtroom."

I felt like someone was choking me. How was I going to be able to say all those horrible things—the truth about what this husband and father had done—knowing that they were there to hear them? Why did I have to be the one who was responsible for taking their loved one away from them?

Kristine did testify on Tuesday, April 11. We all drove to the court-house together. My father called, just before his workday was ending, to wish us luck. He hadn't been able to take any more time off, and I was glad that he wouldn't have to sacrifice time he'd worked so hard for to take a "vacation" spent in a court building.

"Be strong," he said just before hanging up, and then added, "I know you will be."

My American moms and my real mom sat in the courtroom. My mom decided that after the first trial and being in the waiting room and not hearing what had gone on, she wanted to be in there. She understood English well enough that only the legal terms might puzzle her. I'd told her everything about that night, so I wasn't worried that hearing it again would upset her.

Kristine and I waited in the kids' room again.

"At least I won't have to sit here for so long that I'll be able to mem-orize these." She picked up a copy of the children's picture book *The Stray Dog*.

"He's cute," I said, pointing at the cover and thinking of Anette and her dog Enja.

"Yes," Kristine said. I could see her struggling to say something else, keep the conversation going about dogs, or tennis balls, or anything at all but what she was about to face. Her lips trembled and she shook her head.

"Cute," she managed at last with a weak laugh.

I scooted my chair toward hers and we sat face-to-face, our arms rest-ing on our thighs, holding hands, heads bent as if in prayer.

I know that what I was hoping for came true. Within the first hour, the bailiff came to call for Kristine. She stood and smoothed her pants and adjusted her blouse and hair. I stood, and we hugged for a long time, until the bailiff said again, "It's time."

I watched Kristine leave and could tell by her slow and deliberate gait that she was struggling with this situation; she seemed to take a slight pause before placing one foot in front of the other. I hoped she'd turn and look back at me, but she didn't. I stood there until the clatter of her footsteps faded.

I flipped open the book. "It was a great day for a picnic." I hoped that would be true for Kristine and me.

She returned less than an hour later, the relief she felt expressed in her carriage. She stood taller and walked purposefully toward me.

"I did good," she said as she held her arms open for me to embrace her. "I wanted to do that for you."

The next morning, before I had to return to court, I walked with Kristine and Silje from our apartment to SMU.

"I wish that you were coming with us," Kristine said. Then, pointing at her bag that I had insisted on carrying, she added, "You know that's what the freshmen are supposed to do for us."

"I know. It's not that heavy."

"Maybe we can sneak you inside it," Silje said.

"I expect it to be heavier when you get back, with a medal, both of you."

It was bittersweet seeing all of my teammates clustered around the SMU minibus. A few of the girls came up and hugged me, and we exchanged good-luck sentiments for the days ahead.

I didn't want to stand there watching them drive away, but I did, thinking that a very large part of me was on that bus with them. The rest of me ran home and took a quick shower. I had another competition to get ready for.

I felt a familiar mix of nerves and determination as I took the stand shortly after the lunch recess. I looked around the courtroom. Out of the corner of my eye, I saw the judge glancing at some papers in front of her. I looked over at a few members of my team—Kelly and Wenche, my stalwart mother figures, and my own mother sitting between them. In a way this whole experience of testifying again was like running a familiar trail. Those first two women were comforting landmarks along the way, places for which I had comforting associations. My mom hadn't been down this particular road with me, but we'd talked our way through all the events of the rape. I was confident that nothing that I would say would surprise, shock, or hurt her. My mom is the most optimistic person I've ever met, the one that I can always rely on to find some good in the worst of circumstances. I knew that losing her parents had been tough on her, and I admired her for not ever expressing any kind of bitterness over it.

When I was feeling my worst after the attack, it was my mother who told me that I'd been diverted from my path. It was up to me to choose which road I would go down after that. I could be like those men and choose bad over good, or I could find a way to come back stronger than before. She knew that I never would do the first of those, but there was always that middle path—indifference. In her mind that was no option at all, either. I knew that my mother was proud of me, but she also expected me to have the strength to face Zuniga and speak the truth about what had happened.

Brandon led me carefully through the events of the night of December 4 and the early-morning hours of December 5. He had told me it was important that we make it clear to the jury that I understood the role that each of the three men had played, that Alfonso Zuniga was the driver, the man they referred to as the Boss. I explained what the Boss had done to sexually assault me and that he'd also handled the gun. I told how I'd seen that man's face because he was the one leaning out of the car getting my attention in the first place—his were the eyes I met the moment I realized I was being kidnapped at gunpoint.

We also had to make it clear that despite my inability to identify the man who was on trial from a series of photographs, I knew and recognized that man in the courtroom. Brandon asked me how sure I was, and I told him that I was 100 percent sure. In answer to a follow-up question about whether I had any doubt, I blurted out, "I've been trying to delete that face from my memory for a year and a half. It won't go away."

I surprised myself a little when I uttered those words. I continued to answer Brandon's questions, but a part of my mind was working over this puzzle. If these men were going to be receiving a life sentence, was I going to be sentenced to living a life with those images dominating me? Would I always walk around with the feeling that, like the gun pressed against my head, those images could explode into my mind at any time?

The defense attorney's cross-examination was a much less familiar route. Instead of going through the events in sequence, he seemed to jump from one point to the next. I wasn't thrown off by anything he asked, but I couldn't see any pattern to the questions. What was he trying to do? What was he disputing about what I had said? Eventually, I figured out that he was stressing a couple of things: First, he was making the point that his client didn't speak English and therefore couldn't have ordered me around, and second, he appeared to be trying to confuse me about the issue of the gun. We seemed to keep going around and around on who exactly did what and where. I realized that he was trying to make a case that I was confused about who was really there and what they each had said and done. I made it clear that there could be no doubt in the jury's mind that Alfonso Zuniga had participated fully in the crime, that he wasn't just an unwilling participant who drove his friends around while they raped me. I made it clear that maybe those men would not have been able to pick me out of a lineup, and had treated me as an inanimate object, but I was real, and I knew exactly what each of them had done.

I looked at Alfonso Zuniga at several points during my questioning. Unlike Arturo Arevalo, Zuniga at least looked at me, and paid attention to what I was saying. He acknowledged that I was another person and not some doll that he could use and toss away. That was how I'd felt that night, that I wasn't even a human being to those men. But that day in court, I think he saw that I was a person. That was a victory, a small but important one. I wasn't just someone he could stick his fingers and his penis into, slap on the butt, laugh with his buddies about, wrap up in tape, and shove out of his car like I was a discarded wrapper from a fast-food hamburger.

When the judge announced that I could be dismissed, I noticed that the light in the room had changed, that it was now full-on afternoon. Despite how long I'd been on the witness stand, I didn't feel tired at all. I was Brandon's last witness; the prosecution rested its case. It was now up to the defense. I took my seat next to my mother. Because I was done with my testimony, I was allowed to attend the rest of the trial. While I was walking to my seat, I heard the defense attorney, Mr. Jamison, say, "May we approach real quick?"

By the time I sat down next to my mom, the lawyers for both sides and the judge stood at her bench huddling and discussing something.

My mother gave me a questioning look, but all I could do was shrug. I wondered what was up, but I didn't have long to consider the possibilities.

The lawyers went back to their places. I tried to read Brandon's expression, but his face was neutral. All he did was scratch the top of his head before taking his seat and scribbling a few notes on his pad.

The jury came back in, and the defense attorney, Mr. Jamison, stood. I leaned forward in my seat and rested my elbows on my thighs and balanced my chin on my fingertips, anticipating.

Mr. Jamison asked that something about the date of the indictment be read into the record and then he said, "And with that, ladies and gentlemen, the defense rests."

I rocked back in my seat. What was going on?

The defense wasn't going to call a single witness. I knew that the burden of proof fell on the prosecution, but what was the purpose of not putting up any kind of fight at all? Before the trial, Brandon had told me that Zuniga's lawyers were going to make the case that he only did what he did because he was afraid of what Arturo Arevalo might do to him or his family. Brandon had told me about the concept of "duress" and that an accused criminal could be found not guilty if the jury believed that the man legitimately felt that his life or his loved one's lives were in jeopardy unless he participated in the crime. In a way, Arturo Arevalo was back on trial, but Alfonso Zuniga's lawyers weren't going to have anyone there who would testify to how bad a man he was. How was he going to prove duress if he didn't call any witnesses? Was he saying that the prosecution hadn't done their job of proving, so he didn't have to do anything to defend his client?

The judge called for a ten-minute recess. I had a bunch of questions running through my mind, but I knew that Brandon would be busy going over his closing remarks. I tried to calm myself by saying that we'd done the same things at the first trial and we'd won. How could this one be different? I knew I wouldn't be doing myself any good if I stood around with everyone else and fixated on those questions. Instead, my mother and I stepped outside.

"Wonderful," my mother said as she tilted her head up to the sun. "Papa said there's still plenty of snow around at home."

"I know. He told me."

"No matter what, there's always the sun. Funny to think the same one is on him, too."

I nodded and smiled, picturing my dad driving home, squinting into the lowering sunlight.

During the closing arguments, Brandon asked me to stand at one point, to remind the jury of who I was. The woman who stood was, of course, known in the court as Jessica Watkins. I was eager to get on with what I'd done in Norway—coming forward as Monika Kørra and letting the world know who I was and what had been done to me. I was looking forward to walking out of that courtroom and leaving that other name behind.

Both attorneys' remarks in the closing arguments were relatively brief. The judge gave her final instructions to the jury and they left the room. We all stood in the hallway, wondering if we were going to have to wait overnight. We weren't. Less than a half hour later, we were back in the courtroom, and for the second time I felt a thrill of pleasure and relief as the jury foreman read the verdict: guilty.

Unlike after Arevalo's trial, when we had all gathered together and shared a meal, my mother and I went alone to Café Express and ordered yogurt parfaits with granola and fresh berries. We took our food and our coffees and sat in the sun.

I was glad to be alone with Mom, to share this moment of relief and the start of a new period in my life.

"This summer," my mother said thoughtfully, "I think we should do a Texas type of barbecue at the cabin."

"That would be fun."

We went on and on about our summer plans. I still had final exams and other meets before then, but home, after all we'd been through, seemed like a better place to be.

I went back to campus that night and ran, feeling good about how I'd handled myself, thinking more and more about next steps and the strides I'd taken, how I wanted to remember how all of this felt, not take for granted the ground I was covering, the distance that was increasing between then and now.

My thoughts turned down a familiar path. If I had no choice but to live in a world where evil like these men existed and did nothing to offset it, then what was the point of being here at all? If I didn't stand up and tell my story, then what was the point of having suffered? What could I do in the present to help others stop suffering?

At the end of the second trial, I had purchased candles as gifts for all the members of my team. Since that Take Back the Night event, I'd been thinking of ways to relight candles, to bring something positive into the world. I'd attached a note to those gifts explaining how much I appreciated them all reigniting my spirit. Now it was time for me to do that for others.

The next day, I sat in the courtroom as the penalty phase of the trial began. During this, Zuniga's lawyer did present witnesses who tried to show how much of a bad influence Arturo Arevalo was. I was so tired of thinking about Arturo Arevalo. It had been clear to me from that night that he was a terrible and twisted person. I took no satisfaction from being able to say that my assessment of him that night as the Worst One was accurate. As I listened to different people talk about him, I felt uncomfortable. I thought of the conversation that I'd had with my father that first Christmas after the attack. How could I live in a world where people like that existed, where someone like Zuniga failed to stand up to him?

A dull headache gripped me, and I was unable to fully concentrate. The fluorescent lights in the courtroom seemed to hum more loudly. Several witnesses spoke, but I couldn't tell you what they all said. At one point, though, a woman took the stand. She was small and round, and she nervously brushed her hair from her face as she faced the questions asked of her. She looked familiar to me, and as I listened to her testimony, I realized that she was Arturo Arevalo's wife.

She spoke softly, hesitantly. I felt like a sharp knife was being pushed into my heart. She took the stand to tell us about what a horrible man Arturo was. The same man she, in the first trial, supported. Then in fear, now in honesty. She looked so scared, terrified really. But how brave this was of her.

I knew that she now worked against our case, that she wanted to blame it all on Arturo. That was wrong, but at the same time, it felt so good knowing that she now was strong enough to stand up against the man who had been treating her badly for a long time. She told us how she had lived a life in fear of this man, of what he could do to her, to her children.

I cried out loud at that point. There was no way I could hold it back anymore. Her eyes, her children—the knife inside my chest was twisted around and around. How awful this was for so many people. I told myself that I had to get control of myself. I tried to tell myself to hang in there, to keep calm, but the thought of those little kids facing anything at all like what I had faced was too much for me. I had to leave the courtroom to compose myself; I had to go through one night in the presence of this man; that poor woman and those kids had been under his control for a long time. What was going to become of them? I was fortunate to have a large circle of people who supported me, and as I heard the sounds of my footsteps clicking across the tile floor, I could already hear more footsteps shuffling as a few of them followed me out, hoping to offer me comfort, to make certain that I was going to be fine.

As I stood outside the courtroom trying to pull myself together, a number of the reporters who had been covering the case noticed me. Kelly took me aside, and after making sure that I was okay, she said to me, nodding in the direction of all the reporters, "I want you to be sure. I want you to be comfortable with whatever you decide. You don't owe them anything." I'd shared with Kelly my desire to get my story out more widely, and she'd been a great advisor. Seeing how emotional I was, she felt protective of me, and as much as she supported me doing what I felt I needed and wanted to do, she didn't want to see me get hurt again.

The trials had been big news in Dallas, and I had spoken to some of the reporters. They continued to honor the agreement that my real name not be used and that no photographs of me appear that would reveal my identity.

I wasn't happy about how some of the stories had been written. Questions about what I was wearing that night, what was going on at the party and how much I had had to drink, why I was out so late, all seemed to be pointing a finger of blame at me. I didn't like that. One reporter was different—Scott Goldstein of the *Dallas Morning News*. He'd kept the focus of his reporting on what I thought was important: how horrible these men were and how awful were the things they did. Kelly also liked Goldstein's articles, and she'd contacted him, hoping that she'd be able to introduce him to me. Later on, she helped him out by putting Scott and me together. Reporters from other news outlets had also been in touch, and it seemed to me like they were fighting over who would be the one to tell the full story first. I put the rest of them off, telling them that I'd only talk when the trial was over. They were determined to make me honor my word.

Seeing all those TV news crews had me on edge. I didn't want them to get the story in advance of Scott. I had no way of knowing who was who and how they'd reported on the attack before.

As soon as the reporters saw me, they rushed over. I saw Scott shoulder his way past a few of them. I nodded at him, and he stepped forward and ushered me a short distance away.

"You know how hard I've worked on this story. You know that I can help you get the message out that you want. You can make a lot of difference in women's lives. I can help you."

I knew that he was sincere, but at that moment, I was still unsure—not about speaking out, but about the best way to do it.

A reporter from the local Fox News station approached me next. She looked over her shoulder at Scott and said, "He's a great guy, but you know that newspapers are struggling, right? If y'all want to get the word out, then you can get to more people through TV than any other way. Way more. Just think about that."

"I will. It's just—"

I didn't know how to express myself. The scene in the courtroom, now these people seemingly fighting over who should be able to tell my story first—it was all too much. I knew that they had jobs to do and all of that, and they couldn't have known what had just taken place in the courtroom and how I'd reacted. They were using me, but I was using them as well. I wanted to get my message out, and they were offering me a way to do that, but still . . .

"Like I told you before, I sure would appreciate this. You have no idea how much my boss has been pushing me on this. I sure don't want to disappoint him."

She smiled and blinked at me, looking as if her life hung in the balance. I also knew that I was partly responsible for all the reporters coming to me. Saying that I would speak to the media at the conclusion of this trial had fed their desire. But telling me how disappointed their bosses would be if they didn't get the story first seemed unfair. I didn't need to feel more guilty.

Before I could think any more about it, I felt a hand on each of my elbows guiding me away. Kelly and my mother stood on either side of me.

"Monika," my mother said, "we should get you some food right now."

I WAS GLAD that everyone understood me well enough and could read my mood well enough that we didn't talk much about the media while we ate. I pushed a salad around my plate, lost in thought. I was anxious about the sentence the jury would hand down, but even more nervous about what I would say when it was all over, whom I would talk to and whether I would be able to articulate myself in a way that could make an impact on someone else's life.

The jury helped me feel a bit better. They handed down a life sentence. I felt relieved, but unlike after Arevalo's trial, I also felt some twinges of remorse. I couldn't get the picture out of my mind of his wife and his children. What was going to happen to them?

Texas law allows for a victim of a crime to make something called a victim impact statement. That meant that I could stand up in court at the conclusion of the penalty phase and address the convicted criminal directly. I had decided not to do that after the first trial; Arevalo had shown no indication that he would even listen to anything that I had to say. What was the point, then?

With Alfonso Zuniga, who had at least made eye contact with me, I felt like there was an actual human being behind those eyes, someone who had a conscience. I didn't like that he had tried to pass along the blame, but at least he acknowledged my existence. I hoped that by addressing him, I could provide his family with some bit of relief as well.

Yet I had no idea where to start. I was still confused; everything had been happening so fast. He got life; I was free. I was safe. But his wife, his children, had only just begun to deal with the ramifications of his crime. About to cry, I looked at them. I had to take a deep breath not to lose it. I looked over at him, looked him in his eyes. He met my eyes. He looked different now, weak in a way, like he felt bad, like he was sorry for all he had done. I had to talk straight from my heart.

"I just want to tell you one thing," I began, the words crawling painfully out of my mouth. "I don't hate you. I hate what you did to me, but not you personally. I'm not mad, but scared. Scared that you will do this again, to me or to someone else. So I had to do this, I had to testify and tell what you did that night to prevent you from hurting anyone again."

He continued to look straight at me, straight into my eyes. I felt my stomach quiver and then settle.

"By looking at you, by the way you look at me, I can see that you have feelings, empathy."

Tears fell from his eyes, and I tried to take a deep breath, but I couldn't force it past my constricted throat. Seeing him in tears, weak and vulnerable, made me sad in a way that I'd never experienced before.

"I wish all the best for your family; your wife, your children. I hope and pray that they will have a good life. And I hope that you will find peace now."

He didn't let go of my eyes for one second now. He nodded his head and said, *"Gracias. Gracias!"*

I stepped down, and was about to leave the courtroom, when I remembered the media. I was too overwhelmed with feelings to talk to them now. I wanted to talk to my family and my friends first. And I wanted to go for a run; I needed to organize my thoughts. But I felt like I had an obligation to make good on my promise to them to speak out.

I looked out in the hallway. I could see the reporters standing there arguing, yelling at one another. I turned around and walked straight out the back doors. I had just gotten my life back; a man had gotten life in prison; a wife didn't know how she would be able to move on with her life and take care of her children alone. But those reporters, they were standing there arguing about something so small that they didn't even understand it themselves. I didn't feel bad about not talking to them anymore. And they were too busy yelling to see me take the back door out.

Kelly arranged for us to celebrate the end of the trials at the Rosewood Mansion, one of the nicest hotels in uptown Dallas, a place I'd only heard about and never imagined being in. We stood on the veranda drinking champagne before we ate, my cell phone chirping along with the birds that flitted around Turtle Creek. I didn't think it would end, and it didn't. Some members of the media, not all of them, texted me, called me, over and over. I stepped inside the hotel and scanned the barrage of voice mails and texts. After an hour my mom took my phone and turned it off.

"Enough! Let her be!" she said to the night air.

She led me back outside to rejoin the party. Kelly handed me another champagne flute. They all stood there looking at me, and I knew that I was expected to deliver another message.

I raised my glass and said, "This was one of the best days of my life. I owe that to all of you—thank you. *Skål!*" I took a sip and felt the bubbles prickling my tongue and my nose. Everyone laughed at the face I made.

"I'm not used to drinking expensive champagne like this. I'll probably never have anything like it again."

Kelly walked up to me and wrapped me in a big hug.

"Oh, yes you will, Monika. You'll find the man of your dreams, and on your wedding you will realize that it's the best day of your life. Then you'll toast with an even more expensive bottle."

Kelly always knew what to say to make me smile. I stood there on that warm spring evening, the scent of citronella candles and the flowering wisteria bush reminding me again of how sweet my life was and would continue to be.

Going Public

pril 2011 marked an end to the cycle of court cases. Luis Zuniga, the one I'd thought of alternately as the Weak One, had pled guilty to his participation in my kidnapping and assault and was awaiting a sentencing hearing on April 28.

By that time, after spending more than a year talking about this possibility with friends and family, I made good on my promise to the media and shared my story and identity. I was glad that I'd waited. (Strange how my parents always are right.) If I'd done it immediately after Arturo Arevalo was found guilty and sentenced, I would have been doing it partly out of self-interest. I was in a hurry to let people know that I wasn't ashamed of myself for what had happened. I was so eager to put everything behind me, to get back to normal, that I was rushing everything. I'd done a lot of work on myself since the attack and even more in the months following the first trial.

I'd tested the waters by coming out and sharing my story in Norway. I'd taken precise and measured steps, felt in control of what I said and whom I said it to, and was pleased with the results. That might have happened in January, but by waiting until after the April trial, not only was I in a better place, knowing that I wouldn't have any more trials to face and that anything I said wouldn't likely jeopardize the prosecution's efforts, but I'd also built a solid foundation of trust with Scott Goldstein, the *Dallas Morning News* reporter. That was also true to a lesser degree with the rest of the media people. I didn't like how some of them had portrayed me and the case, but I could see later that a lot of my responses to their stories were more reactions. In other words, I was still too emotionally reactive.

Over time, I came to understand better that the media had something I wanted, just as I had something they wanted. If I was going to do some good for other people, I needed allies and not enemies. I didn't want anything to be done in an adversarial way.

I met with Scott Goldstein several times over coffee. He also spoke with my mother in preparation for the article. By the time the second trial had ended, I had known Scott for about one year. In that time, he'd earned my trust. He'd gone the distance with this story and proven to me several times that he was committed to the cause against sexual violence. He wanted to do what he could to help me get my message out. I couldn't predict what the response might be, but I hoped it would turn out as it had in Norway, where my coming forward had received a positive response. So, when the article ran on April 19 of 2011, I had every reason to keep believing that I'd done the right thing. Eventually, I knew that I had.

I'd spent a whole bunch of time thinking about all kinds of issues related to the attack. I was running away from the field in that regard. I just needed to give my thoughts some time to catch up to me, to let my head start to unwind.

It also helped that I had the trials behind me. As much as I hated all the delays and how things had dragged on and on, what Erin and later Brandon had told me, "Trust the system. Let the system work," had proven true. Two men were in prison for life, and the third man, who had helped convict the other two, was soon to be sentenced. For someone like me, who had been spending her whole life trying to go faster, learning to slow down was hard, but in the right circumstances, the rewards for slow could be as great as, or even better than, those for going fast.

As much as I hoped that coming forward would help others, it helped me as well. I didn't feel anymore the low-level paranoia that people might be talking behind my back. I was okay that people knew my name and my face; in fact, once the stories came out, more people came forward to talk to me. They let me know that they cared about me and hoped that I was doing well. They offered me help.

Just before final exams, I logged into my Gmail account and saw an unfamiliar user name in my inbox. I clicked the e-mail open, wary of spam or something else, but as I started to read the message, tears welled up in my eyes. The e-mail read in part, "I know what you've been through. Until I read your story and how you're working to deal with it, I didn't think I'd ever feel safe or good again. I'm ready to take the steps I need to take now, to get back to a normal life. Thanks for sharing."

At that moment, I knew that no matter what else happened, I was glad that I'd spoken out. It reconfirmed my decision to do more for others. It also helped that at that point, everyone on my team was in support of my efforts. My father and mother saw how much better I was; I think it also helped that they'd spent so much time with the members of the support system I had in Dallas that their fears about the consequences of my stepping into the public limelight were much fewer.

There is something called the law of unintended consequences. It mostly has to do with bad things that can happen as a result of an action we take, but in the spirit of my ever-positive mother, I prefer to think that unintended consequences can be good as well.

I thought that going public would make unnecessary the conversation that most people in my position dread—the one about your past with a new man in your life. I met Nick at the gym at SMU in April of 2011, just as the second trial had ended. We were seated side by side on stationary bikes and just nodded at each other at first. I didn't recognize him from around campus, but I did notice his quadriceps, the muscles at the front of his upper legs. I assumed he recognized me; after all, he was an SMU student and *everybody* (at least in my mind) had heard about the cross-country girl who'd been raped.

"You must bike a lot," I said. Only later, when I told Kristine about this opening line, did I realize how close it came to the bar pickup line about coming to this place a lot.

He seemed pleased that I'd spoken first. "I do. Not on one of these usually. Out there." He nodded toward the window that gave a view of the campus and the world beyond. "It's a great way to get around and to get away."

I'd been thinking a lot about getting away, especially with the end of the semester coming up, going back to Norway, and all that entailed.

We talked a bit more. I'm always intrigued by athletes, and seeing someone so clearly more proficient than the usual gym exercise biker caught my eye. Nick was a good-looking guy, and I could tell from our conversation that he was bright, articulate, and incredibly ambitious. But I wasn't in there to flirt. I was at the gym to sweat.

As my cool-down phase began, my pedaling slowed. Nick noticed this and said, "It was really nice talking to you."

I nodded. "You, too."

"You know, Sweden is one of my favorite countries. I was there last summer."

"I like Sweden, too." I was charmed by his efforts, but I had to set the record straight. "But I'm Norwegian."

My heart cracked a little when I saw the look on his face.

I next saw his face a week later. A friend of Kristine's had invited us to go along to dinner with a group of people I didn't know. I was surprised, and pleased, that Nick was among them.

We sat next to each other, and at one point Nick, clearly trying to make up for his mistaking me for Swedish, started talking about Norway and its tradition of great long-distance runners. That made me happy. He'd gone to some effort to study for what I was beginning to sense was not a chance second meeting. He told me that he was majoring in business, and as I got to know him better, it was clear that he was driven to succeed just as I was—just with different end goals in mind.

With the semester ending and Luis Zuniga's hearing coming up, and knowing that I was going back to Norway for the summer, I told myself to be patient. That was easy. I liked Nick, but I wasn't ready to date anyone, and so we kept things friendly. The fact that he was an athlete helped a lot. He seemed to get me in a way that made things easy between us. I liked having someone in my life who was a part of the post-attack/post-trials fresh start I was undertaking.

As the summer progressed and we spent more time together, I realized that Nick actually didn't know what had happened to me. I think he knew about the case, but he hadn't made the connection.

If I hadn't been really starting to fall for him, that wouldn't have been a problem, but I was. I spent a lot of time fretting about how I was going to tell him. I knew that before it got more serious than just being good friends I had to do it. Worse, I was terrified that the ugly truth would ruin what we had spent months building up.

We had gone out to dinner, and we sat in the car outside my apartment. I felt that pre-race buzz circulating through my body. At one point, we lapsed into silence. We both stood looking straight ahead. Nick still sat with his hands on the wheel, staring ahead, as if we were at a stoplight. We were.

"Nick, I have something that I need to talk to you about." I didn't dare pause but just plunged ahead. "I've been trying to tell you for a long time, but I just don't know how. You know that I'm doing good and that I'm happy now, right? But the last few years have also been challenging to me. I'm not sure if you heard about the SMU girl that got raped on the news?"

He shook his head, and I started to tremble. "I'm so sorry, Monika. I feel so stupid. Why didn't I put it all together? I knew it was a girl from your team. But *you*? You're always so happy and always smiling."

He shook his head again and smiled. I felt the squeeze on my heart loosening.

He turned to look at me and took my hand and kissed it. "You're so—" He let go of my hand and shrugged, lifting his hands so that they banged against the car's headliner.

We both laughed.

"You're so *happy*. Nothing. I mean *nothing*, you've ever done or said would have led me to believe it was you. You're incredible."

Nick had never seen me as anything but the happy girl I was, the one who had been telling people for so long that she was okay, but had not been telling the truth in words and actions. I knew then that Nick and I were going to be okay as well, more than okay.

CHAPTER NINETEEN

Perseverance

The morning of April 28, I woke up knowing that, with any luck, this was to be the last time I'd have to set foot in the Frank Crowley Courts Building. If I was nervous about anything that morning it was my upcoming meeting with the president of SMU, who wanted me to speak the next fall at an event welcoming all the incoming freshmen. To burn off some anxiety, I did an interval workout before Sidsel arrived to take me downtown.

With the question of guilty or not out of the way, and with the prosecutor's office having worked out a deal in which Zuniga would serve twenty-five years, this hearing was really more about me. I wouldn't get any say-so or have any influence on his sentence, but I would see him in court and speak with him.

I didn't have a problem with him being sentenced to twenty-five years. I tried to put that in context. I would soon be celebrating my twenty-second birthday. I couldn't imagine being confined to prison and coming out twenty-five years later, at age forty-seven, having missed out on so much of my life. Zuniga would spend the prime years of his life in prison. It wasn't just because Luis had turned state's evidence that I felt like his sentence should be shorter than what the other two men received. He was the one who had seemed to be arguing that they should let me go.

He'd tried to give me back my cell phone and my dress, and his attack was the briefest. He seemed reluctant to participate, and when arrested, he didn't try to make excuses or claim that he wasn't guilty. He cooperated with the investigators and the prosecutors, and though he was given that plea deal, I thought that he did so not just to get a reduced sentence but out of remorse.

He seemed like he could be redeemed, like he could serve his time in prison, come back out, and be a decent person. Maybe that's a very naïve statement, but I believed it. I wasn't projecting that quality of "niceness" on him as a way to make myself feel better. He genuinely was a more compassionate person than the other two, and he deserved to be treated differently from them because of that.

One of the things that I didn't like about the trials was that I felt like I hardly participated in them at all. That wasn't going to be the case during this hearing. In a way, I'd be the one getting my day in court.

THAT DAY, I got to speak directly to Luis Zuniga. Being able to confront him made a big difference to me. I'd always thought that he was different from the other two men.

When he spoke at the hearing, wearing an orange prison uniform, he seemed genuinely contrite. "I just want to ask for forgiveness. I know I'm not going to fix whatever damage or harm we did to you."

He also added, "I wish you the best in life and God bless you."

As important as hearing those words were, I wasn't looking for a simple apology. Anyone can apologize for anything and ask for forgiveness. I needed to know that he was going to change as a result of his experience. I asked him directly if he was. He didn't hesitate for an instant when he replied yes. He then added that he felt as if he already had begun that process. It was a bit strange to have to hear the words in Spanish and then get the translation from an interpreter—I understood what "Sí" meant but not much else—but his body language revealed a lot to me. He nodded thoughtfully and deeply, and his expression softened as I spoke to him. I didn't think that he was an actor capable of making me believe emotions he didn't really feel.

I didn't know much about his life. He was twenty-seven and didn't have a criminal record; again I wondered just what had gone wrong in his life to make him do such things to me. I wanted to ask him why, but that was beyond the scope of the hearing. Instead, I wanted his assurance that he was going to change. I wanted the punishment to have a positive effect on him.

So I said, "I don't think what you did to me that night defines you as a person. I think you made a mistake. You have to promise me that you want to change. You have to hold on to it every day."

When the interpreter finished translating my message, I watched as relief washed across his face. Our eyes met briefly, and I could see that he took my words seriously.

"I forgive you. You still have a lot of your life left."

As I spoke those words, my heart felt lighter. It wasn't as if my for-giving him made a difference in terms of how God would judge him or anything like that, but I did feel that I would be carrying around a burden for the rest of my life if I remained angry. I'd begun to let go of the fear when they were arrested and convicted, and that offered me some com-fort; if I hadn't been able to forgive Luis and to see how he seemed gen-uinely grateful, if I lumped him together with the other two as bad men undeserving of compassion or consideration as individuals, then justice really wouldn't be done.

Luis Zuniga was a criminal and a rapist, but his actions after he was apprehended had shown me that he was deserving of forgiveness, that if he hadn't admitted his guilt and asked for forgiveness and wished me well, then I wouldn't have given him the kind of careful thought I did. I knew that. When he had pushed me out of that SUV, I had felt like I'd been given a second chance, that somehow God had intervened on my behalf that night, and it seemed reasonable then that I do something that could offer this man some hope for change. All our lives had been altered by the events of December 5, 2009, and I was in the process of making my life better than it had been. I wanted to offer to someone else the chance that I had been offered. What he did with that opportunity was more import-ant now than those past actions, just as what I did with the challenges I faced was more important than that night.

Though we don't have an exact equivalent of the term "underdog" in Norwegian, I was familiar with, and a great believer in, the concept. I always liked stories of people who came back from their struggles, who defied the odds, who triumphed in spite of many forces working against them. I wasn't certain that Luis Zuniga's story would end triumphantly, but I at least wanted to be certain that he'd have the opportunity to try to win. I couldn't imagine what it was like to be held in an American prison. I knew a little of how this system differed from ours in Norway, so I had a feeling that Luis Zuniga was going to face many challenges. I didn't feel guilty about that, but I did hope that he meant what he had said about making changes to his life.

With the legal proceedings involving the three men over, I knew that change was possible for me. I felt it instantly. In the wake of the attack, I'd activated a kind of autopilot mechanism. I knew that the pre-rape Monika was a serious student, so I studied like crazy. I was maniacally dedicated to my sport, so that's what I kept doing. I did question that part of my life, but only because my efforts and my results were too frequently a mismatch.

After the Zuniga hearing, I had more time to reflect on how I'd been forced into those patterns of behavior. It took a few days for it to sink in that I wouldn't be appearing in court anymore. This had been like being in a marathon or other long race. Someone once told me that a marathon can't fit inside your head. What that meant was that 26.2 miles was such a long distance that if you started to think about mile 25 and 26 early in the race, you'd never get to those last miles. You'd be so bogged down and plagued by doubts and uncertainties that you couldn't do it. You had to break the race down into smaller increments. I'd been doing that all along as the legal system did its thing.

The adrenaline rush of being done with the court system was fun but short-lived. Immediately after the hearing Brandon had hugged me and said, "This is it."

"It is," I said.

At that moment, I felt like I could have gone out and run that marathon, and it would have fit in my head. A couple of days after, however, I realized how tired I was, mentally and emotionally primarily, but physically, too. Talking with Kristine and Silje helped. They both pointed out just how much had happened between that night in 2009 and the spring of 2011. We'd crammed a marathon-distance set of experiences into a 10K race. "Slow down" was the message I was getting.

For me, that didn't mean stopping completely, but thinking things through with more precision, less hurry-up, and getting real control over the mental game. Nick was helpful with this. After I returned to Dallas in the fall of 2011, we started dating. The physical attraction had been there from the start, but I didn't have space for him as a boyfriend in that life. In my new one, I did. Talking with him helped me sort through the collection of feelings and desires I had.

As much as I didn't want the attack to take over my life and my future, my sense that I could, and wanted to, help others took a stronger hold over me. In a way it worked like this: I had suffered a great deal of pain. In order to truly heal from that, in order for that pain to turn into some kind of gain, I had to do something that extended beyond my own personal needs and desires. Many other lives had been affected by what happened that night. If you placed all that pain, suffering, and worry on a scale, you'd find yourself in need of a whole lot of hope, change, and positivity to even out the scale. But I wanted more than that; I wanted that pain to be catapulted out of the lives of everyone else who had suffered any kind of tragedy.

From the very first days when I thought about coming forward, a phrase had kept running through my mind: "Kill the silence." I knew that by keeping quiet for as long as I had, I'd given the pain and the suffering a bit of a head start. I was confident that I could catch up and outrace it to the finish line. I'd been silent for far too long, and I knew that it was the silence that prolonged the pain for many rape victims; it was a silence whose source was shame and humiliation, a severe form of the desire to be treated as "normal," to not be looked on with pity or, in some cases, blame.

I shared these thoughts with Nick, and the business guy that he was, he suggested that we come up with a plan to make my vision a reality. Over time, he'd help do just that.

In the meantime, I had races to run and personal records to better.

Before it began, Silje, Kristine, and I talked about our goals for the upcoming cross-country season. We'd won our conference title in 2009 and then finished a very disappointing fifth in 2010.

"We know what we have to do," Silje said.

"Nothing short of that will make me happy," Kristine added.

"I'm in," I said. I thought about how proud I was of what we'd accomplished in 2009, how much the watch that we'd been presented as champions meant to me—and how devastating it had felt when the men who raped me stole that watch from me, as well. I knew that I'd never get it back, just as I'd never get back all the time that had been taken up by the men who had robbed me of it and so much more. But winning could make me forget a lot of things.

As team veterans, we set the tone in the first meet of the year. We weren't going to be messed with. Silje, Kristine, and I finished first, third, and fifth respectively in our season-opening meet. But as the saying goes, it's not how you start but how you finish. We were pointing toward the conference championship and the NCAA Championships after that. We weren't going to let anything get in our way. We won again at our second meet, with Silje once again leading the way. She'd go on to win four meets in a row, including a first place at the prestigious Chile Pepper Cross-Country Festival in Arkansas on October 15. I had a top-fifty finish in a field of nearly three hundred, and I was pleased that I was contributing and doing well against such strong fields.

When I was a kid, I hadn't heard of Halloween. At SMU, it was a big deal, and by 2011, it had also caught on in Norway. For the three of us, though, Halloween wasn't about tricks or treats; it was all about getting our jobs done and completing our mission. We traveled to Houston for the Conference USA Championships at Rice University. We were focused on Tulsa's Golden Hurricanes, who had dethroned us in 2010.

Under normal circumstances, I probably wouldn't have even stepped up to the start line. I had come down with some kind of upper respiratory infection that was so bad that I spent the whole week before the race in bed. I was febrile and my joints ached. But I knew that if I could get out of bed, I was going to race. This was the last chance for the three of us to race together as college teammates, and nothing was going to get in the way of me being with the two of them. As the week progressed, I started to feel better, but I was glad that I was so practiced in telling everyone, and myself, that I was okay.

As the starting gun went off, and as much as I was focused on just doing my best, I have to admit that I was keeping my eyes out for Tulsa's white-and-blue uniforms. By the time we reached the two-kilometer mark of the five-kilometer race, the leaders were a thin line trailing a balloon of runners. I focused on the ground ahead of me and on my arm swing, glancing side to side to see who was near me. I knew that Silje was likely near the lead and Kristine likely among that small group at the front. Scoring works like this: You take the finish place of each of your top five runners and add them up. Lowest team total wins the team conference championship.

I had to finish as high as I possibly could. I worked my way up to the top of the balloon as we passed the 3K point, and maybe two dozen runners were ahead of me. I tried to count the jerseys, but with the rolling hills it was tough to be sure. I thought I saw two SMU girls, but a number of other teams were wearing white singlets like the Tulsa girls.

I picked up my pace and told myself to forget trying to count. Just put all your effort into this, I thought, and maybe nearer the finish, you'll have a better sense of where you stand. As the finish line came into view, with about four hundred meters to go, I took a glance around me. No more than a dozen or so runners were ahead of me, and I saw that two white singlets with *Tulsa* emblazoned on them were behind me. I dug deep, determined that no one would get by me at the end, especially those two Tulsa runners.

There are times when you run and you feel everything—the strike of your foot on the ground, your hair whipping you, the flesh of your inner arms and armpits rubbing. But in that last four hundred, I was disembodied. I felt nothing. All I saw was that banner marking the finish. I felt as if I were floating, not the slow-motion *Chariots of Fire* kind of floating, but a sense of my head being disconnected from my body and moving at good speed. I crossed the line, and like a puppet with its wires clipped, I wobbled, let my arms dangle, and then sank to the ground off to the side and meters away from the other runners finishing.

I looked at the clock, and it clicked over to eighteen minutes exactly. I didn't know exactly how long I'd flailed and then tried to catch my breath, but I was pleased with my effort. No one had passed me at the end. I hadn't run a PR, but that didn't matter. I was still not feeling 100 percent, but I'd gutted it out and helped earn the team some points—that was what really mattered.

I found my teammates, the two veteran Norwegian girls, and Mary Alenbratt, our Swedish little sister, and we all threw our arms around one another. A moment later, Kasja Barr, a freshman and another part of the team's Swedish connection, joined us. I looked around at these strong, proud women, our faces a portrait of joy and effort, and let out a huge whooping scream that backed the other girls away from me for a moment before we all collapsed into a pile of exhausted pups.

It took a few minutes for the rest of the finishers to cross the line, but we knew that Silje had led the way again by winning the meet and setting a record. Kristine came in seventh, Mary twelfth, and me in fourteenth place. Kasja finished in twenty-third, giving us a team total of 57. The lowest score would win. We held our breath until Tulsa's score was posted—59!

We'd done it. Once again we all gathered around one another, all five of us whose times had counted and the other four who'd run, along with Coach Casey and other staff. We circled arms and danced as we chanted, "S to the M, M to the U, SMU, SMU—Goooo Mustangs!" I was so choked up with pride and sadness that it was over that I could barely get the words out.

I was so happy that we'd gotten back to the place we'd been in 2009, back to the place I was at just before the attack. I'd spent two long years trying to return to normal, and for me, that meant winning, giving my all, and being surrounded by a group of incredibly talented and hardworking teammates and coaches.

After we had done our cool-down, we put our blue-and-white SMU jackets on and got ready for the prize ceremony. I walked up to receive a watch commemorating our conference championship. As I stood there with the rest of the girls, I only flashed back briefly to the watch I'd received at a similar ceremony following the 2009 season. This one couldn't replace the watch that had been taken from me that night, and I was okay with that. I'd come to understand that none of us ever get back to exactly the point we were before in our lives, that life is one incredible ride, always moving forward no matter what else is happening.

Later that evening, as the three of us sat around the apartment talking about finals and plans for the holidays, I grew reflective. I sat there looking at my watch and couldn't suppress a grin. How funny it was that we were given timepieces to commemorate a conference win. As runners we're so obsessed with time. This was almost like giving an alcoholic a bottle of champagne to celebrate a year of sobriety. I had spent so much of the last several months wishing that time would fly by so that I could get beyond the trials and heal mentally and emotionally. Now I realized that the season and the semester had flown by. For the first time in a while, I caught myself wishing that things would slow down, that everything would stop moving and spinning so quickly. I wanted to savor this moment with my friends, hold these feelings close to me as a comfort and a reminder. I sat there as the second hand swept around the dial of my new watch, turning circles, marking steady progress, always forward in tiny but meaningful increments.

Though I didn't need to receive more tangible proof that I had made great strides that season, I got it. At the end of the fall sports season, all the athletes at SMU gathered together for an awards and recognition banquet. All the girls got dressed up, and we sat at tables grouped together by sport. We all felt so glamorous and giddy, like we were at the Golden Globe Awards in Hollywood, celebrating our individual and collective achievement. With so many sports represented, the evening did drag on a bit.

My thoughts also drifted a bit. The next thing I knew, Kristine was shaking my arm.

"Go up there."

I looked at her. "What?"

Kristine screwed her face up in disbelief. "Go up there. You won."

I still sat rooted in my seat. All around me, I saw everyone else standing. Kristine stood and lifted me up by the elbow.

"Go," she said again. "Shoo!" She burst into laughter, and I finally made my first tentative steps toward the stage.

On a projection screen behind the dais, I read "Perseverance Award 2010–2011."

I stepped onto the stage, and the sound of everyone's applause finally cut through the fog. The athletic director held out the plaque to me, and I took it. Feeling its heft in my arms, and seeing everyone standing and applauding, filled my heart. I didn't care that everyone knew the reason why I had to persevere. What mattered was that I had.

I still had the 2012 track indoor and outdoor seasons to look forward to, and then graduation. It's funny that my being sick just before the conference championship and then persevering through it had helped me better come to grips with my running. I didn't slack off on my training and I didn't give any less effort in the races, but I saw things from a different perspective. These were going to be my last months competing on the collegiate level. I'd helped the team win a championship and that was incredibly fulfilling. I hadn't gone into that race with huge expectations or a focus on running a PR. I just wanted to do my best, and to help the team win, and enjoy the experience.

That was a revelation to me: Enjoy the experience of running again. I know that this is hard to make clear, but I *loved* running. I didn't always enjoy the results; in fact, I too often agonized over them. Heading into the spring 2012 indoor season, I was coming off some of the hardest training I'd done. My results hadn't shown it, but I was trying to shrug that off. It didn't make sense to me that effort wasn't equaling results, but maybe if I stopped thinking about those PRs, then some good would come my way.

On January 27, 2012, I lay in the infield stretching prior to my race. Kristine was alongside me. She must have picked up on my mood.

"Monika, you're better than you think you are," Kristine told me. "You can do this. Just relax."

While I waited for the race to start, I listened to Florence and the Machine's song "Shake It Out" on repeat. One line hit home harder than the rest: "It's hard to dance with a devil on your back."

That was my answer to why training hadn't produced the results I thought I'd earned. How was I supposed to enjoy myself when I was carrying around all this pressure?

I have to let this go, I told myself. It wasn't fair to use my racing as a barometer of my healing. I finally had my epiphany: How fast I ran had nothing to do with whether or not I was going to live as a victim for the rest of my life, and no one but me had ever seen it that way. I was imagining that other people looked at my race results as proof that I was a damaged person. But all along, it was *me* causing the pressure. It was *my* fault that I wasn't racing at my best anymore. And that got me mad. I had expended so much energy on fighting for my mental health that I hadn't had anything left for the fight to race just for the sake of running again.

In that moment, inside the Randal Tyson Track Center at the University of Arkansas, I changed my outlook. I had been thinking about trying to reconnect with the joy of running. Now I was going to do something to allow that to happen. I was going to run this race without staring at the seconds ticking by, without making mental calculations about where I was and where I *should* be, and without being angry with myself about my shortcomings. Before the race started, I did something I'd never done before: I took off my watch.

I took a deep breath, got into position, and when the starting gun fired, I took off. In seconds, I was enveloped in chaos, a tangle of arms, legs, and torsos. I fought off a brief flash of panic. I didn't want to fall too far behind.

One lap.

You have nothing to prove. Just run. That unsettling feeling of uncertainty was subsiding.

Two laps.

Remember why you do this. Remember that you love it. It's time to shake that devil off. Without the pack of competitors around me, I began to settle into a rhythm, not worrying about who was around me but focusing on my breathing and my stride, settling into that good rhythm.

Three laps.

Let the pain give you energy. You're a fighter. Fight for this race. It's yours. I felt as if the parachute of tension that I'd been carrying around my shoulders had fallen off and was no longer dragging me down and restricting my movement. Free and easy. Free and easy.

I didn't even look at the board as I passed each lap. I tried to forget it was even there, and I started feeling good. Free. It was as if I were leaving the shadows behind me on the track. For once, as I had done before I had ever started competing, I ran for me.

On the last lap, I finally looked up at the board: I had to run the rest in forty seconds if I wanted to beat my personal record. And all at once, I knew I could do it. This was going to be my comeback. In my mind, I heard my coach telling me to "Dig deep, dig deep."

I sprinted faster than I ever had before, passing multiple people in the last two hundred meters. I noticed, but that wasn't why I was running that day. It wasn't about beating other people. It was about running that devil off my back, digging deeper even when it got painful. In a normal race, I would lose some speed toward the end, but this time, I just got stronger and faster all the way through the finish line. I let out a yelp of joy.

I beat my record by eight seconds. I don't remember what place I came in and it doesn't matter. My coach ran over to congratulate me, and I fell on the ground, sobbing. It felt like such a long road to get there. I took a long cool-down by myself, just letting the emotions bubble up in bursts. I was still me. I hadn't lost my edge after all.

Those three men had not stolen it from me.

Using the same let-go-of-the-pressure-and-enjoy-the-experience approach, two weeks later, on February 11, at the Iowa State Classic, I got into that proverbial zone that all athletes hope to enter. I set another PR, improving my time by nineteen seconds in the five thousand meters. I was on a roll, and though I knew that the chances of running PR after PR weren't good, I'd learned something really useful and enjoyed the deep feeling of satisfaction those races gave me. Little did I know that they were to be among the last races I would run for SMU.

Shortly after competing in the Iowa State Classic, I started to feel a lingering tiredness that wouldn't go away. When that was joined by a high fever, I went to the doctor and learned that I had developed mononucleosis. Heading into the spring 2012 outdoor season, knowing that these were going to be among my last meets running with my friends Silje and Kristine, I remembered how I'd felt looking at the watch we'd all received. I couldn't actually slow down time, but I could take the time to really savor these last few months of college life and college athletics. We were there to learn and to run, and I was finally able to learn something about how running could best fit into the rest of my life. I wasn't going to focus so much on a PR time as I was on a different kind of personal record—like a CD or an MP3 file—a way to preserve in my mind and my heart the memories I could make with people I had come to care about deeply and who felt the same way about me.

I was incredibly sad about not being able to compete, but as time went on, I came to terms with my disappointment. I'd said all those things about not focusing on PRs and just running for the joy of it, but the truth was, I still fixated on my performance—just to a lesser degree than I had before. Being knocked out of competing by mono was my body's way of telling me that I needed to slow down. I got sick because I was pushing myself too hard. With no track to focus my attention on, I turned to academics. I earned a 4.0 GPA (numbers still mattered) and at the end of the year received an award from the Athletics Department for most improved academic performance. I looked back on that span and felt really good about what I'd done—two PRs on the track and one in the classroom. Not bad for a young woman who was learning to let go of her competitive streak and focus on her happiness.

When I stood next to Kristine at the conclusion of our graduation and tossed my cap into the air, I wasn't thinking that I needed to toss mine higher than everyone else's. I was so proud of what I'd accomplished. My parents had flown in, and it was wonderful for them to be there for something other than a legal trial. Mostly, I was pleased because it seemed to me that my efforts in the classroom had equaled the rewards.

Kristine and I decided to extend our student visas and remain in Dallas the following year. We wanted to see what life in the U.S. could be like without what we referred to as the "bubble" of college life to protect us—ironic, I know, given what had happened to me. We also wanted to stay near to the men in our lives. Nick and I had grown closer during my imposed break from competing, and I needed to know if my future was here with him or back home in Norway. I was eager to find out, and I had plans already in place to make a difference in the world and in the lives of others.

CHAPTER TWENTY

Mediation

I had known for a long time that in order to really heal from the rape, I had to do something to help other people. Before I could do that, I also sensed that there was more I needed to do to help myself so that I could be in a better position to help others. Fortunately for me, I didn't have to come up with the whole plan on my own. The Texas Department of Criminal Justice instituted a program called the Victim Offender Mediation/Dialogue (VOM/D) that allowed a victim/survivor to request a face-to-face meeting with the person who had harmed them.

Erin had told me about the program at a brief meeting we had just prior to Luis Zuniga's sentencing hearing back in April of 2011. She told me that this was something to think about but not act on immediately. Some people felt better after being able to speak directly with the person or persons who had done them great harm. She didn't use the word "closure," and I was glad about that. Even back then, I knew that the concept of closure wasn't realistic. The attack and its aftermath would never come to a close, but it could be managed; I could adapt and heal, but the act of doing so just demonstrated that this thing, the attack, was still an active presence. How much that presence exerted its influence on my actions and my beliefs was up to me. I could close off how and to what extent those men controlled me.

By August of 2011, I still wasn't willing to commit fully to the idea of sitting down and having a face-to-face interaction with any of my attackers, but I didn't want to eliminate that possibility entirely. Something told me from the start that this was something that I should do, as soon as I felt ready for it. I felt, in a way, obligated to follow up on Luis to make sure that he had kept his promise. So, that month, after having interned at DARCC (Dallas Area Rape Crisis Center) and discussing the idea with everyone from my parents to friends to some of my colleagues at DARCC, after a year of contemplating the decision, I decided to sign up to be considered for eligibility.

We both had to qualify for the program by first answering lots of questions about our values and beliefs, what we hoped to gain by participating in this exchange. He couldn't be forced to participate, and I could, essentially, ask him anything that I wanted, but whether he answered at all, or how he answered, was up to him. Most everyone I talked to about the program said that I should just let things stand as they were. What did I have to gain from speaking to him? Why should I allow him the opportunity to speak with me? Why put myself through even more of an ordeal?

I understood their points, but disagreed with the premise that it was of no value for me to go through with it. If I was going to do the kind of work I hoped to do through a foundation I was considering starting, I had to gain a better understanding of just what had happened that night as well as in Zuniga's life prior to the crime and since his conviction. In a way, it was like wanting to see an entire movie instead of just a few scenes. I wasn't interested in just what happened, but why it happened, and whether or not Luis Zuniga had followed up on his words that he was going to become a changed man.

In October of 2012, I finally heard from someone involved in the administration of the program. Luis and I had been accepted. My first meeting would be with a mediator, a trained professional who worked for the program and would be in touch. I thought that maybe I'd have to wait a long time, but the call came shortly thereafter.

The mediator explained how the program worked. In addition to the broad guidelines I already knew about—he could be forced neither to participate nor to answer my questions—I learned that the first step would be for me to submit a series of questions I wanted to ask Luis. This was because the program was designed to be a benefit to victims primarily, and they didn't want the in-person interviews to be too free-form.

No surprises. I kept hearing this refrain again and again. Modest expectations. This was kind of like getting back on the track and taking a different approach from thinking about wins and PRs. I spent some time thinking of questions and consulted with members of my inner circle—the usual suspects, like Anette, Kristine, my mother, Kelly, Sidsel, and Nick, among them.

I was also told that one of the goals of the program was to help victims better understand what the lives of prisoners were like.

Most of my initial questions were about what Luis could recall of that night. I submitted my questions and then forgot about the program for a bit. I was still in Dallas and still thought that was where I wanted to be. It was really nice to have Nick there with me. Still, I was feeling a bit adrift. By October, Kristine had decided that she'd spent enough time in the U.S. outside the bubble and returned to Norway. I missed having her with me. Nick was deeply engaged in developing his career, and that entailed the usual long hours and distractedness that come with being driven in any area of your life. I understood, but being on the other side of that kind of intensity and focus had me a bit off balance. I wondered if maybe I should have done what Kristine had done and just left.

But still. My parents were struggling to come to grips with the idea that I remained in the States. In a sense, they had bought into only one way of reading my story. Small-town Norwegian girl comes to the United States to live out her dream, experiences a nightmare, and claws her way back. Hadn't I done enough in the States? Hadn't my dream of running here served a purpose? Couldn't I do what I was doing here while back home among family and longtime friends? Anette and Jonas were married. They were planning a family. Didn't I want to be a part of that? What hold did Dallas and the U.S. still have on me?

I didn't want to hear those questions. I kept telling myself that this was a place where I felt I belonged. Nick made it clear that he had no intention of going to Norway to live. Success for him meant a big job here in the States. The equation was made simple. If I wanted Nick, and I did, then I had to want to stay in the U.S. In a way, this was where the difference between being stubborn and persistent played a role. I didn't want to give up on the relationship with Nick, even though I knew that this wasn't how I wanted things to be between me and the man I loved.

I was so used to working hard at things that I told myself it was normal that you had to work hard at a relationship to make it great. Even if some of your core values were different, that didn't matter. You had to be persistent to succeed, but you shouldn't have to change fundamentally who you were and what you believed in. I was frightened by the idea of leaving Dallas, the place where I'd been damaged and healed, and one of the key people who helped me put that experience into perspective and make it into something beneficial.

Leaving would have been the safe and easy way out, and I was tempted. But I was used to taking risks, and I had to take a chance on me.

One day I came back from a late-afternoon run and was leafing through the mail when I saw that, among the assortment of bills and ad papers, was an envelope from the Texas Department of Criminal Justice. I knew immediately that it contained Luis's written responses to my questions.

Instead of tearing it open, I decided to wait. I had dinner to make; Luis Zuniga wasn't going anywhere, so he could wait. I scanned the news headlines on my smartphone while I ate. I thought of calling my mother, but our last few conversations hadn't ended well. Not that we ever argued, but there was something about the underlying tension, like we both had something we should talk about but intentionally ignored.

After doing the dishes and cleaning up in the kitchen, I took a shower. I knew that Nick was working late, so the evening was going to be mine. Settling into my pajamas and curling up on the couch, I slit open the envelope and started to read.

It was an odd and unnerving experience to read Luis's account of what happened that night. I'd always had my version in my mind, and though his didn't differ in any significant recollection from my own, I was once again struck by how random it all was. That was true about not just how I became the one taken, but also how Luis had wound up in the SUV at all.

I was pleased that his account of the events of that night coincided with mine. That assured me that my memory of that night was solid and that he was being honest with me.

I wasn't surprised to learn that drugs played a big role in the attack and in the lives of each of the men. Luis admitted that he had taken heroin that night and was a low-level drug dealer and consumer of narcotics. He believed that if it weren't for being impaired, he would not have participated in the attack. The more he told me about that night and his life before and after, the clearer it became that Arturo Arevalo was a truly evil human being. In one of his responses to my written questions prior to the meeting, Luis revealed that he had moved from one prison to another because Arturo had threatened him. He didn't feel safe being in the same prison with him.

He told me a bit more about his prison life, some of which I already knew because I had taken a tour of the prison as part of the program. I was surprised by how difficult life was there. The prisoners woke at four in the morning, had twenty minutes in which to eat each of their three meals, and sometimes worked as many as twelve hours a day.

During the prison tour, the officer guiding us produced a set of index cards. I was asked to choose at random from the pile of ten cards. The officer then read off a brief history of the man whose life and criminal record were briefly summarized there. Time after time, no matter which card I chose, those stories involved drugs. Worse, six of the ten revealed that the individuals had committed some kind of sexual misconduct against children.

"And that," the officer said, "is one part of the ugly truth of all this."

I'd always been vehemently opposed to so-called recreational drugs, and it saddened me to hear just how pervasive their use was. And the fact that so many of these men had committed sexual misconduct against children sickened me.

I wondered what kinds of influences Luis was being exposed to while in prison. How do you make positive changes in your life when such horrible people surround you? That made me even more certain that I was doing the right thing by participating in the program. At least I could show him that the world wasn't made up of just the worst kinds of people.

Before I could do that and meet him face-to-face, I had to complete the rest of the VOM/D program. I met with my mediator a total of four times and completed homework assignments to help prepare me for the

eventual meeting. At first they focused on me, helped me better understand who I was, my values, my feelings about the rape, as well as why I
wanted to participate in the program and what I expected to get out of
the meeting. The mediator evaluated my answers and discussed with me
whether or not I was truly ready for the experience. I also worked on
refining the other questions I would ask Luis Zuniga.

Finally, the date arrived when I would meet with one of the three men
who had kidnapped and raped me.

I could feel my pulse throbbing in my neck, and the familiar sensation
of being submerged in water coated my ears and my mind. I swallowed
and looked up at the man who sat across the table from me. Like me, he
held in his hands a few sheets of paper. His were shaking; mine were still.
Next to him sat an interpreter. Next to me sat one of the two mediators
who were part of the program. A pair of female guards, one of whom had
asked me to participate in a brief prayer outside the prison conference
room, stood outside watching us through the spiderwebbed glass.

At first I couldn't figure out why Luis Zuniga's appearance was different. I recognized him, even though eighteen months had passed since
his sentencing hearing, but he had walked in with his shoulders hunched
around his neck, his gaze not leaving the ground. Even when he sat across
from me, he failed to make eye contact with me. That was it. He wore
glasses now, and when he did look up briefly from the floor, the overhead
light caught in the lenses, obscuring his eyes from my vision.

After the mediator finished his introductions and made a few brief
remarks thanking both of us, Luis began by reading a letter he had written to me. He spoke in Spanish, and his words were halting and uncertain
at first even in his native language. I read along with him, reading a version in English that had been prepared for me.

He began by thanking me for the opportunity to meet with him. I
smiled when I got to the part when he read, "I can only imagine how
difficult this will be for you, as you are the person who was hurt. You
know what? I admire you a great deal because you are very courageous.
You are very brave to go through with this program. I do not deny that I
feel a little nervous, but I cannot pass up the opportunity you are giving
me to apologize, to ask for your forgiveness personally."

He went on and answered a few of the questions I had asked him. I was sorry to hear that he had lost all contact with his son. Child Protective Services had denied him any kind of custody at all. That made him very sad. He hoped that God would fill my heart with light and love and also that someday he would be able to forgive himself for what he'd done.

I read a letter that I had prepared. I let him know that I was there to check up on him, to see how he was progressing with his promise to me that he would change. I also let him know that I would continue to check up on him, that I wanted to be certain that when he was eligible for parole in 2022, he would be ready to live a new and better life.

When I finished, he seemed relieved.

Throughout my previous contact with him, in person and in the preliminary questions he responded to, he never used the word "rape." He always said or wrote something like "what I did to you." That troubled me. It fit into the larger pattern of people not speaking out directly and honestly about the crime. I didn't want people just to not be silent; that kind of whispering, not facing the issue head-on and with clear and precise language, was only going to make it more difficult to solve the problem of rape victims feeling like they are less than other people.

Words do have meanings and associations that convey messages we may or may not intend. I wanted us to be able to have a conversation about the subject that was as honest and as beneficial as it could possibly be. Sometimes we need to acknowledge the ugly truth. I was so tired of hearing and using all the filters we have in our language. Rape is rape— it's a cruel, horrifying, and disgusting act. The words we use to talk about it *should* shock us, should shake us up a bit. That's the only way that I can see people taking the issue as seriously as it needs to be taken.

From the very first speech I did after deciding to come forward, I had in my mind the idea of killing the silence. I knew that was a violent word, but it best described what I wanted to do. Ending it wasn't enough. It was going to take something more drastic than that, something that had more finality then merely ending. We had to be more active than passive. I also knew the word "killing" might trouble some people, but that was okay. Some people needed to have their attention grabbed, to see that this was so serious to me that merely tapping someone politely on the shoulder and saying, "Excuse me, but have you ever thought about the effects that sexual crimes have on this society?" wasn't going to be enough. We'd tried subtlety and indirection. There was nothing subtle about rape.

For that reason, I continued to press Luis Zuniga throughout the remainder of our conversation. That started with getting him to look at me. His translator was his link to me, but he wasn't me. At several points I asked Luis to look at me, and each time he did. I finally wore him down enough that he was no longer looking at the translator when I was speaking. When I felt like his answers weren't as direct as I wanted, I'd ask him again, stressing that he needed to be honest with me. He squirmed a few times with impatience and frustration. I didn't need an interpreter to help me discern what his sighs, slight head shakes, and eye rolling meant.

Each time I asked him what he had done to me, a look of confusion took over his face. He'd glance at the interpreter, but I suspected he knew what I was getting at by asking him what seemed obvious. It was really important to me that he use the word "rape," that he acknowledge that he did something more specific than harm me or hurt me. He hadn't backed his car over my bicycle and damaged it. Finally, he took off his glasses, rubbed his eyes with the palms of his hands, and then rested them facing upward as if offering a prayer and said, "When we," his hands twitched and he sighed, "when I raped you." I didn't need to hear the end of the sentence. I'd gotten the acknowledgment I'd come for.

I didn't want to rub Luis's nose in his crime, but I did want him to fully acknowledge what the starting point of his change was—he was a convicted rapist.

I also saw more clearly that what I wanted out of this mediation conference was a way to make clear to me, and later make clear to others, that it wasn't enough for Luis to be in a place where he wouldn't be able or willing to harm others. That's important, absolutely, but for me that wasn't enough. I was after that next step, like not just winning a race but setting your own personal record.

We need to not stop hurting one another, but also to start, and to continue, helping other people. That began with helping ourselves and knowing ourselves better, but it couldn't end there, not for me.

CHAPTER TWENTY-ONE

I Am Monika Kørra

Meeting with Luis Zuniga was just one part of the larger direction I wanted my life to take. Seeing him made me realize how difficult the issue was, but it also made me determined to become more active in the sexual assault survivor community, to help kill silence by speaking out about my experiences and getting involved with efforts to help others heal. I can't say I enjoyed meeting Luis Zuniga face-to-face, but I'd gotten through it and felt strong as a result. I understood more that I could take on this mission. After all, since my decision to go public, I'd been pleased that people had contacted me and I felt like I'd been helpful.

However, that felt like a passive approach—I was relying on them to come to me and not actively doing anything myself. I'd discussed this with Anette, and later with Nick. Just as was true throughout my experiences, I found myself a part of another team, with many people providing me with valuable resources. Nick was particularly helpful. He wasn't one to let an idea languish in the incubation stage for very long. If you wanted to do something, then you got started doing it immediately.

He—and his family—helped me realize that I could make my desire to help a more formal proposition by creating a foundation. I once again found myself requiring help in navigating the American legal system. I had no idea what was involved in creating a not-for-profit foundation. I knew that I couldn't just start asking people for money to establish some program, but finding out what I'd have to do to make sure the foundation was operating within the laws and guidelines was something I'd need help with.

Through Nick, I met a lawyer by the name of Pieter Tredoux. He let me know that in order for the Monika Kørra Foundation to become a formal 501(c)(3) nonprofit, I was going to need three things—time, money, and expertise. He was willing to provide me with his time and expertise and wouldn't charge me for his efforts. Another lawyer, John A. Bonnet, eventually also volunteered his time and legal training, and he ultimately became one of our board members.

Before we could get that tax-exempt status, we had to demonstrate that we were doing things within the community to realize our mission. As a result, with the help of Kelly and others, I got put in touch with Courtney Underwood. Like me, Courtney had graduated from SMU; she was also a rape victim, in her case, at age fifteen, more than a decade before I met her. Courtney became active in rape awareness after taking years to reveal even to her family what had happened to her. The year I was sexually assaulted, 2009, she was already active in trying to overcome a problem that I didn't even realize existed. In Dallas County at that time, Parkland Hospital was the only hospital in the entire city that kept on hand rape kits—the means to collect evidence admissible in court. That meant that if a raped individual went to another hospital for treatment, he or she would then have to go to Parkland in order to be examined again and have the "official" rape kit used. I had been taken directly to that hospital because the police who found me that night knew to do so, but I don't know if I would have had the strength or the patience to travel to another hospital, do all that waiting, fill out all that paperwork, and endure another round of questions and physical handling. But evidence collected anywhere other than Parkland couldn't be used at trial. Courtney was trying to right that wrong. She didn't believe that there should be any more obstacles placed in the path of a rape victim that might prevent him or her from reporting the crime and getting the perpetrator arrested and convicted.

By the time I met her in 2011, she'd managed to get one additional hospital, Presbyterian, certified as a rape kit exam center. She created a program called SANE (Sexual Assault Nurse Examiner), which trains nurses to do the exams of sexual assault victims. That was part of a $2 million grant Courtney was instrumental in securing to upgrade Presbyterian's treatment programs for sexually assaulted individuals. I was amazed at what she was doing and how committed she was. She was invaluable in educating me about the various issues surrounding sexual assault. I knew that in some ways my goals were more modest than hers. I wanted to end the silence that victims endured. I wanted to share my story in hopes that others would be more willing and able to come forward to share their experiences and to report the crime to the proper authorities.

Maybe this was a way in which my obsession with times and numbers was a good thing. I wanted to reduce these two horrifying statistics: Nationally, 60 percent of rapes go *unreported*; 97 percent of rapists never spend a day in jail. I was both troubled and grateful to learn those two facts. I knew how lucky I was that the men who'd assaulted me were arrested, tried, convicted, and incarcerated, but I didn't realize until later just how rare that was. Initially, my main focus was on getting out and doing public speaking engagements. That seemed a modest and attainable goal. I remembered how moved I was by the Take Back the Night presentation I attended, and I hoped that I could have an impact on people by sharing my story in the same way. I knew that the problem on college campuses was likely as bad as, if not worse than, it was outside them. I knew that I could relate well to women my age and younger, and that was my original focus.

Developing a mission statement, creating a website, the mechanics of creating a presence and a vision, took a lot of time and effort. We eventually settled on this as our statement: "Our mission is to kill the silence surrounding rape and abuse in society and to assist survivors and others impacted by any kind of violence, loss, or other traumatic event in the prevention of prolonged suffering and potential disorders, and in completely healing, through education, exercise, and other tools." What was easiest was selecting a board of directors to serve with me. I'd first shared the idea of formally doing something to help others with Anette, and she'd been an enthusiastic supporter from the beginning. She was also a dedicated teacher of children and had done volunteer work with HIV/AIDS patients in South Africa through AIDS Heaven, along with other volunteer work with the Red Cross and Adults for Children. She is currently writing her master's thesis on trauma, lingering physical symptoms, and recovery. Her husband, Jonas, was also trained as a teacher, and when I was at home, one of the things I loved to do was to go to his family's farm. There, he and his parents and siblings hosted children who had been taken in by Child Protective Services in Norway. Seeing those kids whose troubled lives had them at risk come alive and enjoy themselves on the farm was always a highlight of my visits home. Anette and Jonas were very dedicated to being of service, and the three of us would make a great team.

We got under way working under the umbrella of the Communities Foundation of Dallas. By being associated with them, we could continue our work toward getting our tax-exempt status and enjoy utilizing some of the resources they provided. The logistics of launching the foundation were much more complicated than I'd expected, and it took a long time before we were able to actually get started with any of the work I was hoping we could do. I was using my newfound powers to take it slow, to be patient, and to let the systems do their work, but I was still eager to hit the ground running and do all kinds of innovative and exciting things to help raise awareness. I was anxious to get started, but Nick kept reminding me that we were taking all the right steps, and that in due time we'd see a big payoff.

AS TIME HAS passed and the Monika Kørra Foundation has allowed me to spread this message of hope, healing, and accountability, I've managed to do what it took me many years of running and training, succeeding and failing, to accomplish. I'm not obsessed with my mission to kill the silence and to speak out to help others. It fits into the larger context of my life. When I speak, I try to set an example for the people in the room, whether they are other survivors or not. I make it clear that yes, I was raped, but I'm not a victim of rape. It doesn't define me. It's just another fact about my life, along with other facts, like that I'm blond. I'm also blue-eyed and a lifelong athlete. I'm Norwegian. I'm optimistic and I'm driven. I continue to run. I've dated other men. I've become an aunt. I've found a new direction in which to utilize my education as a yoga instructor, and I coach young athletes in running and skiing, and make public speaking appearances raising awareness about sexual violence.

I want to give others, especially young people, the shield I was given by being an athlete growing up. It gives you a kind of defense to help you meet head-on the challenges being sent your way in life. Physical and mental well-being and toughness can take you through the greatest challenges—and these are gained, learned, through sports. I've realized that sports provided a balance, a harmony, flexibility, breathing techniques, and a consciousness of my body, a heightened awareness of self—and that these tools were very powerful in my recovery. They helped me find the strength to survive those awful early days, to push through the difficult months, and then to find the words to fight for the changes that I want to see in the world.

For a long time, I worked to reject the notion that I was raped and tried to put the experience behind me. That wouldn't have killed the silence. In order to best do that, I had to integrate that part of my reality into a whole outlook on life and a completeness of being that had for so long escaped me.

A few months after I first spoke out, I was back in Dallas at the grocery store, the same one where I'd struggled with the idea of a clerk being so friendly and offering to help me out with my groceries. That notion had seemed so foreign to me when I first came to the U.S. Now, as I stood in the produce aisle, standing on tiptoes to reach to the top of a mountain of avocados, I saw a hand extend beyond mine.

"Is this the one?" a voice behind me said, offering an avocado to me.

I turned to thank the woman. I could tell by the bracelets that ringed the arm that it was a woman's hand that offered up the fruit to me.

"I have a hard time telling which ones are ripe."

"Me, too." She smiled, and then her brows narrowed.

"You're Monika Kørra, aren't you? You run for SMU?"

I nodded and said, "Yes. I'm Monika."

She took a step back and said, "I just have to let you know how appreciative I am of what you've done for women, for people really. Your speaking out is going to make a huge difference for lots of people. Thank you, Monika."

With that she shook my hand and walked back to her cart. "You take care," she said.

"You, too."

I stood there smiling. I had no idea if the avocado I held in my hand was any good, but I was certain of one fact. I was Monika Kørra, and more and more people were going to learn that same, simple, but incredibly gratifying truth about me.

Afterword

November 2013, Løten, Norway

Leave it be," my mother said. "It will catch again on its own."

I smiled and watched the sparks and fragrant smoke climb into the night sky. My father took his stick and poked at the small blaze in the fire pit, trying his best to return it to its roaring state.

"I'm doing it for the little one." He poked the glowing end of the stick toward me. "She's no longer used to such cold."

I lifted my chin and nose out of the collar of my jacket and shook my head. "That's not true." I paused for a second and looked over at Anette and Jonas, who both playfully sneered at me. Anette was ready to give birth any day, and I had to smile as her tongue protruded from her full and flush face. I had heard people say that pregnant women have their own kind of beauty, and I had to agree it was true.

I sat up straighter. "But I do appreciate your efforts, Papa."

I inched my chair closer to the fire.

"Is that better? Are you happy now?" he asked.

Was I happy? I thought about my father's question. In Norway we use an expression that I think best explains what that means to a Norwegian. The single word is *"Hverdagslykke,"* but it conveys more than you might imagine.

It means "everyday happiness." In Norway that is the way we live; we are very good at being in the moment and seeing what we're doing on a daily basis as the truest form of happiness. We know how to enjoy and appreciate the little things in life—which truly are the big things. We don't always search for more. We take great pleasure in having a calm mind, in focusing on the beauty of the life we have, the people we love, and the environment surrounding us.

Of course, I can't say that everyone here is at peace, but generally people are happy—even though they're not millionaires or business owners. I think life is challenging in that way; it is easy to lose track of what's most important; it's easy to always want more. We talk about doing something to our heart's content, and our hearts can be content, but our minds, our minds, well, that's where we get into trouble. Sometimes it is best to keep things simple.

That's not always possible, and my dad's question wasn't just about the fire or about the rape; it was more complicated than that. Only months before, I was still living in Dallas, racing to launch my foundation and to obtain tax-exempt status, hustling to hold fundraisers, and racing between speaking engagements, all good things and all in an effort to be success-ful at my latest passion: spreading the word about rape and hoping to kill the silence. Yet, it was not enough. I was not happy. Truth was, I was lonely but was too busy to realize it. Kristine had been in Dallas for one year after graduating, but now she was gone. Silje? Gone. The rest of my teammates and friends? Gone and involved in their own lives and their own careers.

Maybe I shouldn't have wished to get back to normal. Maybe all of the things I was experiencing were what happened to every college gradu-ate. My parents knew something wasn't right and confronted me after a fundraiser, which had gone very well. I didn't really realize it until then. Even though things were going well for my mission and for me, I was not happy. My relationship with Nick was on the ropes as well, and both of us knew it. And so I ultimately decided to go back to my roots, to my family and to my childhood friends and to familiar trails and slopes. I moved home to Norway. Going home, finding comfort in the people who know you best and love you the most, felt right.

I also felt that way on the night of the rape. When I was put in that situation—between life and death—the only thing I could focus on was how much I just wanted to go back to my normal life—to drink just one more cup of tea with my sister, to get one last piece of advice from my mom, to finish up the last few miles of skiing with my dad, to stand on the starting line of one last cross-country race holding hands with Kristine and Silje, to be able to see my godson, to kiss Robin good night one last time. Those were the thoughts that sustained me in those horrific hours. Nothing could measure my success in life better than to be able to do just this—to be able to be present in the moment with those wonderful people. Over time (in my desperate attempt to find my way back to a normal life), I lost track of that simple truth and what really made me happy.

As I write this, just after coming in from the campfire, I'm glad to be back in Norway. Maybe it's because I spent so much of my life running in circles on the track and in loops on roads and trails, but it feels exactly right to me to be back where I started. I've completed my journey of healing in a way—it wasn't until I returned home to my loved ones that my world finally stopped spinning and I felt at peace.

It's been a long road to get here, but in a way it's been beautiful too. I've learned a lot, about myself, about others, about life. I feel safe now, I know exactly who I am—and I'll stay true to my unique self for the rest of my life.

I've also found my mission in life, and I will do my very best to make a difference. I know where I belong and who my truest teammates are—together we can get through anything. I've been asked a lot of times if I would go back in time and choose a different path after high school. The answer, crazy as it might sound, is no! I would never go back in time and change my decisions, all of the things I've learned, the people I've met, the opportunities I've been given, the moments I've shared with friends, family and teammates.

I wouldn't give that up for anything—not ever.

I followed my dream, and it led me on a new trail—a trail that was meant for me. Now I won't be looking back any longer, but ahead, into my future. I have work to do. I want my story, my message of hope and healing, to be shared with the world. I hope and pray it will help others who have been through trauma of some sort in their life. I travel frequently to the United States to give speeches and attend foundation events. And I hope to be able to do so all around the world. As I write these words, my parents, my sister, and Jonas are resting up after working many hours in preparation for a race against rape and abuse to raise awareness and help support the Monika Kørra Foundation. I also continue to run and compete, simply because I love to. I'll never lose the desire to go faster, but I've learned to slow down and enjoy the ride as well.

For me, it's all a matter of keeping things in perspective and doing the things you love with the people you love.

BEING RAPED ALTERED my life forever. It served as a catalyst, and in time I came to realize that though the attack initiated changes in my life, I was the one in control of whether the catalytic reactions were good or bad. It also taught me so many things about myself and about life. It reinforced in my mind something I had known and felt very nearly on the cellular level since I was a young child: Movement is good. Whether you're moving backward or forward, just being in action is good. But the new concept I learned was that not only was it okay, it was sometimes better, to be still, to not be in motion. Once we get our body and our mind together, then we can take steps in the right direction. Without them working together we can stumble and fall or simply quit.

When we're in crisis we feel like we're being clamped down in place. That's uncomfortable at first, and sometimes for a long time after, but we need to take the time to slow down, to be still, to assess, to heal, and to move forward when our hearts, our minds, and our souls tell us it is time. When I think back on how I approached my healing, I realize that I was in almost constant motion, rushing from one uncomfortable physical, emotional, and spiritual position to another. I was so determined to get back to being the girl I was before the attack, and then I was so eager to see who I was going to become after, that I had no real sense of who I was in the present. I looked for evidence of my progress in terms of GPA and times in races.

I never wanted to stop to look at myself or how I really felt. That would have been painful, but, I realize now, it would have been productive. I was so frightened that life, like the literal runners I competed against, would pass me, that I had to keep moving, keep driving, keep digging deep. The rape was going to transform me, but I made the choice to turn myself into a machine. I was responsible for losing the harmony among my body, mind, and soul. I was interested in producing good results, and I did, but at the cost of really being happy, really taking the time to enjoy the moments I spent with people I loved.

It's funny that it wasn't until I began writing the end of this book, after I'd had some time to slow down and reflect more deeply, that I remembered my meetings with the mirror. I could fool myself for weeks, pretend that I was fine, but when I would take the time to stand still in front of a mirror and look straight at myself, my eyes would always tell me the truth. They would express sadness, anger, fear, and so much more. Seeing what was reflected there, the truth of what I was experiencing and feeling, I gave myself permission to let those feelings out. For months and months, I'd periodically hold an impromptu mirror meeting. Finally, one day, I stood still and saw happiness, pride, optimism. The anger, the sadness, the fear, they were gone.

I also realize now that most people saw me the way I wanted them to see me all along, as unaffected, as strong and determined. I was strong, but no matter how strong we are, tears and feelings are allowed, never forget that. In the end, the only one I kept fooling was me. But that's when the beauty of good relationships came into play and turned it all around. Family, friends, your loved ones—believe me, they are the ones who can help you put everything into perspective and show you what truly matters. They will remind you of who you are. To be surrounded by love will help you surrender, it will help you let go of the ideal you and accept the real you. It's okay to let your guard down, to share your pain, fear, and feelings of gratitude. Let a crisis bring you closer together; don't let it create walls between you and your loved ones. Openness is the key; let them into your world, and they will help you back to the real world.

I know one thing that really helped me: I was accustomed to dealing with physical pain. And to a certain degree running had exposed me to emotional pain as well. I know that we all fear emotional pain, and it is far harder to deal with than physical pain. Fear is a natural response. As athletes, from an early age we are encouraged to make physical pain our friend. We are told things like "pain is temporary, quitting is forever." There is a lot of truth to that. Pain sucks. I don't enjoy it, but I accept it because I know that after the pain comes healing and improvement. We need to allow ourselves to feel the emotional pain a crisis brings. There is no way around it if we want to eventually let go of it. We can hide the pain inside, refuse to take hold of it and accept it, but instead of healing, we will only make the damage worse. Pain tells us that we need to slow down, to get treatment, to let others assist us. Accept the pain and share the experience of it with others.

Unfortunately, I can't offer you a guaranteed set of steps to follow that will help you heal from whatever challenges you face. You have to find your own way of true healing; your unique way to slow down the waves in your mind to find the answers you need. To me, a big part of the answer was communing with nature, exercising, and practicing yoga. Counting my heartbeats and listening to my breath helped me slow down and find inner peace. No worries, no stress, just letting myself feel alive and to be grateful for it. To you, it might be playing an instrument, singing, writing, cooking, working on your car. It can be anything, just something that you are passionate about. Something that lets you forget time and place, that calms your mind, that lets you lose yourself and find yourself at the same time. Turn to your passion—it will guide your way.

It also helps to put some trust into the world, try to accept what has been and believe in the future. Try to envision the future: graduation, marriage, becoming parents, grandparents—all the things you dream about. They can put a smile on your face in the darkest of times. I can't count the number of times I envisioned Kristine and me throwing our graduation hats up in the air, or Robin and me getting married. It's okay to daydream, whatever it takes to keep your head up, leading you on to better times.

In the end, when you feel ready, try to forgive and let go. To forgive can mean different things to all of us; in some situations it may be impossible to forgive those who brought about the harm, but at least then try to forgive the world, the universe, your god as you believe, and yourself. It is a great relief to get there. Do it for yourself, let it go!

I truly believe this saying: "There is one emotion that is stronger than fear, and that is forgiveness."

I know that my transformation isn't complete and that it never will be. I will continue to grow, I will continue to dream, and I'll continue to succeed. More important, I'll take the time to still my mind, my heart, and my body to enjoy exactly where I am, who I am, and who I'm with. If you're not in a race, there's no finish line, just miles and miles to enjoy doing what you love.

So, I can give you the same answer now that I gave me father that night around the fire. Yes, I am happy, truly happy.

ACKNOWLEDGMENTS

I would like to express my gratitude to the many people who have helped me regain my life and made my dream to share my journey of healing with the world come true.

Mom, Dad, without your everlasting love, support, and belief in me, I wouldn't have been able to fight through that horrific night and all the nightmares that followed it. And when you told me, by phone, the very next day that we would make it through this together, I no longer had any doubt in my mind. I've kept that message in mind ever since, and I gain new strength from it every day. The way you raised me gave me the tools I need to fight back against any obstacle; thank you for always encouraging me to keep moving forward, to continue to learn, experience, and grow, and to never let my fears hold me back in any way. I know it was tempting to tell me not to speak out publicly or to share my story in details with the world, not knowing how others would react or the strain it would put on me, your own daughter. You felt I had been through enough, but when I decided to go forward anyway, you still believed in me and trusted that I knew what I was doing. Instead of trying to hold me back, you decided to join me on my journey, allowing us to fight back, together, against sexual assault. And here we are, this is our book; "when together, nothing can break us."

My dear sister, Anette, my mentor in life, thank you for teaching me what life is all about. You assured me, throughout our childhood and as we grew, that the much-used term "Lille Monika" says nothing about me other than my stature. Together, we dare to dream, and if I'm in doubt you shake your head and get me on the right track. I got your back and you got mine for the rest of our lives. Jonas, you've been a brother to me since you fell in love with my sister. The way you've supported us all through this and how you now work with us at the Monika Kørra Foundation is admirable; thank you!

Kristine and Robin, my two soul mates, thank you for standing by my side, day and night, during the most challenging time of my life. You never questioned if I would make it through; you made me hold on to my dreams and believe in the future. You both held me as I cried, and you brought my smile back time after time. You encouraged me to fight to reclaim my life; to meet my fears and to fight through them. Knowing that each of you would be there, holding my hand on every step of the way, made it possible to get back up on my feet; it made every little fight worth fighting, my life worth living.

Ida, through ups and downs, we walk through this life together. A friendship like ours is irreplaceable. All the conversations, the laughter and tears; I cannot describe in words the value of our time together. Your mentality and rule of life— *"Jeg får til det jeg vil"*—has been an inspiration and reminder to me through all of my ups and downs and will continue to be.

Some friendships are established during our childhood, others in the strangest ways throughout life. My Texan family, the way you reached out to me during my college years, and gave me the kind of love and support that you usually only find within a true family, helped sustain me and give me hope during the darkest days of my life; Sidsel, Wenche, and Kelly, thank you for being there for me, my friends, and my family through a challenging time and for continuing to be our beloved friends.

Thank you to everyone at the Dallas PD and the Dallas County DA's office who contributed to the arrest and prosecution of my offenders. A special thanks to Erin Hendricks and Brandon Birmingham. Without your hard work and professionalism I would have lived a life of fear. The guidance, support, and motivation you gave me helped me stay strong and determined to take the witness stand; to stand up for myself and others; to be the one leaving this part of my life with my head held high, knowing that I did all that I could to make sure my offenders received the punishment they deserved.

I would like to thank everyone at SMU. The athletic department, Coach Wollman and Coach Casey, all of my teammates, my professors, the health professionals, and all of my college friends. You all made it possible for me to make the decision to stay in Dallas and complete my studies despite my fears. The way I was taken care of at SMU, not only as a student and an athlete, but as a valued human being, is admirable.

I am forever grateful for the book I received from my friend Olivia's coworker at Lululemon, a book with the title *Begin* on the cover and nothing but blank sheets on the inside. That's where it all started; My thoughts became a diary and my diary became my book—my journey of healing.

Thank you everyone at Dupree Miller & Associates, and a special thanks to Jan Miller and Nena Madonia. You read through my diary and let me know right away that we were going to share my journey with the world in the form of a book. Thank you for all the support, guidance, and help on every step of the way to get there.

Thank you, John Bonnet, my advisor and trusted friend! Thank you for all the support and advice you've given me and my family and for working with us on the Monika Kørra Foundation.

Thank you everyone at Penguin Random House, for believing in me and my story, for all the work you've laid down to create this book and for sharing it with the world. A special thanks to my editors, Leah Miller, Michele Eniclerico, Diana Baroni, and Tina Constable, and to the publicity marketing team, Christina Foxley, Tammy Blake, and Rebecca Marsh.

Thank you, Gary Brozek and Jenna Glatzer for being my ghost writers, for all the time you've spent reviewing my notes, talking them over, and helping me organize them all into this book.

It's been a long road to get here, but together, we made it—this is our book, teammates. Let's Kill the Silence.

About the Author

Monika Kørra is a native of Løten, Norway. She attended Southern Methodist University on a full scholarship in 2008, where she was a member of the cross-country team, which was the 2008, 2009, and 2011 winner of the Central Conference Championship. In 2012 she graduated with a Bachelor of Science degree in Applied Physiology with a minor in Psychology. She is now a yoga teacher, cross-country skiing coach, personal trainer, and a certified advocate for rape victims through Dallas Area Rape Crisis Center's volunteer training program. Monika was the keynote speaker at the eighth annual Conference on Crimes Against Women, as well as the speaker for Take Back the Night at the University of Texas and the Pikes Peak Domestic Violence Summit. Her nonprofit organization, the Monika Kørra Foundation, provides significant services and referrals for rape and abuse survivors and their loved ones. You can visit her at MonikaKorra.org.